BIBLE AND SCIENCE

By the same author

Les tendances nouvelles de l'ecclésiologie

The Relevance of Physics

Brain, Mind and Computers
(Lecomte du Nouy Prize, 1970)

The Paradox of Olbers' Paradox

The Milky Way:An Elusive Road for Science

*Science and Creation: From Eternal Cycles
to an Oscillating Universe*

*Planets and Planetarians: A History of Theories
of the Origin of Planetary Systems*

The Road of Science and the Ways to God
(Gifford Lectures: University of Edinburgh, 1975 and 1976)

The Origin of Science and the Science of its Origin
(Fremantle Lectures, Oxford, 1977)

*And on This Rock: The Witness of One Land
and Two Covenants*

Cosmos and Creator

Angels, Apes and Men

Uneasy Genius: The Life and Work of Pierre Duhem

Chesterton: A Seer of Science

The Keys of the Kingdom: A Tool's Witness to Truth

Lord Gifford and His Lectures: A Centenary Retrospect

Chance or Reality and Other Essays

The Physicist as Artist: The Landscapes of Pierre Duhem

The Absolute beneath the Relative and Other Essays

(continued on p. 223)

Stanley L. Jaki

BIBLE AND SCIENCE

Christendom Press

Published by

Christendom Press
Front Royal, Va 22630

1996

© Stanley L. Jaki

Jaki, Stanley L. (1924-)
Bible and Science

1. Biblical world view. 2. Christian origin of science. 3. Major
biblical miracles.

ISBN 0-931888-63-8

Printed in the United States of America

CONTENTS

Introduction

In 1893, two years before his death, T. H. Huxley wrote a preface to a collection of his essays, *Science and the Hebrew Tradition,* in which he declared: "Wherever bibliolatry has prevailed, bigotry and cruelty have accompanied it." Bibliolatry, or blind reverence for the literal veracity of each and every phrase of the Bible, forced some men of the cloth to take lightly, or even to disregard, scientific evidence. This in turn, Huxley went on, prompted "the man of science not to waste his time upon circle-squarers and flat-earth fanatics."[1]

Taking the cosmogony of Genesis 1 and the story of the Flood at face value was for Huxley the principal illustration of a biblical fanaticism blind to science. Actually he viewed as leading to fanatical blindness any effort, however sophisticated, to make Genesis 1 look concordant with the sciences of geology, paleontology, evolution, astronomy, and physics. The efforts, known as concordism, had become a vogue by the 1890s. Outside of theological circles little was heard of those who began to see that in interpreting Genesis 1 a totally new approach was needed.[2] Whether the Bible retained any veracity at all in its statements with respect to the physical world was not a topic which Huxley would have felt obliged to explore. After all he did not think that the Bible gave a

---

[1] T. H. Huxley, *Science and Hebrew Tradition* (London: Macmillan, 1893), pp. ix and 231.

[2] Among them William Clifford, the Roman Catholic Bishop of Clifton, and F. Hummelauer, professor of Old Testament exegesis at the Gregorian University in Rome. H. Gunkel's insistence, that Genesis 1 should be read as a myth, bespoke the same uneasiness among Protestants. See on this ch. 7, "The Age of Scientific Cosmogenesis," in my book, *Genesis 1 through the Ages* (London: Thomas More Press; New York: Wethersfield Institute, 1992).

reliable account even of historical events. In excoriating "flat-earth fanatics" Huxley dismissed the Gospels themselves as historical records.

A curious dismissal indeed, as archeologists had by then unearthed much evidence on behalf of the historical reliability of the Gospels. Huxley had been dead for only two years when no less an archeologist than William M. Ramsay vindicated the Acts of the Apostles as an outstandingly accurate document.[3] Archeological evidence about the historical reliability of the Old Testament had steadily increased during the last three decades of Huxley's life and has continued to grow by leaps and bounds during the last hundred or so years.[4] A good deal of the evidence consists in texts, carved in stone or baked in clay, many of them with profound relevance for the interpretation of both Testaments. It is, of course, most doubtful that latter-day Huxleys would appreciate the magisterial analysis of those texts as offered, for instance, in books whose authors combine the full rigor of the historical method with the principle, philosophical and theological, that Revelation is both possible and did in fact take place.[5]

Archeology is, of course, a science, but it is not the kind of science which is correlated in this essay with the Bible. The science in question is exact physical science, such as astronomy, physics, and geology. In Huxley's time those sciences appeared to be in particularly sharp conflict with various biblical statements even when these were seen in a perspective free of fundamentalist prejudices. The seriousness of the conflict largely derived from renewed efforts, at times with great competence in those sciences, to

---

[3] In his St. Paul the Traveller and the Roman Citizen, first published in 1896.

[4] A survey of the results is given by P. R. S. Moorey, A Century of Biblical Archeology (Cambridge: Lutterworth, 1991).

[5] To cite only two: W. F. Albright, From the Stone Age to Christianity: Monotheism and the Historical Process, first published in 1940. It is the second revised and enlarged edition of 1946 that saw widespread circulation through a paperback edition in 1957. The other is The Two-Edged Sword: an Interpretation of the Old Testament, by John L. McKenzie, first published in 1956.

establish a concordance between the steps of the six-day creation story and the major phases of the astronomical and geological past. Huxley would have also been right in dismissing some more modest efforts as well. He was no longer alive when there appeared a memorable example of the latter, the booklet, *Astronomy in the Old Testament*, by G. Schiaparelli, director of the Brera Observatory in Milan. To be sure, Schiaparelli admitted that the Bible contains no astronomy, properly so called. But he also claimed that the Bible abounds in "fine passages" out of which "there emerges beyond all other considerations the admiring and enthusiastic contemplation of the heaven, the earth, the abyss, in short, of the whole grand fabric of the universe."[7]

In claiming this, Schiaparelli suggested much more than one would be entitled to say on the basis of knowing the five planets visible to the naked eye, five constellations, and elements of the lunar calendar. Such were the chief items which Schiaparelli could glean from the Bible as evocative, if not of science, at least of scientific interest. Positively misleading are his words about "the great fabric of the universe" as given in the Bible. Its picture of the universe should, when honestly considered, appear an inept fabrication compared with even the least advanced forms of world views that can be considered scientific. Apart from this, all the biblical dicta, however carefully laid out, can in no way be construed to suggest that the Bible contains so much as an incipient astronomy.

Schiaparelli could have easily obtained the information that the Jews did not principally rely on celestial observations in order to keep their lunar calendar in step with the seasons. The intercalation of the extra month, *Veadar*, between the two spring months, *Adar* and *Nisan*, could be decided on grounds wholly extraneous to science. Thus a rabbi from Palestine wrote to a

---

[6] The Italian original, published in 1903, was quickly followed by a German translation in 1904, and a year later by the English translation, still more improved and approved by the author (Oxford: Clarendon Press, 1905). A Spanish translation appeared in Buenos Aires in 1945.

[7] *Astronomy in the Old Testament*, practical. 10.

community in the Diaspora: "The lambs are still too young and the chickens too small, and the corn is not ripe. So we have decided to add a month to this year."[8] Since fresh ears of barley had to be ready for the Passover, the calendar was adjusted accordingly, though, in this case, not mainly because of careful observations of the phases of the moon.

Huxley was entitled to smile at apologetic efforts that multiplied in the wake of the publication of Darwin's *Origin of Species* and *The Descent of Man*. It was no difficult task for his wit to turn the tables on the Anglican bishop Samuel Wilberforce who, at the meeting of the British Association for the Advancement of Science in Oxford in June 1860, challenged Huxley to declare whether he was descended from a monkey on the side of his grandfather or of his grandmother. Huxley could also show that there was no saving grace for Genesis 1 if its phrase about the creation of plants and animals "according to their kind" meant species, as understood by biologists. Huxley succeeded in blunting the edge of St. George Jackson Mivart's *The Genesis of Species*, the foremost of early criticisms of *The Origin of Species*. Huxley did so by showing that, contrary to Mivart, statements of some Church Fathers and of some Scholastics, especially of Suarez, could not be construed as containing the idea of evolution, that is, the basic instrumentality of one species in the rise of another.[9] By catching Mivart in a minor error Huxley effectively drew attention away from Mivart's main argument, which cast a pallor over Darwin himself.

Huxley had no problem rebutting those who tried to reconcile the Genesis 1 account of man's special formation from the earth's dust with the evolutionary vistas of Darwin's *Descent of Man*. Already within a year of the publication of *The Origin of Species* Huxley could confidently write: "Extinguished theologians

---

[8] Quoted in H. Daniel-Rops, *Daily Life in the Time of Jesus*, tr. P. O'Brian (New York: New American Library, 1964), p. 180.

[9] Huxley did so in his essay, "Mr. Darwin's Critics" (1871), reprinted in *Darwiniana: Essays* (New York: D. Appleton, 1896), p. 126-47.

lie about the cradle of every science as the strangled snakes beside that of Hercules."[10]

To be sure, Huxley, unlike most Darwinists then and now, conceded that science was incompetent about absolute origins, or creation in short. This concession could not, however, be of any benefit to religion and theology if Huxley was justified in his agnosticism concerning matters essentially non-scientific. Such a matter was, for instance, the biblical doctrine about God's absolute independence of anything. Instead of coming to grips with this doctrine which, in itself, could be handled in purely philosophical terms, Huxley threw a red herring. He did so by arguing that the Bible did not contain the doctrine of creation out of nothing, because the word *bara* could only mean the shaping of something from something already existing.[11]

Regardless of whether Huxley was right or wrong about *bara,* a word that will be discussed later, he unerringly perceived a crucial point. A God that needed pre-existing matter in order to create could not be ascribed absolute sovereignty over things. But if God was not absolutely independent of things, what merit could there be in the idea of a supernatural revelation? Was not such a revelation the very soul of the Bible? If supernatural revelation and the Bible were not the same thing, did it matter if theologians could shore up here and there the reliability of the Bible with respect to this or that historical, geographical, and archeological detail? And what of those theologians who celebrated Higher Criticism as a liberation from the task of reconciling the Bible with the facts of history and science?

Higher Criticism certainly was not endorsed by the Rev. G. Rawlinson as he delivered, in 1859 (the year of the publication of Darwin's *Origin of Species),* a series of Bampton Lectures, whose long title spoke for itself.[12] But he acknowledged that through

[10] T. H. Huxley, "The Origin of Species," in *Darwiniana. Essays,* p. 52.

[11] T. H. Huxley, "Mr Gladstone and Genesis," in *Science and Hebrew Tradition,* p. 187.

[12] G. Rawlinson, *The Historical Evidence of the Truth of the Scripture Records Stated Anew, with Special Reference to the Doubts and Discoveries of Modern Times* (London: J. Murray, 1859).

"the birth and growth of a new science—the Science of Historical Criticism— . . . the whole world of profane history has been revolutionized."[13] He did not, however, seem to realize that natural science had revolutionized man's knowledge of the physical past even more. Physics, astronomy, geology, and paleontology looked immensely farther back in time than the historical past, whether identified with biblical chronology or not. It was therefore self-defeating to argue that the Pentateuch's accounts of the six-day creation and of the Deluge might be considered as having come from the hands of Moses, who in turn might even have had pre-deluvian documents at his disposal. For even in this case the problem loomed large as to what to do with statements in those accounts that touched on the physical world.

Since in that respect Rawlinson was as brief as possible, he clearly exposed himself to most serious objections as he endorsed the principle that truth is one, that "truth of one kind cannot possibly be contradictory to truth of another." What he meant was that "Faith, real and true Faith, greatly loses by the establishment of a wall of partition between the sacred and the profane, and the subtraction of the former from the domain of scientific inquiry."[14]

The problem with this statement lay with the meaning of Faith, which Rawlinson left unspecified. Did he mean the propositions to which one was to assent with faith, or merely the subjective act of that assent? Had he clearly meant those propositions, and not the biblical texts in general, he might have spotted the crucial issue that was acting as a revolutionary solvent in his day. The issue was indeed a very specific aspect of the oneness of truth: If any statement (biblical or credal) contained data that could be empirically (and especially quantitatively) verified, then empirical and exact science must have the final word about all such data.

Now, if the theologian agreed to smile at the naiveté of pre-critical histories, he had no choice but to smile at the facts of

[13] Ibid., pp. 5-6.
[14] Ibid., p. 7.

nature as naively stated in the Bible. But the theologian who left the term Faith in a convenient vagueness, exposed himself thereby to devastating criticism. Rawlinson was still alive when in 1890 he was made the object of such criticism by a master of it, Huxley himself. Rawlinson, by then Canon of Canterbury Cathedral, could draw no comfort from the fact that Huxley also took for his target the Rev. H. P. Liddon, Canon of St. Paul's Cathedral, London, who had just preached there on "the worth of the Old Testament."[15]

On reading Liddon's sermon Huxley could have done what he did on hearing, thirty years earlier, Bishop Wilberforce's challenge. Then Huxley muttered to someone next to him that he felt as if the Lord himself had delivered the Bishop to him in the same way that the Amalekites had been delivered to David. For Canon Liddon urged that the reading of the Old Testament be done in "the light of Faith" in view of the fact that Christ's uses of the Old Testament assured its total veracity. As a particular example, Canon Liddon mentioned Christ's words that after Noah entered the Ark "the Flood came and destroyed them all" (Lk 17:27). This meant, for the good Canon, that the authority of divine Faith supported the view that all mankind except Noah's family perished in the Flood.

One wonders the extent, if any, to which Canon Liddon realized that the drowning of all mankind in the Flood was an empirically and quantitatively verifiable claim. It mattered not that a hundred years ago paleontology had far fewer pages than today. What mattered was that verification was, in principle at least, possible. Huxley saw clearly that the Canon's oversight on this point opened a breach in his defenses of the light of Faith. With no holds barred, Huxley exploited in full his opportunity. He did so by conjuring up a future Bampton lecturer who would discourse in terms set by Rawlinson and Liddon about the relation of the physical world, as given in the Bible and as unveiled by science, and declare: "Time was—and that not very

---

[15] Quotations from this sermon are given by Huxley in his "The Lights of the Church and Science," in *Science and the Hebrew Tradition*, pp. 208-09.

long ago—when all the relations of Biblical authors concerning the whole world were received with ready belief. . . . But all this is now changed. . . . No longer in contact with fact of any kind, Faith stands now and for ever proudly inaccessible to the attacks of the infidel."[16]

Such would have been a self-defeating shoring up of the Faith, writ large. Those who came to advocate it, seemed to ignore the many who refused to buy it, precisely because it appeared intellectually dishonest to them. One of these was Charles Wilson, who eventually became Churchill's personal physician and, subsequently, Lord Moran. He could easily have had Canon Liddon in mind as he recalled his years as a young physician: "I drifted away from churchgoing because the literal interpretation by the Church of what was surely meant only as symbols threatened to interfere with my own belief that scientific materialism does not explain everything."[17]

It would have been, of course, too much to expect from an overburdened physician, however eminent, to disentangle subtle components in a complex problem. He clearly meant to say that parting with scientific materialism implied, among other things, that the just demands of science be fully respected. But this is precisely what could not be done in the approach advocated by Canon Liddon. By demanding too much, Liddon lost the ground for claiming anything. Hence Charles Wilson and many others felt that everything the Bible stated about physical miracles was just a set of symbols. But then there came the frightening prospect that the delight of anyone brought up on "the splendid utterances" of the Bible and the Book of Common Prayer was "no more than a love of words."[18]

There is no similarly penetrating insight in all the learned theological writings of R. Bultmann who later in this century succeeded most in giving a perverse academic veneer to a

---

[16] Huxley, "The Lights of the Church and the Light of Science," pp. 237-38.
[17] *Churchill. The Struggle for Survival 1940-1965. Taken from the Diaries of Lord Moran* (Boston, Mass.: Houghton Mifflin, 1966), p. 44.
[18] Ibid.

misguided tactic. He dismissed all biblical miracles as if Science, writ large, had proved that miracles were impossible. Such was the essence of his famed "demythologization" of the Bible. He merely wrapped the Bible in the myth that a dubious philosophy parading as Science was Reason itself. Thus did Bultmann sell Reason short in order to secure Faith. Theologians, whose anti-intellectualism had already been on the rise, readily swallowed Bultmann's rhetorically brilliant but logically inconsistent *aperçus* about the Gospel narratives. They were not bothered by the fact that Bultmann relied not so much on Heideggerian existentialism as on the magic of the word Faith, which he had imbibed from his Lutheran background. Armed with that magic, Bultmann easily convinced others no less in its grip that they could safely separate the science of biblical archeology as well as the physical sciences from their reading of the miracles recounted in the Gospels, because Faith alone mattered. Such was Bultmann's rescue of "biblical" Faith from the challenges of historicity and from the grip of questions relating to the credibility of physical miracles.

But Faith, or any faith which is not blind, was not meant to work as a solvent that dilutes hard facts. And regardless of how large a role is attributed to the sociological, psychological, and cultural conditionings of individual scientists in their search for facts, many of the facts or data established by them are facts in a very special sense. They can be measured, weighed, timed—in short, they can be stated in quantitative terms. This is of crucial significance in dealing with science. Theories about science and scientific method may be generated almost to excess. Huxley would be bewildered by the overcomplicatedness and the emotive characteristics of those theories now in vogue. But whether science is a chain of abrupt revolutions; or a series of psychologically-powered paradigm shifts; or a succession of intricate research programs, of conceptually overloaded images, and of endless falsifications, quantities alone can make exact science. Quantitative data, or facts prone to quantitative evalua-tion, whether they are biblical or not, cannot be demythologized, or else one must espouse the principle of double truth or even endorse plain duplicity.

Scientists themselves may feel rightly irritated by sundry methods urged on them by philosophers of science. The latter should indeed feel utterly dismissed when a physicist disgusted with those methods declares that to do science is to do "one's damndest with one's intellect."[19] And even in such "damning" moments, scientists, unlike philosophers of science, can always have recourse to an island of clarity: the domain of measurements and, on what they rest, quantities. There are no two ways about quantities. Quantities are a very special conceptual breed. Concepts relating to beauty, values, justice, and even to reality as such, do not have what quantities do: strict contours. Unlike concepts relating to the realm of the humanities, quantities do not have a suppleness to be readily abused by those eager to escape their grip. Quantities have a truthfulness of their own, however elementary, a truthfulness which pierces heaven itself.

The sharpness of this metaphor is meant to put in bold relief a basic truth about Revelation insofar as it comes from a truthful God. To no such God can be assigned any statement that would contradict a truth clearly perceived by plain reason. And plain reason perceives nothing more clearly than quantities. Nowhere does the principle of the oneness of truth impose itself with greater force, and nowhere does the principle of double truth give itself away more devastatingly than in respect to quantities. Truth, in general, can be carried by a great variety of conceptualizations. But whenever a truth contains a quantitative aspect, obvious limits are set to indulging in those varieties, or "interpretations."

This is especially true in science. Speculations can go on endlessly as to what is electricity or what is gravitation. But in both cases the inverse square law, as a quantitative proposition, secures a firm standpoint. Conversely, a theologian may have some leeway with the proposition that the earth was made by

---

[19] P. W. Bridgman, "The Prospect for Intelligence," *Yale Review* 34 (1945), p. 450.

God. He may claim that the proposition merely means an utter ontological dependence, even though the biblical parlance suggests a specific action on God's part. But if the theologian takes the earth for a body that has preceded the formation of the sun, he has on hand a problem that lends itself to quantitative formulation and verification. The same holds true of the propositions that God fixed the earth firmly on the seas and that the earth is flat—which it certainly is in the Bible. Such propositions imply quantitative parameters, as do the Bible's references to the firmament and to the age of the earth. Such parameters can be investigated and decided by reason with the special certainty quantities convey. Our understanding of Revelation must especially conform to that certainty in this age which science instructs with stunning measures of quantitative exactness about the physical realm. Even the slightest disinterest in that conformity would discredit the basic theological claim that Revelation has its source in an infinitely rational God and is directed at human minds created to His very image.

Plain blindness to that discredit readily profits people like Huxley who are far from utterly frank, at least in public, as to why they are so fond of dwelling on alleged contradictions between science and the Bible. In the glare of publicity they give the impression that a satisfactory resolution of those quantitative conflicts is all they are interested in. It is only in private that they usually make it clear that a satisfactory outcome is of little interest to them. Very instructive in this respect is Huxley's admission to a friend: "Whether astronomy can or cannot be made to agree with the statements as to matters of fact laid down in Genesis—whether the Gospels are historically true or not—are matters of comparatively small moment in the face of the impassable gulf between the anthropomorphism (however refined) of theology and the passionless impersonality of the unknown and unknowable which science shows everywhere underlying the thick veil of phenomena."[20]

[20] Letter of April 30, 1863, to the Rev. Charles Kingsley. In *Life and Letters of Thomas Henry Huxley*, ed. L. Huxley (New York: D. Appleton, 1900), vol. 1, p. 258.

Brave assertions often pass for proofs. What Huxley did was to demand that others accept without proofs his agnosticism, a word specially coined by him. Yet it was easy to show that science found everything passionless only because its tools and methods are blind to anything which is not quantitative. And this holds true also of branches of science, not yet sufficiently exact, that have for their main objects sensory data. For all such data are, in principle at least, translatable into quantities. Only those who are unmindful of this self-limitation of the scientific method will place undue trust in it and take science for a proof that whatever cannot be grasped by it is purely subjective, a category further demeaned by calling it anthropomorphic.

Huxley himself provided a classic example of the stultefying measure to which this exclusive trust in the scientific method can be carried. The context was his son's death at the tender age of seven. When the Rev. Charles Kingsley, chaplain to the Queen, tried to comfort him by referring to personal immortality as anchored in belief in bodily resurrection, Huxley brushed him aside: "I know what I mean when I say I believe in the law of the inverse squares, and I will not rest my life and my hopes upon weaker convictions."[21] Huxley should have rather considered that the very fact of his exchanging arguments with Kingsley was the kind of reality that alone could secure certainty for turning the inverse square law into a communicable proposition.

Whether Kingsley was a theologian alive to basics in logic and philosophy is doubtful. Huxley may have derived some satisfaction from the philosophical poverty of not a few theologians of his time. This poverty is hardly diminished today, especially among exegetes. It is not an accident that some of them are hankering for an epistemology-free exegesis. In doing so they dabble as philosophical circle-squarers and cognitive flat-earth fanatics.

In the present book no space will be wasted on exegetes who take aphoristic phrases for rigorous thinking. Nor will any

---

[21] See *Life and Letters of Thomas Henry Huxley*, vol. 1, pp. 217-18.

sympathy be offered for those theologians who do not see the inanity of the fideistic boast: "I did not invent the faith and therefore I do not have to defend it. I can only swear to you that it is true."[22] No space will be wasted on scientists who still emulate Huxley in his blind worship of the method of science. No attention will be paid to those who a hundred years after Huxley still find creditable his dismissal of the unreliability of the Bible as a historical record, and do so in their capacity as Huxley lecturers.[23]

However, in surveying the Bible full attention will be given to what follows from the special truthfulness of quantitatively verified and verifiable facts. Huxley and his latter-day camp followers will have to be fully satisfied that a complete harmony between the Bible and science can be articulated without doing injustice to either of them. But no less attention will also be paid to articulating an additional proposition that, if made in his day, would have outraged Huxley. The proposition is that, although no quantitative (or empirical) datum can be culled from the Bible from which science could ever benefit, science still greatly profited from the Bible, as a depository of Revelation. Indeed, science owes to that Revelation the very spark without which no accumulation of empirical and technological information could have turned into science.

Of course, no such proposition would have come from the relatively few who in Huxley's day busied themselves, often in a rather amateurish way, with the history of the exact sciences. It was typical of many of them to recount that history as an unrelenting conflict[24] or warfare that would cease only by

---

[22] Whether rightly or wrongly attributed to Karl Barth, the phrase accurately reflects the stance taken by many a theologian today.

[23] Thus Sir Edmund Leach, who declared in 1980: "I agree with Huxley that the Bible is not true as history." This startling statement may appear more natural on recalling that it came early in a lecture on "Why did Moses have a sister?" See E. Leach & D. A. Aycock, *Structuralist Interpretations of Biblical Myth* (Cambridge: Cambridge University Press, 1983), p. 33.

[24] As done by J. W. Draper (1811-92), professor of chemistry at New York University. His *A History of the Conflict between Religion and Science*, first published in 1875, was already in its 25th edition by 1895. The God approved by Draper could

unrestricted acceptance of a fully rationalist approach to the Bible.[25] And even those very few among historians of science, who discussed their subject matter with some sympathy for the Christian religion, would have found absurd the suggestion that science had greatly benefited from supernatural revelation as deposited in the Bible.

Exactly a hundred years after Huxley had viewed as entirely negative the relation of the Bible and science, the very possibility of a positive relation could still be dismissed in such a way as to amount almost to a vote cast on Huxley's behalf. A case in point is the statement of James Barr, a distinguished exegete of the Old Testament, who in his recent Gifford Lectures, *Biblical Faith and Natural Theology*, wrote: "The idea, sometimes fashionable, that science had its roots in the Bible, must be considered to have been an oddity of our century."[26] It would be difficult to dismiss the idea in question more effectively than with Barr's dictum. Its studiedly light touch delivers a heavy blow indeed.

In the context Barr referred to an essay of his, published in 1973, as containing in detail his negative view on the connection between science and the Bible.[27] In the concluding pages of that essay Barr granted, however, that four considerations may put that connection in a somewhat positive light: The first is the insistence in Genesis 1 on the goodness of everything. The second is the picture in Genesis 1 of the world as something ordered. Both considerations are, of course, in consonance with what a scientist must assume to make his work meaningful. Thirdly, Barr found Genesis 1 helpful as a reminder that man should use responsibly his power (or ultimately his scientific and technological tools) over the physical environment. Finally, Barr

---

not, of course, interfere in nature and much less give a supernatural revelation about human destiny.

[25] As insisted upon by Andrew Dickson White, President of Cornell University, in his *A History of Warfare of Science with Theology*, first published in 1895. This two-volume work was an even greater publishing success than Draper's work.

[26] Oxford: Clarendon Press, 1993. For quotation, see p. 176.

[27] J. Barr, "Man and Nature—The Ecological Controversy and the Old Testament," *The John Rylands University Library Bulletin* 55 (1972-73), pp. 9-32.

admitted the presence of some "incipient science and technology" in the Wisdom literature.[28]

The substance of Barr's essay is contained in the answers he gave to two questions. One was "the historical question whether the connections which have been established between the Bible and modern science or technology are the result of a fair interpretation of its interests and tendencies."[29] Somewhat removed from exegetical expertise was the other question, whether a mentality steeped in biblical thinking played an important part in the rise of science in modern times. With hardly a trace of hesitation, Barr answered both questions in the negative. In other words, Barr said nothing less than that any positive view on the connection between the Bible and modern science implied both a misunderstanding of science and a misreading of the Bible.

Twenty years later, in 1993, Barr said the same thing, though with a twist whose significance he seemed to overlook. What he called "an oddity of our century" should seem particularly striking for two reasons. One relates to the immense advances made by science in this century of ours, far beyond anything Huxley could have dreamt of. The other is that only in the twentieth century did the study of the history of science begin to transcend the level of avidly cultivated half-truths, especially in respect to the question of the very origin of modern science. Thus in 1906 Bergson could expect no criticism for his dictum that modern science, as the daughter of astronomy, "has come down from heaven to earth along the inclined plane of Galileo."[30]

Yet just about then momentous evidence was being disclosed that the descent in question had much to do with God's revealed word. Much more evidence was available by 1973, let alone twenty years later, about the medieval (and, therefore, Christian and biblical) antecedents of Galileo than suggested by

---

[28] Ibid., p. 31.

[29] Ibid., p. 18.

[30] H. Bergson, *Creative Evolution*, tr. A. Mitchell (New York: Random House, 1944), p. 364. The French original was published in 1906.

Barr's two publications. Already in the late 1930s quaintly odd, and certainly antiquated, should have appeared Archbishop Temple's artfully vague view which Barr quoted, thirty and again fifty years later, with full approval: "It may be too much to argue, as some students of the subject have done, that science is a fruit of Christianity, but it may be safely asserted that it can never spontaneously grow up in regions where the ruling principle of the Universe is believed to be either capricious or hostile."[31]

Did this vagueness indicate wise caution, lack of information, or failure of nerve? The burden of the present essay is twofold. One is to take a close look at the "interests and tendencies" of the Bible insofar as they may touch on science. The other is to consider the possible historical role of the Bible in sparking the rise of modern science. For once those two points are secured, there will be no need to waste time on minutiae, let alone on rebutting vagaries. These are still fomented by those who, with their advocacy of a "young earth," try to cast Genesis 1 into a textbook on science. In doing so they bring ever fresh discredit on the Bible. A reliable relation of science and the Bible can be argued only by establishing a framework within which equal justice is done to the dictates of natural science as well as to those of supernatural Revelation. Moreover, this is to be done in compliance with the respective manners in which one and the other have become a historical reality. For just as the Bible registers, among other things, a vast series of historical events, so its relevance for science can best be seen against the unfolding of science through its history.

---

[31] Barr quoted (pp. 18-19) from *Beginning Now* (London: Collins, 1971, p. 124) by J. D. Davies, who in turn quoted from C. A. Coulson, *Science and Christian Belief* (London: Collins, 1958), where Temple's dictum occurs on p. 61 (not on p. 80 as indicated by Davies).

I

BIBLICAL ISSUES

1

Some Plain Irritants

A flat and fixed earth

If asked about his physical surroundings or about the physical world at large, the typical Israelite would have given a reply very irritating to the modern mind. It is irritating to say the least to hear that the earth is a flat disk, the sky an inverted hard bowl, and that the two form a vast tent-like structure. Of course, other inhabitants of the ancient Near-East would have given similar answers. But if our Israelite would have been pressed a little further about the stability of such a structure, he, as if bent on irritating modern man, would have ascribed it to some supernatural force. To be sure, much the same would have been done by a typical ancient Egyptian or Babylonian. They were no less religious than the Israelites insofar as religion means what its etymology conveys: the action of re-tying *(re-ligare)* the things of earth and heaven, and of tying man's affairs and destiny to religious powers, usually called deities.

But the Israelite would have outdone them in dispensing his irritants. For he would have been adamant in tying the things of earth and heaven, and himself, not to a plethora of gods, but to a single God who is immensely superior to all forces of nature. This is what really irritates the modern secularized mind that boasts of having been shaped by science. Such a mind finds no major stumbling block in those other gods taken for mere personifications of various natural forces. For in the measure in which those forces became depersonalized under the influence of science, those gods could be readily ignored. But this could not be done with a God whose very singleness or oneness puts him above Nature, writ large, while the same Nature remains in utter subordination to Him. It is the ubiquitous presence of such a God in the Bible that locks, in some scientific eyes, the Bible in an irritating conflict with science.

It is with reference to such a God that our Israelite would have stated that the earth, or the cosmic tent, was stable because, though floating on water, it was fixed there by God himself. He would have also attributed to God's direct actions not only some extraordinary physical events (such as volcanic eruptions and earthquakes), but also the very ordinary ones (such as rain and wind). To that Israelite, Nature, in its wholeness as well as in all its parts, was subject to a God incessantly involved in all natural processes without ever being part of them. It was this kind of tying of nature and man to God that has always appeared to be the most characteristic expression of what is usually called the Hebrew genius.

That genius could boast of no achievement in technology or in the arts. Its chief contribution to culture was a concretely lived monotheistic religion. The most lively expressions of that religious genius are, of course, the Psalms. Indeed, as our Israelite gave those answers, he would have instinctively used phrases from the Psalms, without, of course, taking the Book of Psalms for a source-book on science, or even for a book on theology. But he would have readily taken the Psalms for a book that contained all he had to know and to voice about the ultimate origin and destiny of everybody and everything. More than any other book in the Old Testament, the Psalms were both the vital expression and formative factor of the Hebrew religious genius. To the Psalms, insofar as they were not only a form of poetry but also of prayer, fully applicable is the rule which in Patristic times obtained the hallowed formulation: "Let the norms of prayer set the standard of what is to be believed."[1]

The standard, as embodied in the Psalms, was the fruit of an organic growth. No other book of the Bible had been in the

---

[1] ". . . ut legem credendi lex statuat supplicandi." *Praeteritorum Sedis Apostolicae Episcoporum auctoritates de gratia Dei et libero arbitrio*, Cap. XI, Indiculus de gratia, in Migne PL vol. 51, col. 209.

making for so long a time as was the Book of Psalms. While some of the psalms hark back to pre-Davidic times, and not a few of them were composed by King David himself, psalms were still being produced in post-Exilic times. Most importantly, if exception is made for the summons, "Hear Israel, the Lord is our God, the Lord alone! Therefore, you shall love the Lord, your God, with all your heart, and with all your soul, and with all your strength" (Dt 6:4-5), the scriptural passages best engraved in Jewish memory came from the psalms.

But just as that summons, passages of the Psalms too had an authoritative ring to them. Herein lies a most obvious rub in speaking about the Bible and science. For little if anything may appear to remain for science to do in face of statements such as these: "It is he [the Lord] who set it [the earth] on the seas; on the waters he made it firm" (Ps 24:2), or "The earth you made firm not to be moved" (Ps 93:1), or "The world he made firm in its place" (Ps 96:10), or "You founded the earth on its base, to stand firm from age to age" (Ps 104:5). And if one looked for a justification, he was referred to the wisdom of the Lord "who fixed the earth firmly on the seas" (Ps 136:6).[2] Could an earthling try to fathom a wisdom that "could not be measured" (Ps 147:5), precisely because it was the wisdom of a great and almighty Lord?

The earth's occasional trembling in the sight of God, referred to in Psalms 96 and 97 as well as in Psalm 68, did not, of course, detract from the earth's overall immobility. Nor was the hardness of the sky taken to be weakened by its "melting in the presence of God" (Ps 68:8). The hardness of the sky, but especially the immobility of the earth, had to appear all the more a divinely ordained physical fact as, according to the Bible, a mere man, Joshua, could be authorized by God to stop the sun and the moon in their tracks and, apparently, for a whole day (Jos 10:12-13). This biblical perspective of God's direct involvement in the

---

[2] The earth's immobility is also stated in 1 Sm 2:8 (Hannah's song), an indication that the fixity of the earth was readily taken for a principal reason to praise Yahweh's power and providence.

earth's immobility could be so overpowering as to demand that scientific reasons against it be dismissed. The dismissal was contemptuous in the case of Luther, who gained the dubious distinction of being the first to call Copernicus a fool. And the words, *eppùr si muove*, put in Galileo's mouth years after he had died, have become the battle cry of those bent on showing that science made the Church of Rome look forever foolish.

Continual interferences with nature

Yet the once-and-for-all divine action whereby the earth was made firm, never to be moved, should seem an innocent affair compared with biblical assertions about endless interferences by God in the course of natural events. Psalm 104 is particularly expressive in this respect as it goes well beyond the erstwhile making of the world. There God is celebrated as one directly behind a vast range of frequent and infrequent, regular and irregular natural phenomena: It is the Lord who makes springs gush forth in the valleys, waters the hills from his dwelling in heaven, makes the grass grow for the cattle, makes prey available for various animals, and spreads darkness at night. God's presumably stern look is taken there for the cause of earthquakes and his touch of the top of mountains for their occasional eruptions as volcanos.

God's endless involvement in ordinary physical processes is rendered in several psalms in embarrassingly picturesque detail. In Psalm 66 one finds ascribed to a special application of God's strength the fact that mountains stay in place and that stormy seas are stilled time and again. There God is cast into the role of letting more or less water descend to earth from his river above the firmament. In Psalm 147 the freezing of waters is attributed to the touch of his hand and the same is stated about the descent of snow and frost. Clouds come and go at his summons, rain falls once he produces lightning, winds can blow only when released by him from his heavenly storerooms; so states Psalm 135.

Conviction about God's continual and direct involvement inspired the view that the Lord's fulminating voice is heard in the severe thunder and lightning that shatter the cedars of Lebanon, rend the oak tree, and strip the forest bare (Ps 29:5-9). The same involvement transpires through the celebration of God as one who "rides on the clouds" as well as "on the heavens, the ancient heavens" (Ps 68:5 and 34). A variant on this is Amos' reference to God as striding on the heights of the mountains (4:13). A God so picturesquely close to nature is described in the same context as the one who makes darkness and dawn with the same immediacy as "he declares to man his thoughts."

Compared with these continually intimate involvements of God in the course of nature, relatively unembarrassing may seem God's occasional interventions in nature, even though on a grand scale. Unlike the sudden storm described in Psalm 18, where God is thanked for lowering the heavens (clouds) and wreathing the mountains in smoke to make it possible for David to rout his enemies, those interventions involve a physical miracle. They remain, of course, pseudo-problems for science as long as one denies that God can intervene in nature, let alone that God exists. But they pose scientifically valid challenges to those ready to admit miracles.

Examples of such challenges, that will be treated separately, are the plagues inflicted on Egypt and the circumstances of the crossing of the Red Sea and the Jordan. And even more scientifically challenging are the interventions that seem to involve long-term consequences for celestial dynamics. Such are Joshua's miracle already referred to, Isaiah's making "the sun come back the ten steps it had advanced" (Is 38:8), and the darkness that covered "the entire land" while Christ was hanging on the cross. Scientifically challenging also are the star that led the Magi and, of course, the rainbow, if it really was a physical phenomenon not yet on hand prior to the end of the Flood. The latter poses, of course, problems of its own to geology.

These special interventions put in sharper focus God's will, which in the Bible is thought to be at play in all ordinary or

regular events of nature. It is in reference to them that Psalm 135
declares that God "does whatever he wills." There is indeed a
strong voluntaristic strain in the Bible insofar as it presents God's
relation to nature. Such a strain is hardly evocative of the
impersonal, non-volitional consideration of nature as presup-
posed by science. This is not to suggest that the will in question
is capricious or that it has no redeeming characteristics with
respect to a genuinely scientific study of nature. But even if one
looks at the very product produced by that will, problems
remain far beyond what has been obvious for a long time.

An unscientific world-tent
Obviously, to modern eyes dazzled by space rockets cruising
along "world lines" set by Einstein's four-dimensional cosmology nothing could seem more jarring than the Bible's physical
world, which is little more than a glorified tent. To that tent the
Bible assigns the sky as its cover and the earth as its floor,
though hardly in a consistent way. In Genesis 1 the sky is a
firmament, that is, a hard metal bowl, whereas in Psalm 104 and
Isaiah (45:24) it is more like a canvas that can be stretched out.
In the latter case it is even more difficult to picture the openings
in the sky through which God lets the upper waters descend, in
the form of rain and clouds, upon the earth (Gen 7:11, 8:2, Is
24:18). Again nothing specific is said about the joining of that
sky with the earth at its extremities. The same is true about the
pillars of the earth that are said to jut into the lower waters (Ps
75:4). The Psalmist's interest is focused on God's upholding those
pillars even though the earth and all who dwell in it may rock.
In the Bible the waters that envelop the world-tent above and
below and on all sides are not assigned boundaries. In general,
the cohesion of those waters is of no concern in the Bible. The
declaration that God "collects the waves of the ocean and stores
up the depths of the sea" (Ps 33:7) does not indicate that some
ultimate confines are thereby meant or what those confines are.
     Herein lies one of the non-trivially unscientific aspects of
the world as described in the Bible. This point was altogether

overlooked by Fred Hoyle as he dismissed the biblical world picture as a "merest daub" in comparison with the world view of modern science.[3] Of course, one does not need to combine *à la* Hoyle scientific expertise with robust atheism in order to feel a grudging sympathy for his dictum. Well before the advent of modern science, and indeed of heliocentrism, the contrast between that biblical world-tent and the world of Aristotelian-Ptolemaic geocentrism had to appear enormous.

A universe bounded with the sphere of the fixed stars, with a spherical earth at its center, had a genuine scientific consistency. The measuring of a relatively short distance (from Alexandria to Syene along the Nile) on the earth's surface of a relatively minute part (the earth) of that universe could logically lead to quantitative estimates about the very size of that universe. Only a generation separates the measurement by Eratosthenes of Cyrene of the size of the earth from the computation by Aristarchus of Samos of the relative and absolute distances among the earth, the moon, and the sun. These great scientific achievements made around the middle of the 3rd century B.C. need not be reviewed here. Three centuries later they greatly helped Ptolemy calculate the minimum distance which, within that universe, the sphere of the fixed stars must have from the earth.[4]

One did not have to wait for heliocentrism to be struck by the enormous size of a universe encompassed within that sphere and the relative smallness of the earth in it. Very puny should have appeared the earth's radius if about twenty thousand times larger was the distance to the fixed stars. Moreover, any educated person of Late Antiquity (including such Church Fathers as Basil and Augustine) could readily follow the geometrical methods that yielded those data and estimates.

Nothing scientific of this sort could be done with the biblical world-tent. Neither in the east-west nor in the north-south

---

[3] F. Hoyle, *The Nature of the Universe* (New York: Harper and Brothers, 1950), p. 138.
[4] For details, see A. Van Helden, *Measuring the Universe: Cosmic Dimensions from Aristarchus to Halley* (Chicago: University of Chicago Press, 1985), pp. 16-17.

direction could one guess the true extent of the dry land by measuring some distance on it. Ignorance about the true extremities of the dry land also made it impossible to guess the diameter of the firmament. The firmament itself offered no clue about the extent of the waters above it. Nor could an estimate of the horizontal dimensions of an essentially flat cosmic floor, the earth, imply anything about its thickness or about the depth of waters under it. Another sign of that non-scientific perspective is the Bible's fleeting interest in the pillars which supported the firmament (Jb 26:11). The openings (doors) in the firmament must have appeared rudely non-scientific even in pre-modern times. The search which some Church Fathers made for the firmament (Augustine looked for it in a vaporous layer in the orb of Saturn[5]) never included a search for those doors through which rain as well as the manna (Ps 78:23) were said to come down to the earth. It seemed that it was better to remain silent about those openings.

Job's scientific trials

That the physical world as presented in the Bible does not lend itself to a scientific exploration is not, however, its most unscientific feature. What may seem fundamentally unscientific in the Bible is a theme which is an integral part of the main and final argument in the Book of Job. The argument adds to Job's physical and psychological torments something that may best be called Job's scientific trial, a trial invariably overlooked in commentaries on that book.

The author of the Book of Job does not merely argue that God knows infinitely more than Job does about his own actions and intentions, and that therefore Job should submit to God's decree about him. This may be understandable enough. But Job, or man as represented by him, is confronted with a scientific trial in the additional two-step claim about man's knowledge relative to nature. In the first step it is argued that actually man knows

---

[5] See my *Genesis 1 through the Ages* (London: Thomas More Press; New York: Wethersfield Institute, 1992), pp. 92-93.

much less about nature than God does, which is not something to be overly upset about. But in the second step it is also claimed, and by God himself, that man cannot even hope to learn much about nature. This argument is wholly distorted when presented as "the self-revelation of creation,"[6] even if that phrase means the witness of nature as something created.

The argument turns up briefly in the principal charge which Job's three friends make against him. They, of course, reject Job's pleading of innocence mainly on the grounds that suffering is punishment for sins and that no evil-doer fails to receive his desserts. The latter point can easily be challenged by anyone, like Job, unaware of any serious transgression and yet subjected to excruciating trials. Job finds a far more exacting intellectual challenge in his friends' occasional references to God's unfathomable knowledge, particularly evident when one considers His power over nature. Job indeed fully concedes this. He does so in two ways: One is to ascribe to God a power which does away with the regularity of nature on the vastest possible scale: "He removes the mountains before they know it; he overturns them in his anger. He shakes the earth out of its place, and the pillars beneath it tremble. He commands the sun and it rises not; he seals up the stars." The other is to characterize God's superior power and wisdom in ordering everything in nature to be such as to be never fathomed by man: "He alone stretches out the heavens and treads upon the crests of the sea. He made the Bear and Orion, the Pleiades and the constellations of the south; he does great things past finding out, marvelous things beyond reckoning" (Jb 9:5-10).

To be sure, Job is ready to turn these considerations against his friends. This happens when he finds that his friends suggest some lack of clarity in nature, as seen by God, in order to defend their claim about Job's sinfulness, though the latter may not be transparent. Job retorts by stressing that nothing in nature can block God's view as He acts, certainly not that empty space over

---

[6] The title of ch. ix in G. von Rad, *Wisdom in Israel* (London: SCM Press, 1972).

which He stretches out the firmament, or that void over which He suspends the earth. If the full moon is not wholly visible, it is only because God spreads clouds before it (Jb 26:7-9).

This, of course, implies that man can and does indeed know certain things about nature even in a way that may beckon science. But the rest of Job's reply is a mixture of remarks of which only one is intriguing scientifically, suggesting as it does a circular, though not spherical, confine to the ocean: God "marked out a circle on the surface of the deep, as the boundary of light and darkness" (26:10). In Job's other remarks thunder is seen as a vehicle for God's rebuke, and the same is true of flashes of lightning which He hurls relentlessly against the waters. With those flashes in his hand God is seen "to pierce the fugitive dragon" that tries to escape from His grasp. This is a trace of the vision, especially strong in Psalms 74 and 89, about God being engaged in a battle with Rahab (Leviathan), the symbol of unruly forces in nature.

God's overwhelming power manifest in a storm is a chief support of young Elihu's argument against Job's reluctance to admit his guilt. In the measure in which God appears to be directly involved in various aspects of the storm, the room for potential scientific considerations becomes limited: "Out of his chamber comes forth the tempest; from the north winds, the cold; with his breath God brings the frost, and the broad waters become congealed" (37:9-11). Such are some of the events about which Elihu states: "God does great things beyond our knowing; wonders past searching out" (37:5). To make matters even more dispiriting for a scientific approach, the author of the Book of Job makes God say much the same, and to a much greater extent. Once more the portrayal of God's power in creation and in the subsequent course of natural events is aimed at revealing Job's ignorance and indeed his lasting inability to ever see into the workings of those events.

From our actual and accurate scientific understanding of the formation of hail and raindrops in clouds, of the path of thunderstorms, of the gestation period of mountain goats, it is almost embarrassing to see poor Job being lectured that all this can only be known by God (38:25-30). Again, while even modern biology does not fully understand by what discernment the hawk soars and spreads its wings toward the south (39:26), it is not at all scientific to assume that God's direct command or guidance is involved whenever an eagle takes off to build its nest aloft (39:27). And what has been learned about the physiology of the hippopotamus and the crocodile makes the entire chapter 40 of the Book of Job rather uneasy reading. There, between the lines which state that Job knows nothing of those matters, lurks the suggestion that man as represented by him would never know anything much either.

Of course, to read that chapter and the immediately preceding ones with scientific eyes would be to read them with highly distorting glasses. But such glasses may be worn even when one looks in the Book of Job not for something scientific but for the distinctly theological, which is certainly there. A case in point is Norman C. Habel's *The Book of Job*, an exegesis as vast as it is meticulous. There the source of Job's problem and its resolution are placed in the lack of a symmetry between two orders. Whereas "the natural order is amoral," the realm of human actions is distinctly moral. In the context of the Book of Job this means that a cause-and-effect relationship operates unfailingly only on the physical level; on the moral level there is no unfailing retribution. Since Habel calls the unfailing retribution a "mechanical operation," the inference is inevitable that the physical order operates in a mechanical, that is, scientifically meaningful, way in the Book of Job.[7] But then Job's agony over the suffering of the innocent can only be aggravated if it is true, as Habel would have it, that God's speech to Job is a defense of the mechanical operation of the "cosmic design" created by Him.

This interpretation of God's speech injects a distinctly scientific consideration (mechanical causation in nature) into the world view of the Book of Job, which in fact contains nothing of

---

[7] N. C. Habel, *The Book of Job: A Commentary* (Philadelphia: The Westminster Press, 1985), p. 65.

the sort. A case in point is chapter 38, which Habel presents as God's defense of his cosmic design. But what God defends is not so much a design, which would be after all primitive and summary. No details of that design are disclosed by God's declaration that he alone stretched a measuring line over the earth and that he alone knows where the earth's pillars were sunk. Nothing is disclosed about the doors with which God hedged in the sea, except that he alone did it. The same is true of his clothing the sea in robes of clouds and of his fixing its bars and doors (Jb 38:5-11). While this implies that there is a world-edifice with a mechanical and quantitative structure which any edifice, however primitive, should possess, there is nothing there about a mechanical interaction among its parts.

This becomes even more evident as God's discourse further unfolds. Nothing causal is stated by Him as He recalls the daily sequence of darkness and night, or the sequence of various phenomena of the Heavens and the atmosphere. Nowhere is it stated there that a physical factor, and not Yawheh's direct action, leads forth certain constellations in their seasons. Nowhere are clouds as such credited there as being instrumental in producing rain and lightning. It would clearly be futile to credit the Bible with a mechanistic insight on reading Yahweh's question: "Who tilts the bottles of heaven when the dust melts into a mass and clods cleave together?" (Jb 38:37-38).

Should one attribute a mechanistic protoscience to any primitive culture familiar with the fact that mud is produced whenever water and dust come together? Almost everything said in the Book of Job about the workings of nature constitutes a harsh lesson given to Job about his own hopeless ignorance and about the enormous limitedness of human knowledge in general in such and similar matters. We are very far from even a scintilla of what is not even science but merely a modest encouragement of that curiosity on which science feeds itself.

In fact, the question quoted above about the tilting of the bottles of heaven makes it all too clear that in the Book of Job as well as in the rest of the Hebrew Bible God is not said to operate *in* nature through secondary mechanistic causes, but rather to use bits *of* nature to intervene in nature to influence human affairs. He is said, time and again, to be the sole and supreme cause of natural events, ordinary as well as extraordinary. Even in the Book of Job, which contains the longest passages in the Hebrew Bible about physical phenomena, this theme of God's power over nature is not taken up even as a subject of natural theology. This is not to say, however, that natural theology is not visible here and there in the Hebrew Bible. Indeed, when that theology transpires there, it reveals grounds of knowledge that are godly in the deepest sense.

2

Godly Grounds

God's power, eternity, and wisdom

The main message of the Hebrew Bible is about God's ethical action in human history, and especially about the unfailing efficacy of that action. This ethical aspect of God's work dominates whenever more than cursory references are made in the Bible to nature. It is to stir up faith in God's power to carry out his plans in history that Isaiah gives his emphatic portrayals of God's power over the entire world, a power that puts God in a class totally apart from anything or anyone else. Thus Isaiah raises the rhetorical question of whether someone else but God cups in his hands the waters of the sea, marks off the heavens with his span, holds in a measure the dust of the earth, "weighs the mountains in scales and the hills in a balance" (40:12). A little later, Isaiah recalls as an age-old dictum that "since the earth was founded God sits enthroned above the vault of the earth, . . . and stretches out the heavens like a veil, spreads them out like a tent to dwell in" (40:22). That Cyrus would effectively carry out God's program of liberating his people is supported by the prophet's making God declare that he is the one "who made all things, who alone stretched out the heavens," that no one was with him when he "spread out the earth" (44:24). Again, the unfailing outcome of salvation history is the thrust of Isaiah's insistence that it is none other than God who forms the light and creates darkness (45:7), that his hands alone stretched out the heavens and he alone gave order to all their host (45:12). In sum, he is the sole creator of the heavens and the designer and maker of the earth (45:18).

This coupling of the reliability of salvation history with God's exclusive power over nature is present also in the Psalms.

This is particularly true of the passage in Psalm 33 where that power is extolled through the assertion that its exercise implies no effort whatever on God's part, despite its spanning over the greatest conceivable distance, that is, the gap between non-being and being. God merely has to utter His words and the heavens are made. The entire earth has to fear the Lord and all who live in the world revere Him, because "he spoke; and it came to be. He commanded; it sprang into being" (Ps 33:6 and 8-9).

The repeated references to God as "the maker of heaven and earth," that is, the maker of *all* (Ps 115:15, 121:2, 124:8, 134:3) obtain their full meaning in the form "who *alone* made heaven and earth, the seas and all they contain" (Ps 146:6). Such an emphasis on the Creator's exclusivity is a further aspect of Old Testament monotheism. The latter, insofar as it implied a total transcendence of God over anything visible, was immensely superior to Akhenaten's short-lived sun-worship, with a very visible and changing object at its center. Moreover, it is clear that references to the Sun as the sole creator in the celebrated Aten hymn are so many clichés, borrowed from the Amun cult within which other deities are very much tolerated.[1]

The exclusive status which the Hebrew Bible accords to God implies more than meets the eye. For the elimination of rival gods means the elimination of any power that could conceivably undercut the efficacy of God's decrees. This is implied in the celebration, found everywhere in the Bible, that those decrees have an eternal validity. The God of the Bible is, above all, faithful in all his work. He is a God whose love has no end and endures from age to age. In Psalm 117, the shortest of all psalms, all nations are asked to praise God simply because he is faithful forever. The next psalm begins with the repeated acclamation that God's love has no end.

---

[1] As pointedly noted in *Documents from Old Testament Times,* translated with introductions and notes by members of the Society for Old Testament Study and edited by D. Winton Thomas (1958; Harper Torchbooks, 1961), p. 149.

Being *hallel* psalms, or beginning with an alleluia, they were sung at the conclusion of the Passover meal,[2] and were therefore particularly effective in engraving on Jewish memory the enduring character of God's saving work. This is a point well to keep in mind in connection with still another *hallel* psalm, Psalm 111, in which the theme of God's eternal faithfulness is articulated in detail. There God is thanked for his great works, that is, for giving food to those who fear him and for keeping "his Covenant ever in mind," for giving precepts that "stand firm for ever and ever," for having "established his covenant for ever." Through this repeated assertion of the endurance of that covenant, its stability is conveyed. And since the just man is a constitutive part of the covenant, he is celebrated, in still another *hallel* psalm (112), as the chief beneficiary of endurance. The generous and upright man is one whose "justice stands forever," who "will be remembered forever," and, again, whose "justice stands forever."

God's work being eternal, it has to reflect the quality of being well designed, a quality always connected with endurance. That the maker of heaven and earth is also a designer of it is one of the shafts of light that pierce through the non-scientific hue of an apparent capriciousness in the Hebrew Bible. Something of that light appears, for instance, in Psalm 33. To be sure, the assertion that God's "designs shall stand forever and the plans of his heart from age to age" refers directly to God's actions in history, though in close connection with his world-making. But that world-making too is preceded by the statement that all of God's works are "to be trusted" (Ps 33:4 and 11). Clearly, the God in question is so far from being capricious as to deserve to be looked upon as supremely, infinitely wise. This is a further aspect of those godly grounds that underlie the biblical world view and give it features that far outweigh its irritatingly unscientific character.

---

[2] In mentioning that "after psalms had been sung they [Jesus and the apostles] left for the Mount of Olives," Matthew (26:30) and Mark (14:26) referred to the *hallel* psalms.

In fact, whenever that non-scientific hue is implicitly countered in the Bible, the context is usually a celebration of God's wisdom in designing the universe. Very learned and arcane disputes about the true status of that wisdom with respect to God[3] leave wholly intact the point that the cosmos produced by that wisdom has to display the rationality which is the purposeful coordination of parts. It is precisely on this point that the notion of wisdom in the Hebrew Bible stands apart from the wisdom celebrated in Babylonian and Egyptian literature, where it denotes skill in cult and, above all, in magic.[4]

In the famed passage of the Book of Proverbs (8:22-31) Wisdom is described as a craftsman who assisted God in the formation of all the main parts of that cosmic tent, with several references to the measurements without which there is no architectural craftsmanship. Wisdom was present "when he [God] marked out the vault over the face of the deep; when he made firm the skies above, when he fixed fast the foundations of the earth; when he set for the sea its limit, so that the waters should not transgress his command" (8:27-29). Moreover, it is also stated that all that cosmic engineering was an act of intellectual delight, a sort of play, on the part of Wisdom. Primitive as that cosmic tent may appear to modern eyes, it has a hardly primitive quality because it is the work of God. This quality, which is another of those positive shafts of light, can be translated into physical features such as stability, coherence, regularity, and permanence.

Those features should seem especially remarkable against the background of repeated warnings by the Prophets about the eventual collapse of all cosmic structure on God's great judgment day. Of course, for the prophets that collapse was not a return to a chaotic state but the phase immediately preceding the establishment of a "new heaven and new earth," or the culmination of

---

[3] B. Vawter, "Prov. 8:22: Wisdom and Creation," *Journal of Biblical Literature* 99 (1980), pp. 205-216.

[4] See J. L. Crenshaw, *Old Testament Wisdom: An Introduction* (Atlanta: John Knox Press, 1981), p. 212, and, of course, the standard work by W. G. Lambert, *Babylonian Wisdom Literature* (Oxford: Clarendon Press, 1960).

God's always purposeful plan. This is implied even when God's eternal permanence is given as the backdrop against which the stability of the cosmic order appears to be bordering on a state of decay: "They [the heaven and the earth] will all wear out like a garment. You will change them like clothes that are changed. But you neither change, nor have an end" (Ps 102:27-28). In the prophets such vistas of the eventual passing away of the present physical order are tied to an eschatological view of a restoration of all to a state, the new heaven and new earth, which in stability and beauty would immensely surpass those qualities displayed in the present physical world.

Stable nature, secure salvation
No wonder that the view of an eventual decay of the present stability of the world and the dictum about the infinitely superior quality of God's permanence do not undermine a most significant religious use of the stability given by God to the actual physical world. Indeed that stability is assumed to be so obvious to the human mind as to be used as a proof that the same stability characterizes also God's plan of salvation. Being parts of a Psalm, quite widespread had to be familiarity with the words: "Your word, O Lord, forever stands firm in the heavens: your truth lasts from age to age, like the earth you created. By your decree it endures to this day, for all things serve you" (Ps 119:89-91).

These verses could not fail to shape minds and hearts far beyond their immediate significance, which may seem today to cut both ways. Taken by themselves they could be seen to undercut their message about a stable, consistent order of things by tying that consistency to a seemingly literal fixity of the earth. But those verses clearly had a dynamic ruled not so much by the apparent physical fixity of the earth, but by the decree which could only give consistent commands much broader in potential meaning than what was immediately perceived. That broader meaning is conveyed whenever the same Psalm celebrates the unchangeable, perennial validity of God's commands: "The justice of your will is eternal; . . . long I have known that your will is established forever; . . . your word is founded on truth, your decrees are eternal" (Ps 118:144, 152, 160). In view of this it is possible to see beyond the fixity of the stars, as announced in Psalm 148, and all the more so because that fixity is tied to a "law which shall not pass away."

This insistence on the unchangeability of the divine will and its decrees is not, however, without close ties to nature even in Psalm 118 itself, a fact especially remarkable in view of the preoccupation there with legal observances. Only if reference to nature's unchangeability was something very natural to make, can one understand the sudden appearance there of the lines: "Your truth lasts from age to age, like the earth you created" (Ps 119:90). In other words, it was very biblical to consider the fixity and stability of the natural order as a starting point to illustrate, indeed from which to infer, the unchangeability of God's moral or legal decrees.

Clearly, there has to be more to the stability of the earth, the moon, and the sun than what primitively could be assumed when it can be used to support confidence in the stability of God's spiritual designs. A case in point is Psalm 72, where the permanence of the rule of the Messianic King is asserted in terms of the sun's and moon's endurance and with an eye on the impossibility that the moon should fail (Ps 72:5, 7, 17). That David's, that is, the Messiah's throne would last is stated in Psalm 89 with an eye on the stability of the natural order: "I will establish his dynasty forever, make his throne as lasting as the heavens. . . . In my sight his throne is like the sun; like the moon, it shall endure forever, a faithful witness in the sky" (Ps 89:30, 37-38).

Being in all likelihood of Davidic origin, Psalms 72 and 89 may seem to be tainted, on at least a cursory look, by the optimism generated by the rapid rise of David's throne. But it is precisely in view of one of his major setbacks that David invokes in Psalm 89 nature's stability as established by God to stir up faith in the unshakable certainty of the Covenant which God made with him. Moreover, if upheavals of sacred history could seriously shake that confidence based on nature's stability, the trauma of the Exile would have certainly achieved this. Yet exactly the opposite happened. Jeremiah finds no more effective way of stirring up the faith of the exiled in the unfailing character of God's promise about their eventual return than in an appeal to the unfailing workings of nature!

Those workings are, of course, the effect of an eternal decree of God, which has to be the case if God's relation to nature is a covenant. It is the unfailing character of God's covenant with nature which Jeremiah takes for an assurance that God's covenant with his people would not fail: "If you can break my covenant with day, and my covenant with night, so that day and night no longer alternate in sequence, then can my covenant with my servant David also be broken . . ." (Jer 33:20-21). The same reasoning is immediately repeated, though with an explicit assertion that the covenant with nature is a law, strongly evocative of a law of nature: "When I have no covenant with day and night, and have given no laws to heaven and earth, then too will I reject the descendants of Jacob and of my servant David" (Jer 33:25-26).

That the rather modern meaning of laws of nature is near on hand is recognized by all those biblical scholars who render Jeremiah's account of God's direct involvement in nature as issuing in "natural laws": "Thus says the Lord, He who gives the sun to light the day, moon and stars to light the night; who stirs up the sea till its waves roar, whose name is Lord of hosts: If ever these natural laws give way in spite of me, says the Lord, then shall the race of Israel cease as a nation before me forever" (Jer 31:35-36).

Such a projection of the idea of natural laws or laws of nature into the Bible will surprise only those who are unaware of an important factor in the development of that idea. The factor is that many moderns projected their own agnostic or pantheistic philosophies into science. This was particularly the case during the nineteenth century when the laws of mechanistic physics were taken for a priori verities. But with the demise of that

physics, those philosophies proved to be insufficient to secure
objective meaning to the laws of nature. As a result thinking
about those laws often degenerated into taking them for convenient coordinations of data of observation. Neither of these
extreme forms of the laws of nature can be found in the Bible.
For the God of the Bible is an infinitely faithful, therefore
consistent (rational) Creator who, by creating, lets entities thus
produced share something of those qualities. Thus creation is an
imposition of regularity as well, in a manner akin to the enacting
of a law. It is therefore unbiblical to say, and especially while
discussing biblical miracles, that "the concept of nature and
natural laws is foreign to the religious literature of the Bible."[5]
Such a statement runs counter to a number of biblical passages,
among them, most conspicuously, the reference to the making
(by divine command) of the sun, moon, and stars: they were
"fixed forever," because God "gave [them] a law which shall not
pass away" (Ps 148:6).

Such a biblically stated natural order, without which neither
scientific laws nor miracles (biblical or not) make any sense,
underlies Jeremiah's argument. His is a conviction that man can
know with certitude that there is a high degree of regularity and
stability in nature, qualities that evidence God's very existence.
In fact, those qualities support the demonstrative strength of the
"magnalia Dei," or God's momentous interventions, such as the
plagues against Egypt, the crossing of the Red Sea, etc. Those
interventions are not invoked first whenever reference is made to
nature's witness about the existence of God. Invariably, nature's
witness is celebrated first before attention is turned to those
"magnalia." The declaration that "the heavens declare the glory
of God and the firmament proclaims his handiwork" and similar
references to nature's workings in Psalm 19 precede there the

[5] Y. Zakovitch, "Miracle OT" in *The Anchor Bible Dictionary* vol. 4. K-N (New York:
Doubleday, 1982), pp. 846. Such scepticism about the presence of the idea of laws of
nature in the Bible goes together with the claim that any unusual natural phenomenon, as indistinguishable from a miracle properly so-called, can function there as a
sign of God's intentions. See on this also p. 178 below.

encomium of the Law's ordinances bearing on salvation. Several other psalms are indeed structured on the same sequence.[6]

Nature and mind

What is on hand, thereby, in the Bible is plain natural theology, the contentions of Barth and his disciples notwithstanding. Not that the Bible would contain a treatise on natural theology, let alone a knock-out demonstration of the existence of God. Those who composed the Bible knew all too well about that human frailty for which proofs, however demonstrative, often fail to be convincing. Indeed, the entire Bible is, in a sense, about the difference between a proof or demonstration (either by reasoning or by deeds), however valid, and their concretely convincing character. While the latter can be vitiated by resistance to plain evidence, the evidence itself retains its validity.

That plainness of evidence is in turn resting on plain direct knowledge of reality. Such a knowledge alone translates itself into recitals that everywhere are marked with keen attention to concrete graphic details. 1 and 2 Samuel abound in such recitals too well known to be recalled in detail. Suffice to mention David's sparing of Saul, Joab's murder of Abner, Uriah's refusal to play into David's hands, Ittai's cursing of David, the list of provisions brought by Shobi to David's troops, the manner in which Absalom's death was announced to David, and the circumstances of the pestilence consequent upon his ordering a census.

From 1 and 2 Kings, it should be enough to recall details of the Temple building as well as the particulars of the furnishing of its interior; of Solomon's chariots and concubines; the sacrifice of the priests of Baal and of Elijah; the murder of Naboth; Naaman's healing; the assassination of Jezebel; the Temple repairs by Jehoash; the list of places of false worship destroyed by Josiah. Last but not least, there is that concluding chapter of

---

[6] Thus, for instance, Psalms 24, 33, 94, 95 and 136. For further details, see my article, "The Universe in the Bible and in Modern Science," in *Ex Auditu*, vol. III (1987), pp. 137-47.

2 Kings, with its gripping details of the destruction of Jerusalem and the two deportations.

Try as one may to read mere mythical imagination into a number of other stories in those four books, the recitals just listed will not fail to witness to the realism of the Hebrew mind. It was a mind fully aware of the fact that to know all those real details, it did not need to be strengthened by a special revelation. They could be known through direct evidence. Such a mind, if any philosophical label is to be put on it, was not idealist, nor pragmatist, not even empiricist. It was plainly realist, and in a metaphysical sense, because it was convinced about the mind's ability to go far beyond mere empirical or sensory evidence. Indeed, all too often, God, or some quality of God, is the target which is to be reached by that ability. Moreover, time and again, there is a subtle scientific touch present.

To see this it is enough to ponder the mental dynamics behind the phrase that God's "greatness cannot be measured" (Ps 145:3) and that "his wisdom can never be measured" either (Ps 147:5), or that one has to praise God's "surpassing greatness" (Ps 150:2). Such a dynamics has a philosophical vitality which is genuinely metaphysical, because it takes one beyond that physical which is always measurable. It makes no difference whether that dynamics is executed in sophisticatedly articulated steps or not. In both cases the naturally metaphysical ability of the mind is at play.

Actually, one may wonder whether any of the Greek philosophical poets, or philosophers in their poetical moods, could have shown a more genuinely philosophical touch than the author of Psalm 139. That Psalm proves that the Hebrew mind found nothing contrary to its genius in celebrating divine omniscience about man both in graphically metaphorical and in unmistakably philosophical terms. In Psalm 139 metaphorical is the darkness which is not dark for God and the night which for God is as clear as the day. Metaphor is still on hand in reference to God's eyes that see all human actions, but philosophy makes a grand entrance with what follows: "Every one of my days was decreed before one of them came into being." And no Greek reasoning about God could have transcended philosophically the lines: "To me how mysterious your thoughts, the sum of them not to be numbered!" Modern mathematical speculations about transfinite numbers do not have the clarity of what follows in that Psalm: "If I count them, they are more than the sand, to finish, I must be eternal like you" (Ps 139:16-18).

More remarkable still is the fact that these statements about God's infinite knowledge are not voiced in the form of a special revelation from God. While God can declare his own eternity, and in the form of a divine oath, "To the heavens I raise my hand and swear; as surely as I live forever . . .!" (Dt 32:40), man can voice the same as something very clear to his own reasoning. A case in point is the declaration that unlike clothes that are changed and are changing, "You [God] are the same, and your years have no end" (Ps 102:28).

Yet, although these evidences of a realist metaphysics in the Hebrew thinking should be easy to spot, scholarly status has been accorded to books in which the Hebrew and the Greek way of thinking are set up in radical opposition to one another.[7] The results are at times stupefying, such as in *Hebrew Thought Compared with Greek* by Thorlief Boman.[8] Since thought is always expressed in language, Boman had to insist that Hebrew was "a language exceptionally unusual in our experience and to our manner of thinking."[9] The trouble with this related to the word "our." Whatever it meant to denote, it did not fit the experience of leading linguists. In fact, it was the study of African, Asian, and American languages that made it clear to a prominent

---

[7] While this dichotomy is affirmed by D. B. Macdonald in his *The Hebrew Philosophical Genius: a Vindication* (New York: Russell & Russell, 1965), he also attributes some philosophical insights to the Hebrew mind. Only the philosophy is not specified.

[8] A translation (London: SCM Press, 1960) from the 2nd German edition, *Das hebräische Denken im Vergleich mit dem Griechischen* (1954).

[9] Ibid., p. 27.

linguist that "Hebrew is by no means extremely divergent from a European point of view."[10]

Fortunately, Boman unfolded some such consequences of his own claim that amply reveal its fatuity. Thus after trying to prove that, unlike the Greeks, the Hebrews of old "offered no visual image of a man, a building, or an object," Boman found it most surprising that they did so with respect to the world. Of course, after putting the Greek and the Hebrew thought in mutually irreducible categories (static versus dynamic, space versus time, etc.), Boman had to declare that the Hebrew image of the world is visual only in appearance. Consequently he had to insist that, for instance, the "windows" (Is 24:18, 2 Kings 7:2, Mal 3:10) and "doors" (Ps 78:23) of the sky are religious notions. According to him those "windows" and "doors" are not physically real and visualizable because in each case God opens them.[11]

The confusion which is caused by such a preconceived approach to plain texts is preceded by Boman's assertion that "the creation of the world is a historical event; thus it does not belong to any sort of natural (scientific) category. It represents no primitive explanation of the world (i.e. cosmogony); it is the

---

[10] H. A. Gleason, Jr., "Some Contributions of Linguistics to Biblical Studies," *Hartford Quarterly* 4/1 (1963-64), p. 52.

[11] Boman, *Hebrew Thought Compared with Greek*, p. 177. Such is the very extreme of disregarding plain natural reality whenever one obeys the logic of the claim that Hebrew thinking is radically "religious" as opposed to viewing the world scientifically, that is, as being causally connected in its parts. Protection against such extremes demands much more than giving mere lip service to ontology as done, for instance, by L. Gilkey in his "Cosmology, Ontology, and the Travail of Biblical Language," *Journal of Religion* 41 (1961), pp. 194-205. Nor is the remedy really on hand through the acknowledgment, as made by J. Barr in his *Biblical Faith and Natural Theology* (Oxford: Clarendon Press, 1993), that there is genuine natural knowledge (and therefore naturally religious knowledge, including natural theology) in the Hebrew Bible. It merely points in the right direction to note, as Barr does, that the syntactical structure of biblical Hebrew is far from being so different from the "rational" Greek as is often claimed. What is needed is an honest facing up to the dictates of a realist epistemology and the metaphysics based on it, as absolutely indispensable in interpreting the Scriptures, whether Hebrew or Greek.

beginning of history."[12] But not only is the creation of all never a subject matter of science, creation cannot even be part of history, although it makes history possible. Apart from this, it remains to be shown that anything religious can be said about the world, the *all*, or about anything at all, unless it exists in the first place. Or should we say that the Bible imposes on its devout readers the duty to espouse the trickery of putting the cart before the horse?

Similar, though more directly exegetical, problems arise as Boman, motivated by the same exaggerated opposition between Greek and Hebrew thought, further asserts: "The idea that God created the world became known only in later times; it is not an axiom of the Old Testament but a conclusion drawn from it. The creation of the world by God, in the Old Testament, is not an absolute fact important in itself; rather creation is thought of as the inauguration of history."[13]

However, if such were the case, the learned rabbis, who composed Genesis 1, failed to understand themselves as they put Genesis 1 at the head of the Scriptures. It must have been all too clear to them that, compared with the "historical" character of the second creation story (Gen 2:4-3:24) and the patriarchal narratives, Genesis 1 is very "ahistorical." Indeed, Genesis 1 has resisted all attempts to see in it a cosmic history along patterns which science keeps unfolding. Nor did Genesis 1 cease to strike one with its systematic and matter-of-fact diction, a far cry from the style of myths.

The realism of Genesis 1

The "ahistorical" and "unscientific" character of Genesis 1 reveals much about the philosophical acumen of the Hebrew mind. This is all the more significant because Genesis 1 is a religious document above all. Philosophy has nothing to do with the observance of the sabbath, the very point Genesis 1 is largely

[12] Ibid., p. 172.
[13] Ibid.

about.[14] But considerations germane to metaphysical realism are subtly present in the device whereby God is cast in the role of a worker in order to underline the importance of the sabbath observance.

To cast God in the role of a worker who rests on the seventh day must have had very strong motivation behind it. And since Genesis 1 is, on stylistic grounds alone, a patently post-Exilic document, that motivation is not difficult to find. The trauma of the Exile had made the sabbath rest a central proposition in reconstructing Jewish identity. Genesis 1 was meant to function as a special help in promoting compliance with God's plan of salvation in which specific ordinances played a pivotal role. Next to circumcision, the sabbath-rest was supreme in importance in that respect. Otherwise Nehemiah would not, in the concluding chapter of his book, have warned against infractions of the sabbath-rest with a reference to the destruction of Jerusalem as punishment for past infractions of that kind. The nine mentions of the sabbath in a mere eight verses (Neh 13:15-22) make that section a startling document of the responsibility which the people had in keeping alive the Covenant by observing a specific ordinance.

Of course, the setting up of God as such a role model imposed on the redactor of Genesis 1 important obligations. God was to be pictured with an absolute superiority over his raw material. He indeed produces everything with a mere command and does it with consummate perfection (implied in the repeated assertions that what he made was good and indeed very good). Further, he was to be pictured as working without the slightest trace of effort or fatigue. God could not be portrayed as toiling, however unobtrusively, as he does in Psalm 104 where he stretches out the heavens or in Psalm 95 where he shapes the dry land with his own hands. As the highest model of those who work, he makes everything by mere commands. Such a God can be said to rest on the seventh day, without suggesting exhaustion

---

[14] See my article, "The Sabbath Rest of the Maker of All," *The Asbury Theological Journal* 50 (Spring 1995), pp. 37-49.

on his part. Quite a contrast to the resting (not on a seventh day) of the gods of Babylon who obtain respite only by making humans, so many slaves destined to cater to their needs and whims.

Most importantly, God is assigned the supreme job, the only job compatible with his status. The object of his work has to be the *all* or the universe. That the *all* is indeed the object of the work assigned to God is voiced at the very start of Genesis 1 through the statement that in the beginning he made "the heaven and the earth." The expression "heaven and earth" is but one of the many cases when, in the Bible, the idea of *all* is conveyed through the rhetorical device of *totum per partes*.[15] The making of *all* is conveyed again by the work of the second and third days: the production of the ceiling (firmament) and the floor (earth) of the cosmic tent reasserts the making of the whole in terms of its main parts. The work of the fourth and fifth days conveys the same message in terms of the main particulars of the main parts of the whole. Thus the technique of stating the whole in terms of the main parts (*totum per partes*) is repeated three times, the classic biblical stylistic device of making the point emphatically, namely, that the *all* is indeed the only suitable target of God's work. This threefold repetition of the production, by God, of the *all* is in Genesis 1 a backbone that lends itself to a graphic representation, as shown in the opposite page. Finally, it is the *all* as made by God that justifies his being portrayed as taking a rest on the seventh day, acting thereby as a role model for the sabbath observance.

Appreciation of the fact that the thrust of God's creative work is the *all*, might, if properly appreciated, have served as a powerful antidote against the ever present lure of setting up a concordance between Genesis 1 and the science of the day. For already in the days of Aristotelian and Ptolemaic geocentrism it should have been clear that what could be said scientifically about the whole, or the cosmos, was much less convincing than

---

[15] See my *Genesis 1 through the Ages* (cited in note 2 to the Introduction), p. 288.

In the beginning God made the totality
(heaven and earth)

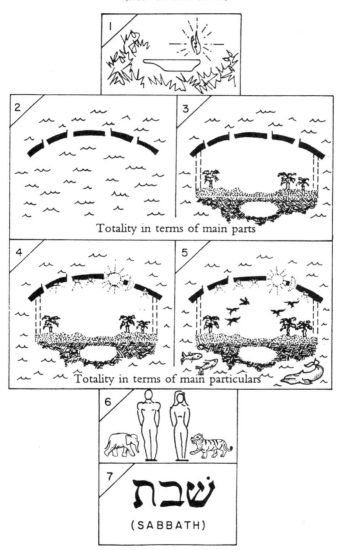

Totality in terms of main parts

Totality in terms of main particulars

(SABBATH)

propositions about the countless details in it. Contrary to ingrained clichés, Newtonian science failed as a cosmology, regardless of its superb handling of a vast variety of gravitational phenomena. It is still to be generally perceived that Einsteinian cosmology (whatever its stunning ability to cope with cosmic details, such as the bending of starlight and the advance of the perihelion of planets) has not coralled that true *all*, which is Cosmos, writ large. Quantum cosmology is no less incompetent about the Cosmos as such and for a reason that derives from the very nature of scientific demonstrations and therefore affects science as such—past, present, and future.[16] It was therefore all the more regrettable that so many bright exegetes yielded to the lure of concordism, which is the hapless effort of setting up a harmony between details of Genesis 1 and scientific details about the evolution of the cosmos. The effort, that maintains itself with an almost blind resolve, has not ceased bringing discredit to the Bible. The latter is not served any better by the present fashionable trend whose protagonists take the story of Genesis 1 for a myth.

The first stage of that sinister resolve can be seen in the interpretation which the great Hellenistic Jewish scholar, Philo of Alexandria, gave of Genesis 1. The Church Fathers followed suit in trying to make it appear that the cosmos and cosmogenesis of Genesis 1 closely parallel the data of Greek science and astronomy. The Scholastics, with Thomas Aquinas in the van, claimed a concordance to exist between Genesis 1 and Aristotle's physics. This mistaken approach was vigorously cultivated by exegetes of the Counter-Reformation and quickly assimilated by Protestants, who, for obvious reasons, could not live with Luther's and Calvin's precepts, to be discussed later, concerning Genesis 1. The nineteenth century, during which concordism became a rule of the exegesis of Genesis 1, produced only blind alleys, both for faith and for science. Much the same is true of latter-day efforts that look to Genesis 1 for an anticipation of Big Bang cosmology.

[16] See my book, *Is there a Universe?* (Liverpool: Liverpool University Press, 1993).

Had Christians resisted the temptation of trying to make Genesis 1 (and the Bible) look respectable by giving it a scientific aura, the story of the interpretations of Genesis 1 would not have become a dismal story indeed.

But to return to Genesis 1 proper. Its principal stylistic device, *totum per partes*, often occurs in the Bible. Examples are the expressions "the little and the great," "low and high," "rich and poor," "the just and the wicked," "summer and winter," "evening, morning, and noon." They all reveal some kind of totality. All movements are meant by "coming and going," all postures by "to walk and to lie down." Psalm 148 is palpably structured on the device of stating the whole by listing its main parts. Thus the essential meaning of that Psalm would be safeguarded by condensing it into the phrase: In the heavens everybody and everything, on the earth everything and everybody praise the Lord!

There is, however, much more in the Hebrew Bible about the *all* (a philosophical notion most worthy of the mind, Hebrew or other) than what is conveyed by various forms of that rhetorical device. That the expression "heaven and earth" means cosmic totality, and not merely the sky and the dry land is, of course, an old truth, but like all genuine truths this too has depths worth probing. For insofar as the expression, "heaven and earth," means *all*, the expression shares in the semantic dynamics which *khol* (all) displays in the Bible. Indeed, Psalms 33 and 145 may seem to be composed to unfold the full range of that dynamics. They make little sense unless the various uses in them of *all* are allowed to be means whereby one is carried beyond an *all* actually known and ever knowable to man.

This dynamic takes on a special expressiveness when human reasoning is caught in utter dependence on God. Job must have meant much more than the particular examples set forth in God's speech to him, when he surrendered with the words: "I know that you can do *all* things" (Jb 42:2). Much earlier, Hannah's praise of an *all*-knowing God (1Sm 2:3) testified to the presence of that mental dynamics among ordinary people. In face of a humanly hopeless undertaking, Esther turns for help to that God who knows *all* things. She echoes a more articulate supplication of Mordecai of whom it would be patently wrong to assume that he did not look beyond the visible sky as he cast his and his people's lot with God's omnipotence: "You made heaven and earth and every wonderful thing under the heavens. You are Lord of *all*, and there is no one who can resist you, Lord. You know *all* things!" (Esther C:4-5). In view of all these "Hebrew" examples, very Hebrew should seem the words (preserved only in Greek) with which Susanna attests her innocence: "O eternal God, you know what is hidden and are aware of *all* things before they come to be" (Dn 13:42). She seems indeed to echo the words of Psalm 139, to be quoted shortly.

This dynamic mental grasp by both the learned and the simple of an *all* far beyond human enumeration witnesses the eminently philosophical, that is, metaphysical, acumen of the human mind. But in the case of the Hebrews that acumen rested on grounds that, in addition to being human, were godly as well. Such is, above all, the insistence in Genesis 1 that the *all* made by God is good, and indeed very good. That goodness meant much more than, say, the stability of an edifice. It carried the broader meaning which is celebrated, for instance, in Psalm 136, where the assertion of God's goodness is introductory to the repeated assertion that "his great love is without end."[17]

That God does indeed love and can in turn be loved is that most godly ground upon which rests the Hebrew (biblical) understanding of the world. It is a ground that sets that understanding wholly apart from the Babylonian as well as the Egyptian world views, although in its grasp of purely physical details it does not differ from them. There is still to be found a clay tablet to the effect that man is *loved* by any of the deities comprising the Babylonian or the Egyptian pantheon, or by any of the countless Baals of the Canaanites, and that therefore man

---

[17] In the preceding Psalm 135 the two ideas are joined in the call: "Praise the Lord for the Lord is good. Sing a psalm to his name for he is loving." Many other examples could be quoted from the Psalms alone.

has to love them. Moreover, that biblical understanding of the world, as rooted in God's love for his creatures, is the supreme protection against the temptation to assume that behind the all too numerous physical and moral catastrophes there is an evil principle equal in dignity and power to God.

The barring of such a principle (another aspect of the absolute sovereignty of God) assures that nothing can, in independence of him, influence any event or process in heaven or on earth. Hence the emphatic warning against fortune-tellers and diviners of all sorts (Dt 18:10-12), and against astrologers in particular (Jer 14:14 and Ez 13:6-7), as so many abominations that cannot be tolerated among the people of God. Such warnings set apart the biblical lore from any other lore, a separation particularly evident in the struggle against idolatry.

One should, of course, be on guard against ascribing that uniqueness to some "national" character or genius of the Hebrews of old. Once a dearth of true prophets left them to their own natural devices, such as during the long reign of Manassah, the Hebrews of old readily fell prey to the lure of divination and astrology.[18] Resistance to that lure had for its source a prompting or inspiration that was not so much national as biblical, that is, supernatural. So much in way of a corrective to Schiaparelli's admiring words: "It is no small honour for this nation to have been wise enough to see the inanity of all . . . forms of divination. . . . Of what other ancient civilized nation could as much be said?"[19]

Such an admiration is not complete, especially on the part of a man of science, if it does not include the recognition that the biblical struggle against astrology and idolatry completed a basis on which alone it was possible to see nature as divested of capricious forces. For only if the material realm, or nature, and

---

[18] As stated in 2 Chr 33:5-6, Manassah "built altars to the whole host of heaven in the two courts of the Lord's house" and practiced "augury, divination and magic" to the point of letting the lawful ceremonies fall into oblivion.

[19] G. V. Schiaparelli, *Astronomy in the Old Testament* (Oxford: Clarendon Press, 1905), p. 52. See also E. Walter Maunder, *Astronomy in the Bible* (3rd ed.: London: Hodder and Stoughton, 1909), p. 146.

especially its heavenly region, was thought to be free of such forces could man ever presume that he was superior to matter at least in the sense of being able to investigate the forces working within it without continually assuring, by magic, their coopera- tion. The godly grounds were indeed fundamentally useful for the prospects of science.

Those grounds had other aspects as well, aspects decisive for the future of science. One such aspect, which related to the prophets' insistence on the unfailing character of God's work in salvation history, became indeed invested with an eternal significance. This is why scepticism and subjectivism, which deeply penetrated the religious and philosophical writings of the Greeks, failed to make inroads into the Bible. This is why the Hebrew mind could raise itself to the heights of a metaphysics embodied in genuine natural theology. This is why the Hebrew mind, insofar as it was biblically oriented, perceived an absolute beginning and an absolute end, the two being connected with an essentially linear process. That the sacred texts available to Nehemiah or Ezra contained this linear perspective made it all the easier for them to introduce the canonical books with a chapter where the first statement is about a "beginning" and the last is about the absolute end symbolized by God's rest. Since this biblical or linear perspective of all events, human and cosmic, proved itself to be of crucial importance concerning the relation of the Bible and science, it is imperative that a close consideration be given to that perspective.

3

Eternal Horizons

Linear breakout from the circular

The impossibility of counting or measuring God's eternity has time and again for its backdrop the assertion, again as if it were obvious to the mind, that the world had a beginning: "Before the mountains were begotten and the earth and the world were brought forth, from everlasting to everlasting you are God" (Ps 90:2). Hardly less widely known to the Hebrew mind than these passages from the Psalms were the lines from Proverbs about the divine wisdom, as anterior to the beginning of everything else: Wisdom was brought forth "while as yet the earth and the fields were not made nor the first clods of the world." Wisdom was already at work "when he [God] established the heavens, . . . when he marked out the vault over the face of the deep, . . . when he set for the sea its limit" (Pr 8:26-29). The learned rabbi, who after the Exile composed Genesis 1, merely gave a pregnant form to the temporality of everything as he began that memorable chapter with the words: "In the beginning God made the heaven and the earth [everything]."

It would, of course, be rather unscriptural to use those phrases (including the expression, "in the beginning [*bereshit*]"), as a means for deciding the argument whether man can demonstrate the doctrine of creation in time. The phrases in question evidence, however, a clear awareness in the Hebrew mind, insofar as it was a monotheistically religious mind (which it was not necessarily either then or now in the case of each Jew), that there was a cosmic beginning for the *all* or the universe.

Inseparable from that absolute beginning is the idea of an absolute end, or the "new heaven and new earth," celebrated by the Prophets in particular. Connecting those two termini is God's plan of salvation which no opposition, be it the failings of his people or the onslaughts of external forces sent as God's punishment for those failings, can derail from its course. Herein lies the ground for characterizing the Bible's idea of the overall historical and cosmic process as a straight arrow.

If there is anything radically alien to thinking as evidenced in the Bible, it is the notion of eternal recurrence.[1] That notion determined the cosmic world view in all ancient cultures and dominated even their view of human history.[2] While the Bible contains a world chronology from the days of creation, the Egyptians of old restarted their calendar with each dynasty, in subtle indication of their thinking being governed by cyclic patterns that culminate in the idea of eternal recurrence.

The annual Akitu festival in Babylon was a gripping expression of a similar distrust in the linear flow of time.[3] The week-long frenzy and orgy that set the tone of that festival stood for a symbolic

[1] The phrase from Ecclesiastes, "What now is has already been; what is to be, already is" (3:15), is not as much as a momentary endorsement of eternal recurrence. Rather, as shown by its immediate context, it conveys the belief that nothing is futile in God's plan either about man or about the world, because "whatever God does will endure forever; there is no adding to it, or taking from it. . . . and God restores what would otherwise be displaced (3:14 and 15). But was not a sense of futility fueled by the specter of eternal recurrence?

[2] Concerning ancient India, China, pre-Columbian America, Egypt, Babylon, and Greece, see chapters 1-6 in my *Science and Creation: From Eternal Cycles to an Oscillating Universe* (1974; 2d enlarged edition, Edinburgh: Scottish Academic Press, 1986). It is beside the point that in dealing with relatively short spans of time, such as the Persian and Pelopponnesian wars, neither Herodotus nor Thucydides give a glimpse of eternal recurrence. Polybius, who deals with the entire history of Rome, finds, as a Greek, solace in the idea of cyclic destiny: Rome, too, will see its power eventually decline, for such is the fate of everything. As to Greek philosophers, who had to be more speculative than Greek historians, they can be classed in two groups according to whether they believed in endless individual recurrence or only in the endless recurrence of types or classes of beings.

[3] See my *Science and Creation*, pp. 95-96. Strangely, there is no reference to that festival in W. G. Lambert, "History and the Gods: A Review Article," *Orientalia* 39 (1970), pp. 170-77, where linearity is assigned to the relation of Babylonian gods to human history. The same is true of Lambert's "Destiny and Divine Intervention in Babylon and Israel" in *The Witness of Tradition*, the text of papers read at the joint British-Dutch Old Testament Conference held at Woudschoten, 1970. (Leiden: A. J. Brill, 1972), pp. 65-72.

immersion of the catastrophic collapse that threatened a world of which Marduk was merely the shaper but not the Creator.[4] That *Enuma elish,* the confused Babylonian creation story, was read aloud during that festival, witnessing to the sense in which Babylonians of old took that story. The festival revealed much of the pessimism that naturally arose in every culture dominated by the idea of eternal recurrence. In ancient India that idea often took the form of an explicitly eternal treadmill. Wherever that view became dominating, ubiquitous was the use of the *swastika,* a consummate symbol of eternal returns. Ironically, the word etymologically means "well-being," the very opposite to that despondency which is invariably generated by the fatalistic prospect of endless repetitions of the same.

In this age of cultural relativism and religious ecumenism it may not be popular to stress the despondent tone which exudes from the great literary and philosophical documents of ancient China, India, Egypt, Babylon, and Greece. But the record is there, and any perspicacious reader will notice a tone strikingly different from the hope that prevails in the pages of the Hebrew Bible. That hope is at the least a steely conviction that, in spite of all calamities and trials, God's plan will prevail.

Whatever there is borrowed in the Hebrew Bible from Egyptian and Babylonian lore, it is not that hope. This is all the more significant because the borrowing was enormous. The vastness of Egyptian elements in the Hebrew Bible made it possible for a Freud to imagine that Moses himself was an Egyptian. Equally of Egyptian origin was, according to Freud, the monotheism which Moses tried to graft onto a people that Freud therefore had to picture as a Canaanite tribe.[5] So numerous in the Mosaic legislation are the laws that echo word for word lines

---

[4] A point curiously missed by S. G. F. Brandon in *Creation Legends of the Ancient Near East* (London: Hodder and Stoughton, 1963), who downplays, for instance, the differences between creation by mere *fiat* as given in Genesis 1 and in Egyptian and Babylonian creation stories, respectively. See especially pp. 37 and 150.

[5] S. Freud, *Moses and Monotheism*, tr. K. Jones (London: The Hogarth Press and the Institute of Psycho-Analysis, 1939).

from the famed Code of Hamurabi that Freud could just as well
have tried to set up Moses as Hamurabi's resentful great-grand-
son, driven by an atavistic Oedipus complex. Yet entirely missing
in that Code is, for instance, the idea of the sabbath rest.[6]

Whatever art and architecture the Hebrews had, they
borrowed it from their neighbors. The Temple of Solomon was
built by talent imported from Tyre and Sidon. Some of the most
charming Hebrew poems (Psalm 104, for instance) echo Egyptian
lines. But when it comes to essential content and thrust, the
Hebrew Bible stands apart, and certainly does so with its linear
view of history, covenantal and cosmic. That view is based on the
trust that both covenantal and cosmic history will not, in spite of
everything else, be deprived of their promised destiny and are
therefore equally coherent.

Only a Western world already in short supply of that trust
could fail to appreciate that difference when it stumbled upon
the cuneiform tablets of Babylon. This is why much applause
greeted efforts to see in *Enumah elish* a pattern for Genesis 1, even
though no two compositions could have appeared more different,
despite the fact that in some sense both dealt with the same topic.
The same happened after the story of Gilgamesh was deciphered
and taken for the pattern of Job's story. In looking back on the
verbal   obfuscations   practiced   in   the   school,   called
panbabylonianism, the latter may best be viewed as a Babel of
intellectual panic. It was a panic born in the cultural masochism
of modern Western man trying to sever himself from his biblical
heritage.

Those who composed the Hebrew Bible displayed a remarkable ability to separate the genuine from the spurious whenever
they borrowed from Babylonian and Egyptian lore. And they
certainly did not borrow that animism which was the hallmark of
the world view in ancient Egypt. There, in an even more gro-
tesque way than was the case in ancient India and China, the
world was imagined to be an organism, living as a whole and in

---

[6] See my article, "The Sabbath Rest of the Maker of All," quoted above in note 14
to the preceding Chapter.

all its parts.[7] Compared with the crassness of those organismic and animistic world views, in which everything was ultimately capricious, biblical animation of various parts of nature never have a similar connotation. If parts of nature are occasionally animated in the Bible, this is done only to express their utter subjection to God. Thus the heavens rejoice, the earth is glad, all within the sea thunder praise, all the trees of the wood shout for joy (Ps 96:11-12)—but only to express a subjection of theirs which, because it is total, is also joyful. The same is true of similar poetical references to the rivers' clapping their hands and the mountains' shouting with joy (Ps 98:7-8).

Nowhere in the Bible does that personification result in attributing to any parts of nature a volition whereby they could set their course as they will. Nor does the Bible justify a view within which nature lets man commune with it in a pantheistic sense, or (to allow for modernity) in a sense evocative of a living earth as imagined by champions of Gaia.

Efforts to graft, under the pressure of ecological awareness, such an ideology onto the Bible will not succeed in making the graft hold. A far more treacherous and persistent pressure of organismic world views had failed to penetrate the Bible as it was in the making over so many centuries. Enormous indeed should seem the measure of success of the ancient Hebrews to keep essentially intact their non-organismic religious view of the world from powerful neighboring influences. Much of the credit goes to a chain of individuals, called prophets, who, for the most part, did not succeed one another. Some of the greatest of them seem to have come from nowhere and left no notable successors behind. Their sequence is unparalleled in ancient religious history, partly because they did not plan to form a chain.

They were the ones to insist that whatever the extent of human frailty, the Covenant would not go under, though only because God is utterly faithful in his promises and therefore his plan cannot fail. This is the uniform message of the prophets

---

[7] For details, see ch. 4 in my *Science and Creation*.

through six or seven turbulent centuries. The same message was turned into individual and communal testimonies in the Psalms. Yahweh's mercy and promise are believed to triumph over the sins of individuals and their various misfortunes as well as over catastrophes and betrayals involving the nation. Whatever the uncertainties of history, there will always be a Remnant because Yahweh's plan remains unshakable.

To see the relevance of this for science, one need merely realize a markedly non-scientific facet of human experience and predicament. Man's thinking is far more riveted on his experiences with history, individual and communal, than on his encounters with the physical world. Contrary to the claims of modern scientistic gurus, the securities and comforts which science delivered in modern times did not lessen the overriding primacy of the historic experience over the scientific. In fact, the tools delivered by science greatly contributed to keeping history what it has been at all times, a very tragic affair for most human beings. Modern political and cultural history bears out fully what can be gathered from the documents that survive from the millennia immediately following man's prehistory: they form a dark background against the confidence generated by biblical salvation history.

Resisting Hellenism

Prophecy ceased, however, once the Return from Captivity had been consolidated. After that those within the Covenant were much more intent, in line with Nehemiah's instructions, on relying on their own spiritual heritage rather than enrich it with borrowings from the outside. One can only guess the extent to which Nehemiah and Ezra realized that liberation from the cultural cauldron of Babylon would merely be followed by an exposure to the even more alluring cultural threat of Greek and Hellenistic civilization.

Hellenistic culture put particularly heavy pressure on Jews living in diaspora, however close to Judea. Yet the Book of Sirach, written in Alexandria, is remarkably free of borrowing in its passages about nature where Hellenistic learning, or science, for that matter, could have most readily made itself felt. Reflection on already existing Hebrew sacred texts was enough to hold high, in terms of a "measured wisdom" and "accurate knowledge," the wisdom evident in God's creation: "When at the first God created his works and, as he made them, assigned their tasks, he ordered for all time what they were to do and their domains from generation to generation" (Sir 16:23-25). And, of course, the injunction of Genesis 1 given to man whom God created "from the earth," made "in his own image," and "makes him return to earth again" is enlarged upon in what almost immediately follows: "He endows man with a strength of his own and with power over all things else on earth. He puts the fear of him in all flesh, and gives him rule over beasts and birds" (Sir 17:3-4). And immediately, as if to emphasize even more the Hebraic provenance of all this, the topic turns to man's principal task to choose between good and evil and fulfill, by obeying the commandments, "the everlasting covenant" between him and God.

Equally biblical is the other major passage in Sirach about nature where God is praised as the Creator. Of course, that "the works of the Lord are all of them good," can imply more than a basically moral goodness. But in the context moral goodness is meant insofar as God's workings of nature are praised, because "in its own time every need is supplied" and, above all, man's needs in more than a purely physical sense. As in the Psalms and in Job, God's supreme power and direct involvement are praised and the point is made that, because God knows all, there is no "cause to say: What is then the purpose of this?" For "everything is chosen to satisfy a need" (Sir 39:16-21).

Indeed, the purpose is dominated by a moral perspective. Undisturbed harvesting of wheat as well as abundance of honey, milk, wine, oil, and cloth are God's rewards for righteous conduct. Storms are winds whipped up by him to punish evil acts. Clearly, not the regularity of nature, but appropriate time for moral punishment is meant by the "proper time" for which

God keeps in his storehouse "fire and hail, famine and disease." This moral purposefulness involves "ravenous beasts, scorpions, vipers" as tools whereby God implements his moral retribution: "In doing his bidding they rejoice, in their assignments they disobey not his command." It is within this patently non-scientific outlook that the goodness of all of God's work is reasserted (Sir 39:31-35). Of course, the idea of the ontological goodness, that is, non-chaotic orderliness (or goodness for scientific purposes) of all material things is fully compatible with that moral goodness; still, that idea is not to be looked for in this context.

More directly germane for scientific considerations is the lengthy recall of God's works in nature in chapters 42 and 43. There the moral considerations yield to an intellectual admiration of God's wisdom and power. Nature must be assumed to be fully rational if it is true that "the Most High possesses all knowledge, and sees from of old the things that are to come. . . . No understanding does he lack; no single thing escapes him. Perennial is his almighty wisdom" (Sir 42:20-21). The witness which nature brings to God's wisdom is so overwhelming that "even to the spark and the fleeting vision" all his works must look beautiful. They together constitute a fully coordinated whole, the universe, which "lives and abides forever; to meet each need, each creature is preserved" (Sir 42:24).

Particular mention is made of the clear vault of the sky, of the orb of the sun, of the moon which marks the changing times, of the stars adorning the heavens and their utter regularity, and of the majestic sight of the rainbow as so many examples of God's wisdom. When it comes to lightning, storms, wind, and snow, God once more appears as directly involved. There is little there which man can hope to understand. Man's mind is said to be "baffled by the snow's steady fall." The succession of scorching heat and refreshing rain is no less God's plan than the action whereby he "calms the deep and plants the islands in the sea." As to man the seafarer, he is overcome by the variety and size of monsters in the ocean and therefore bows before God's greatness:

"Awful, indeed, is the Lord's majesty, and wonderful is his power." Not only can he himself not be seen, but there are many things hidden beyond what are visible: "Only a few of his works we have seen."

In all this there is no science, not even a direct encouragement to make reflections that indirectly may promote scientific investigation of phenomena. That at least Solomon penetrated much of the workings of nature is stated in the Book of Wisdom, but only generalities are offered there about what he had learned. Written as it was by a Jew in the large Jewish community of Alexandria, the center of all learning (including Jewish learning) in Hellenistic times, it may be that the author was reflecting on his own connection with the Museum there, the great storehouse of information in Hellenistic Antiquity. The style is distinctly Greek as he states, in the person of Solomon, that God's wisdom gave him "sound knowledge of all things" so that he "might know the organization of the universe and the force of its elements." Greek astronomical learning echoes through reference to "the beginning and the end and the midpoint of times, the changes in the sun's course and the variation of the seasons, cycles of years, positions of the stars." Then, after a shorter list of sublunary matters, there follows the general conclusion: "Such things as are hidden I learned and such as are plain; for Wisdom, the artificer of all, taught me" (Wis 7:17-21).

Yet a little later this optimistic, if not slightly boastful, tone yields to despondency about the mind's being weighed down by the body and, in view of the meagerness of what we learn about things on earth, by our practically total ignorance about what goes on in the heavens. Moreover, all this preoccupation with knowledge should seem insignificant in comparison with the kind of knowledge that really counts. The latter is about that special Providence whose object is the People of the Covenant and which was particularly manifest during the Exodus. Water punished the Egyptians, but benefited the Jews. Manna rained down on the Jews, but plagues visited the Egyptians. The Jews were led by a pillar of fire, while the Egyptians were afflicted with darkness. The Jews were spared that which hit the Egyptians hardest: the death of their first-born.

It is, however, in this context, so removed from anything scientific, that one comes across a phrase to which exegetes do not seem to have given proper justice. In speaking of the animals (vermin) that punished the Egyptians, the author of the Book of Wisdom points out that God could have sent "new-created, wrathful, unknown beasts, to breathe forth fiery breath, or pour out roaring smoke, or flash terrible sparks from their eyes." Not only the mere appearance of them would have completely destroyed the Egyptians, but God could have eliminated them "with a single blast" (Wis 11:18-19). But God did not resort to such drastic action because, even as he unleashes his awesome punishments, he shows the moderation of his mercy. To illustrate this moderation, the author departs from the dramatic style of the context by resorting to a phrase almost impersonally mathematical: "But you have disposed everything according to measure and number and weight" (Wis 11:20).

That in running the dramatic course of history God uses moderation in a "quantitative" way may appear strange if the context had dealt with history alone. But immediately attention is called to the fact that God's moderation cannot mean the absence of strength. To illustrate God's strength attention is shifted from salvation history to the cosmic perspective of the creation of the universe: "Indeed before you the whole universe is as a grain from a balance or a drop of morning dew come down upon the earth." Clearly, the "everything" in that foregoing phrase includes that cosmic perspective where the physical universe as such looms large. This is all the more the case as the section about the possible creation of unimaginable beasts begins with the argument that precisely because God's "almighty hand fashioned the universe from formless matter" (Wis 11:17), he was not without means or ability to produce such beasts as well.

In fact, that cosmic perspective remains strong in the rest of that section, which contains several uses of *all* to denote cosmic totality in immediate proximity to references to God's dealing with human affairs: "But you have mercy on *all*, because you can do *all* things; and you overlook the sins of men that they may repent, for you love *all* things that are and loathe nothing that you have made, for what you hated, you would not have fashioned." The cosmic perspective has a depth which is unmistakably ontological: "And how could a thing remain, unless you willed it, or be preserved, had it not been called forth by you" (Wis 11:22-26).

It would therefore do grave injustice to the entire context to downplay the significance of that phrase because it is philosophical and not eschatological in character. Not exegesis but anti-philosophical presuppositions underlie von Rad's lame apology for that phrase: "On one occasion—thinking about the punishment of the Egyptians—the author admits, 'You have arranged everything by measure, number and weight'. This shows once again how familiar this idea was to the thinking of the age. One cannot, however, say that the author's presentation of history was colored by it. It is rather an incidental argument."[8] In view of the cosmological perspective of the context, the presence of that phrase is not incidental at all.

One need not share von Rad's overemphasis of the eschatological or non-philosophical in order to play down the significance of that phrase. Major commentators on the Book of Wisdom did not find anything extraordinary in that phrase as they listed passages resembling it.[9] If not all three terms, at least two of them occur in Isaiah (40:12) with a distinctly cosmic bearing: "Who has held in a measure the dust of the earth, weighed the mountains in scales and the hills in a balance?" Similarly cosmic is the perspective of the passage in Job about the weighing of the winds and the making of rules for the rain (28:25-26).

In times postdating the composition of the Book of Wisdom one finds all three terms in IV Esdras (4:36), though less con-

---

[8] G. von Rad, *Wisdom in Israel*, p. 283 note.

[9] See C. Larcher, *Le livre de la Sagesse ou Sagesse de Salomon* (Paris: Librairie Lecoffre, 1985), vol. III, pp. 684-86.

cisely: God weighed the world in the balance, the times he measured, and the seasons he numbered. Philo seems to have directly quoted that phrase as he opposed Protagoras: "God and not the mind of man measures, weighs and numbers all things, and circumscribes them with bounds and limits."[10]

Similar passages from classical literature are neither numerous nor too impressive. Only in Plato's *Laws* do all three terms occur together, but with a political and not a cosmological relevance. Indeed, Plato frowns on the equality of "measure, number, [and] weight" which can be achieved in any society by the lot, as being inferior to "the true and best equality." Such is one of Plato's ways of expressing his contempt for the democratic idea with its numerical leveling of any and all.[11] This is not to say that Plato had not impressed classical antiquity with his ideas in the *Timaeus* about the quantitative ordering of all matter in the cosmos and with his dictum that God keeps counting. It was indeed the Platonist and not the Aristotelian tradition that encouraged the cultivation of mathematics and geometry and even the kind of skill with machinery that culminated in the famed contraptions of Archimedes. But none of the great mathematicians and geometers of Greece produced a phrase similar in its conciseness to that phrase in the Book of Wisdom. Could not then such a phrase, with its cosmological bearing, eventually make an impact far greater than its author would have imagined?

For the author of the Book of Wisdom could hardly even imagine the answer which was to come fairly soon to his immediate and principal concern, namely, the fate of the just who were victimized by the wicked. Not that his perspective had not extended far beyond that gloomy state in Sheol, the most that the Hebrew Bible allowed concerning a possible individual survival

---

[10] Philo, *De somnio* II. 26. I am quoting from J. Reider, *The Book of Wisdom: an English translation with Introduction and Commentary* (New York: Harper and Brothers, 1957), p. 146.

[11] Plato, *Laws* VI, 757B. See *The Collected Dialogues of Plato*, ed. E. Hamilton and H. Cairns (New York: Random House, 1963), p. 1337.

beyond death. A state diffused with the radiance of genuine peace is conjured up in the Book of Wisdom as its argument about unfailing divine Providence begins: "The souls of the just are in the hand of God, and no torment shall touch them. They seemed, in the view of the foolish, to be dead; and their passing away was thought an affliction and their going from us utter destruction, but they are in peace. . . . Chastised a little, they shall be greatly blessed, because God tried them and found them worthy of himself" (Wis 3:1-5).

To be in peace, and in the kind of peace assured by being in the hands of God, witnesses a belief in personal immortality riveted in a personal union with a very unique God. The author of the Book of Wisdom does not offer a union with Plato's idea of Goodness, nor with Aristotle's Prime Mover, or rather Prime Motion. The union in question is that of a personal soul with a personal God. If on this point the author of the Book of Wisdom could keep a distinctly biblical perspective, he can be assumed to be thinking in an equally biblical framework even when using the very Greek formula of "formless matter" out of which God shaped the world, as noted above.

In fact Plato's memorable use of that formula in the *Timaeus* provides a most convincing backdrop for showing the very different, or non-Greek, thinking of the author of the Book of Wisdom. The latter's use of that formula is part of his celebration of God's absolute power over all as he recounts the *magnalia Dei*, or God's interventions in nature. Not only are such interventions inconceivable for Plato, but Plato's god disdains even the erstwhile shaping of the world from a pre-existing "formless matter." That job is left to a mere underling, the *demiourgos*. Therefore the use of "formless matter" in the Book of Wisdom is an implicit resistance to Greek thought and should be seen as something akin to the *tohu vabohu* in Genesis 1, where the absolute power of God is reaffirmed, as was seen, in thematic steps, over everything and therefore also over the chaos.

Indeed, the biblical thinking was strong enough even for an explicit confrontation with Greek pantheism for which formless matter, eternally existing, was a standing or falling proposition. This is not the place to contend with those who dismiss the story, in the Second Book of Maccabees, of a heroic mother and her no less heroic seven sons as a poetic invention. It is for them to prove that the use of the number seven in a story necessarily puts it into the category of myth or fable. For even if the little exhortation which the mother addressed to the youngest of her seven sons is a literary elaboration, it at least documents the thinking of the author of the Book of Maccabees.

That author, undoubtedly a learned Jew in Alexandria, could not be unaware of Plato's doctrine of shapeless matter and of Aristotle's and other Greek philosophers' contempt for the idea of creation out of nothing. In rejecting this idea as absurd, the Greeks proved two things. One was that the idea could clearly emerge on the horizon of minds not aided by Revelation. The other was that in rejecting the idea as absurd the Greeks acted in conformity with their pantheism, the highest form of religion usually espoused by minds outside the biblical ambience.

The author of the Second Book of Maccabees merely unfolded the biblical doctrine about the absolute superiority of God over nature and of nature's total dependence on God as he made that heroic mother exhort her youngest or seventh son. She reminded him about his being called, by great promises of God to his people, not to break as much as a single Mosaic Law. The upshot of the exhortation is that martyred bodies will be brought to resurrection by a God who has the power to make everything (the universe and mankind) "out of non-existing things" (2Mc 7:28).

Most significantly, this apparently very Greek phrase comes closely united to the reference to the time of mercy at the end of times that will witness the mutual reunion of all who served God faithfully, an idea wholly un-Greek. Further, in the statements of the six elder brothers one finds united such very biblical themes as faith in the Creator of all, his unfailingly just retribution, and the impossibility that he should forsake his chosen ones; that is, his plan of salvation. Most importantly, the seventh son voices the belief that martyrdom has its immediate, personal, eternal reward: "My brothers, after enduring brief pain, have drunk of never-failing life, under God's covenant" (2Mc 7:36). No science here, and nothing to look for by scientists for whom matter and motion, or the world here and now, alone exist. What is on hand is an unabashedly otherworldly perspective within which alone the Covenant makes sense in an all too often senseless existence. The suggestion that such a perspective provided the spark for the only viable birth of science may seem perplexing and all the more so as it is emphatically embedded in the completion of the Covenant.

The Covenant's completion
In speaking of the New Covenant as the completion of God's covenant with man, often not enough attention is paid to its being steeped in the best of the Old. That best included belief in resurrection, a belief widely shared by the Jews of Christ's time, with the exception of the Sadducees, who, in proof of their perennial modernity, prided themselves on representing cultural progress. The Pharisees were not, however, the heirs to the conviction, voiced by the youngest son of that heroic mother, that meritorious death means the immediate tasting of "never-failing life." For them earthly prosperity and satisfaction as rewards for a righteous life were as important as was belief in the resurrection of the just on the last day. For them it must have sounded utterly foolish on Christ's part to assure the good thief, agonizing as much as He did on the cross, that still on that very same day of their equally wretched bodily demise, he would be with Him in Paradise (Lk 23:43).

But this assurance was the culmination of Christ's teaching about the New Covenant. And just as Christ knew himself to be the fulfillment of God's unchanging plan and purpose, so was he seen in the Apostolic preaching. A most eloquent expression of this is the argument formulated by the author of the Letter to the Hebrews, intent as he was to stir up the confidence of those caught in great trials. He recalled God's oath to Abraham by which God wished "to give the heirs of his promise even clearer evidence that his purpose would not change, . . . so that by two things that are unchangeable, in which he could not lie, we . . . might be strongly encouraged to seize the hope which is placed before us." This hope, so the argument proceeds, is now anchored in heaven itself, into which "Jesus . . . has entered on our behalf, being made high priest forever" (Heb 6:17-20).

Christian martyrs drew their courage from that assurance. It made them hold, in conformity with Christ's words, that nothing profits a man if he gains the whole world but in the process he puts at risk his eternal salvation (Mk 8:36-37). This fully otherworldly perspective sets the tone of Christ's two great sermons, of which one, the Sermon on the Mount, with its eight somber beatitudes, marks the beginning of his teaching mission. The other great sermon of his, the one on the final judgment, brings that mission to a close. It is a sermon full of social consciousness, though with nothing socialistic or even humanistic about it. He did not conjure up earthly rewards for feeding the poor and clothing the naked. He offered for reward only an eternal union with him.

Otherworldly he was to the hilt. He extolled the life to come as having a value compared with which everything else in this world was of no more significance than something to be devoured by moths or eaten up by rust (Mt 6:19-20). This otherworldly character of Christ's preaching and of the Apostolic catechesis admits no compromise. Far more than the Old Testament, the New Testament shows no concern that could be described as scientific.

Scientific concern would at the least imply readiness to put ideas and facts on record. Yet, as far as the record goes, Christ does not seem to have ever suggested that his disciples record what they had seen and heard. The full authority he gave them to preach in his name could be taken for a commission to write with full authority. Yet, they never preached with authority on the basis that they had already written with that authority which is divine inspiration. Christ's own apparent disinterest in putting his teaching in writing should seem all the more surprising as his disciples recorded time and again his mastery of the Scriptures[12] and his fondness for referring to them as having witnessed about him.[13] Again, as will be seen later, his disciples, although they quoted the Scriptures as having prophesied about him,[14] did not seem to have been embroiled in the task of deciding which books about him (some of which they authored) could be trusted.

Christ, who did not urge his disciples to do science in the general sense of doing some writing, certainly did not inspire them to do science in any specific way. He did not urge his hearers to develop further the art of predicting the weather as he referred to the physical portent of winds blowing from the south and of clouds rising in the west. Rather he denounced those who stifled a similar predictive ability in themselves to read "the present time," that is, a special divine presence (Lk 13:54-55). He spoke in the same unscientific vein about human ability to perceive the nearness of summer by looking at the leaves of the fig tree (Mk 13:28). In recommending the industriousness of those who invested well the money entrusted to them, he extolled otherworldly perspectives. His praises of the divine Providence that unfailingly clothes the lilies of the field almost sounded as if the cares of this world could be ignored in caring for the world to come. In speaking of the growth of seeds or of the action of yeast, he showed himself observant of the obvious, without the slightest hint that he thereby wanted to inculcate a study of the lawfulness of the processes of nature.[15]

In all this he merely assumed that the lawfulness in question was obvious to his disciples. He assumed that as ones imbued

---

[12] Most notably when he reduced his opponents to silence by his interpretation of the Messianic Psalm 110.

[13] Already at the very start of his ministry in the synagogue of Nazareth.

[14] In various passages of the opening chapters of the Acts.

[15] See on this my article, "Christ and Science," *The Downside Review* 110 (April 1992), pp. 110-130. The statement of the Anglican Archbishop, William Temple, that "Jesus of Nazareth taught men to see the operation of God in the regular and normal—in the rising of the sun, the falling of the rain, the growth of the seed into the plant" (*Nature, Man and God* [London: Macmillan, 1940], p. 46), is clearly misleading.

with the Psalms (and of other parts of the Old Testament), they took the "heaven and earth" for the work of God, a Father in the highest sense. It was not the first part of the Lord's prayer, which began with a reference to the Father in heaven, that sounded novel to the Twelve, but the second half which contained the law of divine forgiveness. His own prayer, "Father, Lord of heaven and earth, to you I offer praise . . . " (Mt 11-25), began with voicing the plain truth about the Father's supreme lordship over everything, the basis of all biblical doctrine about creation.

That he assumed in such a matter-of-fact way that for his audience it was most natural to see beyond "heaven and earth" the Father of all, is, however, of enormous significance. Only by overlooking this is it possible to make the sweeping statement that "the religion preached by Christ and understood by the apostles and the early church *depends entirely upon* history."[16] Had such been the case, Paul would have hardly begun his speech on the Areopagus and his letter to the Romans with an emphatic reference to the witness of nature about the Creator of all. More on this shortly.

Precisely because Christ could assume in his disciples a vivid awareness of that witness, He could disparage the "heaven and earth" that, unlike his words, would pass away (Mt 24:25). In the vein of all prophets he too forecast the eventual falling of the moon, the sun, and the stars out of their places in the sky (Mt 24:29). If not to those steeped in Old-Testament perspectives, at least to all pagans conditioned in the worship of the cosmos, those words of his had to appear a supreme blasphemy, not only religious but intellectual as well.

All educated persons of classical antiquity could sense blasphemy in the special status which John accorded to Christ by calling him the "only son," or *monogenes* (Jn 1:18). The latter term,

---

[16] So stated Gregory Dix in his *Jew and Greek: A Study in the Primitive Church* (Westminster: Dacre Press, 1953), p. 5, in a context in which he extends to early ecclesial times the opposition between Hebrew and Greek thought. Several well-known passages from the writings of the Apostolic Fathers, to say nothing of some statements of Saint Paul, run counter to Dix's statement.

soon to be further hallowed by ecclesial usage, was one which in classical paganism emphatically denoted the universe (*kosmos*) as the only-begotten emanation from the divine principle. Plato, Plutarch, and Cicero were among the notables who spoke in this vein.[17] To all those reared on the reading of their works, acceptance of the emphasis put by John on Christ as the only-begotten meant therefore a fundamental challenge to their thinking about the universe. Educated converts to Christianity had to demote in their thinking the universe from a divine rank to the rank of a mere creature. Actually, the universe could thereby genuinely rise to the level where its parts and its entirety formed a proper object for science, without being entangled in the unscientific inspirations and aspirations of pantheism.

The difference brought about by this new look at the universe could seem almost non-existent from a superficially theological viewpoint. In Cicero's *De natura deorum* there are passages that in some ways are very similar to Paul's declaration that the contemplation of the visible universe reveals "invisible realities, God's eternal power and divinity" (Rom 1:20). Paul, who made similar statements elsewhere (Acts 17:24-29; 1 Cor 1:21) could hardly consider alien to his thinking the statement, with which he undoubtedly was familiar, in the Book of Wisdom that "from the greatness and the beauty of created things their original author, by analogy, is seen" (13:5). But while Cicero had in mind a Creator not different from the universe, in the Christian or biblical view the two were radically distinct. Had this not been the case with Paul, he would not have, in a matter-of-fact way, voiced the doctrine of creation out of nothing in speaking of Abraham's faith in God, a God "who restores the dead to life and calls into being those things which had not been" (Rm 4:17).

Paul's statement certainly asserts the kind of distinctness between God and universe that entails a total ontological dependence of the universe on the Creator. Such a dependence logically implies the idea of a creation out of nothing, regardless

---

[17] The principal classical texts are quoted in Kittel, under *monogenes*.

of whether in time or not.[18] As such an entity, the universe must therefore have features of dependence in a far deeper sense than the features whereby ordinary artifacts bespeak their craftsmen. Only within that biblical perspective of total ontological dependence on a true Creator (a being that embodies truth in its infinite fullness), could the universe be a fact which is artful in the highest conceivable sense. The consequences of this for science were of decisive significance.

But to see the heuristics of those consequences one has to keep in mind that in Paul's statement a strictly supernatural proposition, the resurrection of the body, goes together with another proposition, creation out of nothing, which in principle can be discerned by the powers of the mind. They do so in conformity with many other instances in the Bible. Yet, while those propositions occur together, they do not undermine their respective status. They remain distinct without constituting an opposition. It is that subtle union of the natural and the supernatural that lies at the source of the impact which the Bible, as a *par excellence* reflection of authoritative Christian catechesis, was to have on the fate and fortunes of science.

---

[18] The force of that logic will satisfy those who do not identify philosophical truth with some technical formulation of it. This point, as will be seen in the next chapter, is of crucial importance for a proper evaluation of the Christian development of the idea of creation out of nothing.

II

THE ISSUE OF SCIENCE

4

Greeks, Science, and Christ

Greeks and Gnostics

The Bible, as was seen, embodies a very special view of the universe. The primary function of that view is, of course, religious, and in a sense that puts it apart from all other religious views of the universe. Indeed, only this biblical view of the universe had features that proved to be instrumental in the eventual rise of science. Such an outcome is part of the full meaning of the promise about the necessities of life: "Seek first his kingship over you, his way of holiness, and all these things will be given to you besides" (Mt 6:33). This did not suggest a slighting of industrious hard work in securing those necessities. Nor could it mean an exception to the manner in which the promises of God's Kingdom on earth were to materialize. The manner had to be similar to the quiet way in which the leaven works and to be as much devoid of spectacular displays as the coming of the Kingdom of God was stated to be (Lk 17:20). As with most prophecies, here too the steps of fulfillment can clearly be seen only in retrospect, but the case is no different for the historian who considers the progress of science.

Science was not, of course, spoken of when, in the context of debates touched off by Arius, that very special view of the universe unfolded for the first time something of its scientific potentialities. Neither Arius nor Athanasius nor anyone in their respective theological camps showed interest in science, which should not be surprising. Hellenistic culture, of which they were a part whatever its paganism, imposed on science too its distinctly pagan or pantheistic theology. A result was a heavy mixing of science with magic in general and of the science of astronomy with astrology. In the latter, the Church Fathers (it is enough to think of Saint Augustine) saw a major spiritual threat to Christian faith.

Science as known in the Hellenistic world fell far short of being a means that gave effective control over physical reality. At its best, or in Ptolemaic astronomy, ancient science made possible exact predictions of the position of planets. In Aristotle's biology, science could boast of no more than excellent observations and classifications. The art of mechanics was more of a technique than a science. Other branches of science were dominated by distinctly non-scientific features, even apart from superstition and magic. A chief responsibility for this lies with the overriding impact which Socrates had on Hellenic and Hellenistic culture. It was because of him that science too had become part of a cultural, that is, cultic concern, though with disastrous consequences for a genuinely scientific understanding of the world.

For Socrates was much more than an incisive critic of the intellectual presuppositions of the fashionable views of his contemporaries, especially of the Sophists. By calmly drinking the hemlock, Socrates showed that he truly believed in what he argued in the *Phaedo*. The argument was that adherence to moral principles made sense only if the individual soul had an eternal destiny. Securing that destiny through a righteous life was, according to Socrates, the means of making sense of human existence, of assuring its very purpose. He might have just as well summed it all up by saying that all intellectual endeavor had to be subordinated to the task of "saving the purpose."

Socrates himself gave a glimpse in the *Phaedo* of what this meant for the scientific enterprise. He did so by claiming that the soul's avid search for abiding purpose could be rationally vindicated only if the motion of all physical bodies is seen to be done for a purpose. And since he saw that the mechanistic physics of the Ionians and of Anaxagoras excluded purpose from the physical world, he proposed the formulation of a physics in which all physical bodies were seen as trying to achieve through their motion what was the *best* for them. This thematic vitalization of the physical world fully restored the pre-Ionian organismic view of the universe, very much in evidence in Homer and Hesiod, and also reinforced its pantheistic component. Greek thought had thereby thematically realigned itself with the world view prevalent in all ancient cultures. In all of them the world was conceived as a huge organism and venerated as the supreme pantheistic being. Therein lay the reason for the stillbirth of science in all of them, an outcome particularly instructive in the Greek context.

To oppose the materialism, be it purely methodological, of the mechanistic physics of the Ionians and of Anaxagoras was one thing. It was another to cast doubt on that mechanistic approach. In sum, what Socrates achieved was to throw out the baby (the mechanistic approach to the mechanisms of nature) with the bathwater (the materialistic ideology grafted onto that approach).[1] In either case, the prospects of science suffered greatly, regardless of how much was made of optical and astronomical studies.

The first major proof of this came with that very Plato who forbade entry to the Academy to anyone unfamiliar with geometry. He began the *Timaeus* with setting the purpose of science to "save the phenomena" in terms of geometry. He ended the same work by describing the world in terms of a human organism in which all parts work for the good of the entire body. He also claimed, and most emphatically so, that the pursuit of the Good represented the highest conceivable aim. But motion toward that aim could not appear to be a motion along geometrical lines. Thus a convincing geometrical study of physical motions was not encouraged within the framework of "saving the phenomena." Moreover, Plato argued that only in the superlunary parts of the universe did bodies achieve their purpose. The sublunary part was in that respect a partial failure. In other words, the vitalization of the universe deprived it of a thorough, universally valid orderliness. In spite of his having

---

[1] See my article, "Socrates, or the Baby and the Bathwater," *Faith and Reason* 16 (1990), pp. 63-79.

reduced the four terrestrial elements (fire, air, water, earth) to geometrical figures, Plato was not led thereby to seeing in the terrestrial realm a domain of genuine order.

When interest in geometry was not particularly keen, as was the case with Aristotle, organismic and volitional considerations fully set the tone of scientific discourse. Every page of Aristotle's *Meteorologica* (or terrestrial and atmospheric physics) and many a page in his *On the Heavens* (astronomy and cosmology) are tainted with organismic considerations and at times with very crude ones. Needless to say, Aristotle took the heavenly spheres for something divine and held the universe to be the perfect ultimate being, not really distinct from the Prime Mover.

And even when interest in geometry was very keen, the geometrical (scientific) account of the heavenly motions went side by side with an animistic and astrological, as well as panthestic, interest in them. Thus Ptolemy composed not only the *Almagest*, but also an astrological compendium (*Tetrabiblos*) and still another work, *Planetary Hypotheses*. In the latter he accounted for the harmonious motion of the planets by comparing them to living beings (dancers and soldiers) well trained to execute their motions without bumping into one another. But they were divinely trained, on account of a divine nature attributed to them. Hence Ptolemy's opposition to the heliocentrism which Aristarchus of Samos proposed three hundred years earlier. To remove the earth from the center of the universe was, in Ptolemy's eyes, equivalent to disturbing an order proper to the divine nature of celestial bodies.

Animistic and organismic elements were not lacking even in the physics of the Stoics, who largely determined the cultural tone of thought in the first centuries of the Christian era. In other words, even in doing science, Hellenistic intellectuals tried to contribute to the Socratic task of "saving the purpose," a pantheistically religious or cultic and, in that sense, a cultural task. Such a task was very different from the task which Christianity aimed to achieve through its special way of assuring purpose to human existence. Herein lay a profound reason for

Christians of those times not to be interested in pursuits in which it was very difficult to separate the scientific from the non-scientific, and all too often very anti-scentific, elements.

At any rate, science was far from being a conspicuous feature of life in late antiquity. The number of those who did science was not large at all. Far fewer geometers are known to have existed during the first two centuries of Imperial Rome than during the two centuries prior to Euclid (fl. 300 B.C.). The vast majority of the educated were not at all interested even in that meager freedom which Plato's "to save the phenomena" could, in geometry and geometrical astronomy, secure from volitional and ethical concerns. They were interested above all in "saving the purpose," or achieving some hold on the meaning of existence, a distinctly religious and cultic objective.

Examples of this are the writings of Plutarch, Cicero, and Marcus Aurelius. They show no traces of scientific interest even in that restricted Platonic sense, while they are permeated with pantheistically existential concerns. It should not therefore be surprising that scholarly studies have not failed to register a decline of scientific interest during Hellenistic times. Still fully valid is the observation, now a century old, of Paul Tannery, the foremost student in his day of ancient Greek mathematics, that Greek science had lost its creativity by the time of Christ's birth.[2]

Christians, periodically driven underground prior to Constantine's reign, cannot therefore be blamed for that loss just because they too placed their religious concerns, centered on the meaning of existence, high above any other interest. The merits of their religious concerns should loom large today when so many people are adrift concerning their sense of purpose while being pampered by the wondrous amenities delivered by the latest in science and technology. Christianity had an appeal, then as now, only inasmuch as it held high the sense of purpose taught by Christ. The pivotal point of His teaching was that life

---

[2] P. Tannery, *La géométrie grecque* (Paris: Gauthier-Villars, 1887), pp. 10-11. Tannery was the first president of the International Congress on the History of Science.

really begins with one's death, the most trying test for an abiding sense of purpose. John the apostle gave the most animated echo of that point by repeatedly returning in his First Letter to the personal eternal life, which is the very essence of Christ's preaching and promise.[3] No concession there to the lame conjectures, voiced from Plato to Plotinus and beyond, about a nondescript impersonal immortality.

No wonder that eternally abiding personal purpose, as secured by belief in Christ in spite of bodily death, is the chief thrust of the few extant apologetical works written by Christians during the second century. But this focusing on death made sense only if the life leading to it was deserving of a life after death. Removing oneself into the desert, lest any worldly concern should interfere with one's preparation for eternal life, was far from being the only response. Most Christians had to remain in this world, though intent on not being of this world. A full century before the emancipation of Christians by Constantine's decree, Tertullian registered the full participation of Christians in all sorts of ordinary enterprises: "We [Christians] are," he warned the pagans in 197 A.D. in his *Apology*, "but of yesterday, and already we have filled all your world: cities, islands, fortresses, towns, marketplaces, the camp itself, tribes, companies, the palace, the senate, the forum. We left you nothing but your temples only."[4]

The really important intellectual defense which Christians had to work out was not so much aimed at pagans who were patently outside the fold as at those who claimed to be within, though they were not. Such were the gnostics and then the Arians, both with a program adverse to a genuinely supernatural Revelation. Confrontation with them greatly helped to articulate major characteristics of the Christian understanding of existence.

---

[3] Not satisfied by having stated this twice in his epistle (2:25 and 5:11), he concludes with the warning: "I have written this to you to make you realize that you possess eternal life" (5:13).

[4] Tertullian, *Apology*, ch. xxxvii; in *Anti-Nicene Fathers* (Grand Rapids, MI.: Wm. B. Eerdmans, 1980), vol. III, p. 45.

Reflection, however brief, on those characteristics, can show that they were indeed very useful for the eventual creation of an intellectual milieu germane to scientific interests and pursuits, and for a balanced perspective on the relation of the Bible to science.

To gain a first glimpse of those characteristics it is enough to turn to the major anti-gnostic writing of patristic times, Irenæus' *Against Heresies, or Detection and Overthrow of the Gnosis Falsely so-called.* Irenaeus, who suffered martyrdom as bishop of Lyons in 202, had those gnostics in mind who claimed to be in possession, through some interior illumination, of the right Christian doctrine (knowledge or gnosis) and not simply gnostics who claimed to possess only some form of philosophical knowledge. Thus the gnostics Irenæus had in mind were heretics, that is, Christian groups that had set themselves up in independence of communities gathered around the bishops as sources of proper Christian doctrine. This independence also manifested itself in the gnostics' use of inspired writings.

In battling them Irenæus had therefore to argue not only doctrinal points but also the question of what were the sources of genuine doctrine. He had to make clear that a large number of writings championed by the gnostics were not documents composed by the apostles. While explicitly rejecting false gospels, he quoted 625 times from the four genuine gospels. His strategy was all the more telling as by then most of the six gospels falsely ascribed to the apostles had already been in circulation. And so were ten other gospels that did not claim to be apostolic, half a dozen acts of various apostles, and about the same number of spurious apocalypses.

In insisting on the difference between genuine and spurious Scriptures, Irenæus enumerated various criteria with different values. One was the use of Scriptures in other churches about which he had remarkably wide information, covering all the Mediterranean. He could also claim to have had direct contact with those who knew some of those who had seen the Savior himself. But above all he held high the succession of bishops as the ultimate criterion of truth about everything that related to salvation. Their authoritative preaching would have sufficed even if "the Apostles themselves had not left us writings." Such was a daring supposition, but one that alone could bring out the basic logic of ecclesial reality. That logic was embodied in the living tradition which the Apostles "handed down to those to whom they did commit the Churches."[5] In full consistency with this Irenæus could argue that an error-free reading of the Scriptures depended on remaining attached to "those who are presbyters in the Church, among whom is the apostolic doctrine."[6]

By keeping in mind this role of authoritative teaching in the Church, one will understand that within the early Church even a high-level familiarity with the Scriptures did not encourage the principle of private interpretation. Hence the absence of acrimonious disputes about the list of canonical books. Irenæus was already dead when Origen produced the first list of books that were accepted everywhere by the local Churches. The list, as is well known, contained only 21 out of the 27 canonical books of the New Testament. While authoritative catechesis of the New Covenant had already been on hand in hallowed formulas (such as the Apostles' Creed), an exact listing of all the books of the New Testament was still to come.

All this is important to note in order not to misunderstand Irenæus' heavy reliance on the Scriptures as he argued against various aspects of pantheistic emanationism in which he rightly saw the very essence of false gnosis. This is not the place to recall in great detail the weird forms in which gnostics of all sorts imagined the production of the world. That production consisted in a continual cosmic begetting in line with the gnostics' crudely organismic and animistic views. Their emanationist doctrines ran counter to doctrines about Christ as formulated in the Gospel of John and in Paul's letters. For the gnostics Christ could not be the only-begotten in whom the Father created everything. Yet they

---

[5] Irenæus, *Against Heresies*, Book III, ch. 4. English translation in *The Anti-Nicene Fathers*, vol. I, p. 417.
[6] Ibid., Book IV, ch. xxxii, p. 506.

were busy twisting biblical passages indicating precisely that. In quoting John's words that "through him all things came into being, and apart from him nothing came to be" (Jn 1:3), Irenæus pressed what the expression "all things" implied: From *all* "no exception . . . is stated; but the Father made all things through Him, whether visible or invisible, objects of sense or of intelligence, temporal on account of a certain character given to them, or eternal."[7]

This insistence on the meaning of *all* reduced to the rank of mere creatures all things visible and invisible. Herein lay the ground for ultimately seeing all physical things, be they heavenly bodies, as being governed by the same laws. Also, emphasis on the *all* made no sense if the so-called "unformed matter," a mainstay of all Hellenic and Hellenistic philosophy and cosmology, had not been included in it. Herein lay a crucial difference between a genuinely Christian cosmogony and everything else, whether written by first-rate thinkers, such as Plato and Aristotle, or by a host of epigones, or plainly syncretistic thinkers, many of them gnostics.

The latter were, of course, of a great variety, with only a few of them voicing here and there orthodox doctrines. One of these was Basilides (fl. 125-140), apparently the first writer in early patristic times to speak of creation as a work whereby things were produced from what was not (*ek ouk ontos*). But almost simultaneously, the same expression was used by Aristides and Hermas, who certainly were not gnostics. A generation later, around 181 A.D., the variant *ek ouk onton* is prominent in *Ad Autolycum* of St. Theophilus of Antioch, and immediately afterwards in Irenaeus' work, whereas it failed to gain popularity among gnostics, even though Basilides was one of them.[8]

---

[7] Ibid., Book I, ch. xxii, p. 347.

[8] In his book, *Schöpfung aus dem Nichts* (1978), which has recently appeared in English translation by A. S. Worral under the title, *Creatio ex nihilo* (Edinburgh: T. & T. Clark, 1994), G. May admits that it is not possible to prove that Basilides had inspired in Aristides' *Apologia* (c. 140), and in Hermas' *Pastor* (c. 150) the statements that God made all things from "what did not exist" (*ek tou me ontos*). May did not explain why the gnostics failed to espouse Tertullian's phrase "*creatio de nihilo*,"

Irenæus' work, which, as noted above, is bursting with quotations from the Bible, is equally permeated with warnings about the primary role of the tradition handed down by the Apostles. No wonder that he stressed the primary importance of credal formulas as chief expressions of the authority of those who "have received with the succession of the episcopate, the sure charism of truth, according to the good pleasure of the Father."[9] Herein lay the reason, according to Irenaeus, for the remarkable endurance of true doctrine even among illiterate nations that have come into a Church which included, as he pointedly noted, countless tongues and tribes.[10] This emphasis on the authority of the magisterium vis-à-vis the Bible had, as will be seen, important consequences for the relation which the Bible was to have to science after the latter's real birth.

Irenæus prided himself on having been in contact with those, such as Polycarp, bishop of Smyrna, and others who had seen the last of the Apostles. It was the contact of a future martyr with great martyrs of the immediate past. Yet, it never occurred to Irenæus to trace the authority of the books of the New Testament to the martyrdom of those who composed them. What counted in the eyes of Irenæus was the authors' status as apostles, that is, ones, to recall the etymology of that word, who had been sent, in this case, by Christ. He sent the apostles with authority precisely because He claimed that all authority in heaven and on earth had been given to Him. That the apostles also suffered martyrdom was merely the consequence of the

---

whereas it was immediately recognized by Christian theologians as the most concise way of stating a basic truth about creation. May's principal contention is that the foregoing Greek and Latin expressions, cited in italics, introduced a significant departure from the biblical doctrine of creation, which, according to him, was non-philosophical. Underlying this contention is the claim, far from being proven, that philosophical knowledge is on hand only when technical terms of philosophy are also used. But May's claim itself implies that at least a part of philosophy is always pre-philosophical, because the technical status of a term always postdates its first usage.

[9] Irenæus, *Against Heresies*, Book, IV, ch. xxvi, p. 497.

[10] Ibid., Book, III, ch. iv, p. 417.

truth valid about all disciples, namely, that none of them could be greater than their master.[11]

Irenæus earned his martyr's crown in a major outburst of persecutions of which the third century witnessed three others. From those times on it became customary to recount the words which martyrs uttered when demanded to sacrifice to idols. The Acts of martyrs often bear witness to the primary role which credal formulas—in particular the phrases of the Apostles Creed— played in helping martyrs profess their faith.[12] That role was no less in evidence when the last of those persecutions, the one unleashed by Diocletian, took the books of the Bible as its special targets. In this book, of course, interest in that role relates to the impact it made on the relation of the Bible and science.

Christology and science

Following Constantine's victory the question arose as to what extent the Church, suddenly finding itself in the open dynamics of Hellenistic culture, was to become a part of it. To this question Arius proposed an answer, motivated as he was by the desire that Christians ought to be culturally correct. He felt that an accommodation could be achieved between the pagan world and

[11] This correlation is overlooked in the essay which W. R. Farmer, an evangelical, contributed to *The Formation of the New Testament Canon: An Ecumenical Approach* (New York: Paulist Press, 1983). Farmer took the martyrdom of the writers of the books of the New Testament for the source of their canonicity. The true position of Irenaeus is set forth in the other essay in that book, by D. M. Farkasfalvy, a Cistercian. Mr. Farmer has since become a Catholic.

[12] The hero of one such act is Crispina, of whom St. Augustine repeatedly spoke a century or so later as deserving the same admiration as St. Agnes and St. Thecla. On being requested by Anulinus, proconsul at Theveste (Tebessa), to obey the edict of the emperor and sacrifice to the gods, Crispina, a woman of rank from Thagara and the mother of several children, replied: "I observe an edict, but it is that of my Lord Jesus Christ." Upon being asked whether she would persist in her "foolish frame of mind" and face decapitation, she replied as if she were summarizing her catechetical instructions: "My God who is and who abides for ever ordered me to be born; it was he who gave me salvation through the saving waters of baptism: he is at my side, helping me, strenghtening his handmaid in all things so that she will not commit sacrilege." Quoted from "The Martyrdom of Saint Crispina" in *The Acts of the Christian Martyrs*, introduction, text and translation by H. Musurillo (Oxford: Clarendon Press, 1972), p. 307.

Christianity, and at a price that could seem nominal on a cursory look. What if Christ were to be spoken of as merely the super-eminent creature of God, though still a creature? It seemed to Arius, if one is allowed to reconstruct his strategy, that in this way harmony could be achieved between Christianity and the nobler parts of pagan religion.

Arius could hardly be unaware of Plotinus, a native of Alexandria, who died around 270, or shortly after Arius was born. To a superficial reader of Plotinus' *Enneads,* the cosmic system set forth there could appear monotheistic, with the One on top of a vast hierarchy of lower beings. But on a closer look those lower beings were not creatures but necessary emanations, generated with no beginning or end. There is no evidence that Arius tampered with the doctrine of creation in the beginning. That doctrine was too clearly enshrined in the very first verse of the Bible as well as in catechetical instruction. But Arius thought that better-grade pagans could perhaps be gained over to the idea of a once-and-for-all creation. A product, however super-eminent, of that creation would have been Christ himself, although Arius did not want to turn Christ into an emanation from the One. Arius was no gnostic, nor was he a Plotinian. He was, however, unduly exercized by the fact that for most pagans the doctrine about Christ, the only-begotten, the one equal with the Father, posed the great stumbling block.

If Christ were taken for the noblest and foremost of God's creations, a synthesis with the best in pagan religious culture would be on hand, so Arius seemed to think. Some of his followers fond of Plotinus might have thought that a created being, precisely if so eminent as the Christ of Arius, might invite a subtly emanationist reinterpretation. At any rate, Arius did his best to propagate his strategy of cultural synthesis with no small skill in public relations. Instead of theological arguments, he couched his theology in the seductive vagueness of songs. Being well written, they were quickly gobbled up by many unsus-pecting Christians, ready to be full-fledged members of a society in which at that time they were still very much a minority, perhaps no more than a tenth of it.

Theologically speaking, very treacherous was the use which Arius made of various biblical expressions relating to the Son. Arius and the Arians found it relatively easy to twist any of those expressions to fit their views of Christ.[13] There was only one expression, "of the same substance" (*homoousion* or *consubstantialis*) which allowed them no logical escape from the duty to come absolutely clean as to what they meant. The expression was not biblical, a fact of which the Arians tried to make the most in their efforts to discredit it. In vain did Athanasius argue his orthodox interpretation of all biblical terms relating to the Son. Without the term *homoousion* he might not have carried the day. This is a point which cannot be pondered enough by those who advocate a reliance on the Bible as severed from the authentic credal tradition.

The clash between Arius, the Arians, and semi-Arians on the one side and the orthodox party on the other has often been ridiculed as being a senseless dispute over a mere iota, the difference between *homoiousion* (similar in nature to God) and *homoousion* (of the same nature with God). It is, of course, useless to remind those scoffers about the principal concern of the orthodox party. As Athanasius put it concisely in the most memorable of all his treatises, *De incarnatione*, the culminating point of God's Covenant with man, the sacrificial death of Christ, would have had no infinite value, had it not been the death of God made man. For if Christ was merely a man, however exalted, the satisfaction his death earned for mankind's sins could not be of that infinite value that alone could offset the infinite offense which any sin means in reference to an infinitely holy God.

---

[13] On this subject the best treatment is still Newman's *Select Treatises of St. Athanasaius in Controversy with the Arians. Vol II. Being an Appendix of Illustrations* (London: Longmans, Green and Co., 1897). Newman shows that Arius' opponents fully demonstrated the impossibility of giving an Arian meaning to those terms without twisting their plain meaning again and again.

Of course, those scoffers would not have suspected that the value of the foregoing argument, on which hinged the outcome of the contest between the Arians and the orthodox party, would eventually be of crucial consequence for science. Nor did Athanasius guess anything of the sort as he defended the divinity of Christ, the only-begotten Logos, against the Arians. Still, in retrospect, so indispensable for the historian, one of Athanasius' arguments explicitly contained an outlook on the universe that made science possible.

The argument unfolded some implications of the assumption about the rationality of a truly divine Logos, that is, a Creator-Logos. For the Logos, or the Word, was that very Son about whom Saint Paul wrote that the Father created everything in him (Col 1:16). This was Paul's way of coordinating strict monotheism with the equality of the Son or Jesus with the Father, and asserting thereby the Son's divine status.

If, however, the Father, as Paul argued, created everything in the Son, it was most biblical for Athanasius to argue that the universe made by the divine Logos had to be fully rational. Athanasius was enough of a logician to see that this train of thought worked also in the opposite direction: Only the idea and reality of a fully rational universe enabled one to infer that its cause or origin had to be supremely rational, that it had to be a Logos in the strictly divine sense.[14]

To make this inference, a higher measure of cosmic harmony and rationality had to be assumed than could be gained from Greek and Roman authors. Athanasius had to reject, at least implicitly, a central claim of Plato and of Aristotle (and of the Stoics as well) that partial disorder ruled in the sublunary realm. To unfold in full the consequences of that rejection would have, of course, defied even Athanasius' grasp of the issue on hand.

One reason for this was that the pagan Greeks had emphatically attributed rationality to the universe, or else they would

---

[14] For texts and discussion, see my *The Savior of Science* (Washington: Regnery Gateway, 1988), pp. 76-79.

not have called it a cosmos, or something beautifully ordered. Their celebration of cosmic order could, then as now, easily distract from the fact that they restricted full rationality to the superlunary or heavenly regions of the universe while designating the sublunary realm as the realm of partial disorder. Yet no such restriction mars Athanasius' celebration of the full rationality and orderliness of the universe. This is not to suggest that he explicitly rejects the prevailing views that in the sublunary realm there can be no full orderliness. But his theological argument clearly bars him from exempting the sublunary realm from the sway of full orderliness. Just as foreign to his theological perspective was the classical Greek idea that God was neither free to create the world, nor free to create any kind of world as long as it was fully ordered or rational.

Last but not least, it would have been inconceivable within the orthodoxy Athanasius stood for to imagine that the Father did not have that supreme independence of and domination over the realm which he created out of nothing. By then the expression "creation out of nothing" (*creatio de nihilo*) had become a touchstone of Christian truth. Even today that expression is the only concise means to distinguish creation, as understood in the Old and especially in the New Testament, from an emanationism often couched in sophisticated philosophical and scientific parlance. Tellingly, the orthodox party led by Athanasius quickly became known as the party of *ekoukontoi,* a term derived from *ek ouk onton,* that is, the party of those who held things to have been created from what *did not exist,* that is, out of nothing.

Orthodox theology was not, of course, meant to produce science as if by magic. But in view of the stillbirths suffered by science in all ancient cultures, that theology should indeed be credited with having achieved something miraculous. By steering the mind towards assuming a full order where beforehand only a partial order was seen, orthodox theology had provided the basic conceptual matrix within which alone science could arise. Thus wherever Christian orthodoxy, and with it the right reading of the Bible, prevailed about the divinity of Christ, it was impossible to grant the kind of disorder which is the absence of cause, or the operation of mere chance, in physical processes. While this view of a fully ordered cosmos did not immediately spark the idea that the same set of laws operated throughout the universe, it was pointing in that scientifically indispensable direction.

In some rare cases, when scientific interest, hardly widespread in Hellenistic society, was very keen in a Christian, marvelous anticipations of the scientific future could occur. Such were the arguments of Philoponus (fl. A.D. 520) that the various colors of stars suggested that they were not of some divine matter but of the same type of matter which on earth produces flames of various colors.[15] The implication that celestial and terrestrial matter were subject to the same laws pointed toward the perspective within which the fall of an apple and the fall of the moon in its orbit were seen as obeying the same law of gravitation. Newton and the Newtonians owed much more to traditional Christian orthodoxy than they would have dared imagine. Some of them, including Newton himself, veered towards mere deism, while others, such as Halley, became ill-disguised atheists. In doing so they illustrated the proverbial success of parasites who refuse to make a consistent break with the organism on which they depend.

The surprise of erstwhile Newtonians might have turned into shock had they been informed that their chief pride, the idea of inertial motion (Newton's first law), also had origins in a Bible read in the light of Christian catechesis and credal formulas. That catechesis clearly implied that the world was not eternal. In support of this the phrase, "In the beginning," of Genesis 1 had been regularly quoted long before Philoponus anticipated the essence of inertial motion. The essentially non-inertial motion of everything as advocated by Aristotle and by all others throughout antiquity, including Ptolemy, was part and parcel of their

---

[15] It was not a coincidence that Philoponus was also a most spirited and articulate opponent of the pagan idea of the eternity of the world, especially as set forth by Proclus.

eternalism. On that basis alone, Philoponus' innovation must be seen as due to his having been thoroughly imbued with the idea of creation in time, which by his time had been a hallowed tenet of Christian catechetical instruction. Its decisiveness would stand out even more as science kept unfolding the lure it would exert on readers of the Bible.

5

The Lure of Science

Genesis 1 and science

The havoc which the lure of science could play in reading the Bible was already in evidence in Philoponus' case. For the plain truth is that not all of Philoponus' writings are an unmitigated pleasure to read with modern scientific eyes. Whatever his seminal exploitation of the meaning of "in the beginning," it is in his exegetical work on Genesis 1 that Philoponus sounds most unscientific time and again. No wonder. With respect to matters concretely scientific there was no catechetical guidance, which, after all, was not about how the heavens go but how to go to heaven. It was one thing to take to task Theodorus of Mopsuestia, one of only two patristic writers who took Genesis 1 for a proof that the earth was flat. It was another to see what Genesis 1 really tried to convey. Contrary to Philoponus, it was just not possible to read the spherical figure of the earth into that memorable chapter or into any other chapter of the Bible. But if, as Philoponus knew, one could know with certainty that the earth was spherical, what was one to make of the biblical flatness of the earth?

A very good resolution to that dilemma had already been on hand for over a hundred years in Augustine's great work, *De Genesi ad litteram*. There Augustine laid down the rule that whenever reason established with certainty this or that feature of the physical world, contrary statements of the Bible must be interpreted accordingly. One reason for obeying that rule was to prevent the Creed from being turned into a laughing stock for unbelievers, who, as Augustine stated, often happen to know "with absolute certainty and through experimental evidence about the earth, sky, and other elements of this world, about the motion, rotation, and even about the sizes and distances of stars, about certain defects [eclipses] of the sun and moon, about the cycles of years and epochs, about the nature of animals, fruits, stones, and the like."[1]

Augustine assigned indeed a very generous extent within which scientific knowledge could have absolute certainty. At the same time he allowed no range whatever within which there could be, about natural phenomena, a "Christian account" in opposition to what could be known by science. He viewed such accounts as "most deplorable and harmful, and to be avoided at any cost," because on hearing them the non-believer "could hardly hold his laughter on seeing, as the saying goes, the error rise sky-high."[2] Such was the context of Augustine's enunciating the principle of the unity of truth, a principle which has ever since been central to sound Christian theology and apologetics. There it is held that even God's revelation is not above the principle of contradiction and identity.

Those who would now say that it was far easier to state the principle of the unity of truth than to apply it with skill, would do well to recall a facet of Muslim theology. More than half a millennium after Augustine, Averroes and Avicenna held high the principle of double and even of triple truth: The highest form of truth is known only to philosophers (actually, to slavish followers of Aristotle as they themselves were). A lower form of truth is held by the clergy who voice the Koran. The lowest form of truth is left to the uneducated populace. Muslim mystics, such as al-Ashari and al-Ghazzali, championed a complete dichotomy between truths accessible to philosophical reason and truths channeled by inspired scriptures. In fact they denounced the former as the products of the insanity of philosophy.[3] Compared with them, Augustine's insistence on the unity of truth should

---

[1] *De genesi ad litteram*, Bk. 1, ch. 19.

[2] Ibid.

[3] For further details, see ch. 8 in my *Science and Creation: From Eternal Cycles to an Oscillating Universe* (1974; 2d enlarged edition: Edinburgh: Scottish Academic Press, 1986).

seem particularly incisive and valuable. He took seriously the affirmations of the Bible that God was the God of truth who would not deceive a human mind created to His very image.

So much for the merits of the principle of the unity of truth as enunciated by Augustine. To apply the principle in cases when the attainments of reason were not so much positive (such as in respect to the sphericity of the earth) but negative, or simply a matter of reasonable doubts, was an arduous task. Thus Augustine experienced great perplexity over the firmament as characterized in Genesis 1 and elsewhere in the Bible as a roof that separates the air from the upper waters that descend from there in the form of rain or clouds. For the fact that such a firmament, as distinct from the sphere of the fixed stars, was not found by astronomers did not mean that they would not eventually find it, and much less that it simply did not exist.

The positive truth that the earth was spherical was very different from the negative proposition that no one had yet found the firmament. In seeing that difference Augustine showed the good sense of logic. It was another matter whether it made good sense (exegetical or otherwise) on Augustine's part to take the biblical passages about the firmament at face value and start a baffling search for the firmament. He failed to see that astronomers had already disposed of the biblical firmament as a hard roof upon which rested a huge mass of water and clouds. Nor was the biblical firmament comparable to the ethereal spheres retained either in Aristotelian cosmology or in Ptolemaic astronomy. Whatever those crystalline (ethereal) spheres that carried the sun, the moon, and the other planets, they were very different from the biblical firmament, a point that had to be clear to any learned individual of Augustine's times.

Indeed, Augustine must have thought of this. Otherwise he would not have shown so much perplexity as he was searching for the biblical firmament in the Ptolemaic heaven. He did not sound convincing at all as he went as far as the orbit of Saturn to find it. Since astrology (at that time not really distinct from astronomy) assured him that Saturn was a cold star, he argued that a cold body would not fail to produce a vapory track as it moved in its orbit. He took that imaginary vapory band for the waters above the firmament and this was enough for him to be assured also about the existence of a firmament somewhere in the vicinity of that vapory layer. Augustine did not consider the question whether rain and clouds would come to the earth from a distance that had to appear enormous even to those unaware of estimates, in vogue since Ptolemy, about planetary distances in a geocentric universe.[4]

Augustine's search for the firmament should seem baffling. It certainly seemed to slight the very sound principle he had already laid down in respect to reconciling truths known by reason about the physical world with corresponding propositions in the Bible. But beyond that principle Augustine also laid down principles that even more profoundly witness his utter respect for reason. The one who went down in history as the most resolute champion of the primacy of grace in all meritorious acts, assigned a priority to reason with respect to faith as given by grace. He did this, first, by pointing out that unless "we had a rational soul, we could not believe." Secondly, he noted that although trustful acceptance of a divine mystery can greatly help the intellect in penetrating its meaning, here too "the intellect always comes first, however slightly," inasmuch as it alone can provide the persuasion that the mystery be taken up for consideration.[5]

This respect for what comes logically first figured prominently in Augustine's rebuttal, dating from 397, of an epistle by a leading Manichean, named Fundamentus, who demanded that *his* reading of the Bible be accepted by Augustine. Had the letter not established itself as a major Manichean document, Augustine may not have given so much attention to what is logically the

---

[4] See on this the data given in chapter 1 with reference to A. Van Helden, *Measuring the Universe: Cosmic Dimensions from Aristarchus to Halley* (Chicago: University of Chicago Press, 1985).

[5] "Quantulumque ratio . . . ipsa antecedit fidem." In *S. Augustini epistulae*, 120:3, in *Corpus scriptorum ecclesiasticorum latinorum* [CSEL], vol. 34, p. 707.

first principle in reading the Bible. What Augustine stated in speaking for himself, "I would not believe the Gospel, if the authority of the Catholic Church did not move me,"[6] he meant, of course, to be true for anyone who accepted Revelation. Such was Augustine's bottom-line answer to the Manichean claim that the New Testament alone was a revealed document.

In his analysis of that epistle, Augustine first asked for "very clear reasons" why one should not take the Old Testament too for something inspired. He clearly wanted far more in the way of reasons than Fundamentus' insistence that "he [Augustine] should believe what he wanted him to believe and should not believe what he did not want him to believe." Augustine had no use for anyone who (anticipating the attitude of so many nowadays) under the cover of copious references to the Bible merely preached his own imperious reading of it.

Never satisfied with a negative approach, Augustine set forth the positive reasons why he accepted both Testaments. The reasons were "the general consensus of people; the [ecclesiastical] authority confirmed by miracles, nourished by hope, strengthened by a long past; the succession of bishops taking their origin from the chair of Peter to whom the Lord, after his resurrection, confided his sheep to be fed; the very name Catholic which that Church, in the midst of heretics, alone obtained not by chance and to such a degree that heretics neither call themselves Catholic nor, when asked by a stranger about the Catholic Church, would dare point at their own churches or buildings."

Clearly, Augustine was interested in easily identifiable reasons, free of obscurities or subjectivism and, last but not least, of circular reasoning. In other words, he looked for the reason that could serve as the logically primary reason. He took the view that the reason or consideration that supported all the foregoing

---

[6] "Ego vero evangelio non crederem, nisi me catholicae ecclesiae commoveret auctoritas." This and the subsequent quotations are directly translated from the critical edition, *Contra epistulam quam vocant Fundamenti*, 5-6, in *CSEL* 25: 196-98. A rather dated translation is in *The Nicene and Post-Nicene Fathers. Volume IV. St. Augustine. Writings against the Manicheans and against the Donatists*, pp. 130-31.

reasons was that one was not so much to believe in the Gospels as "in those who preached the Gospel." In asserting that he would not believe the Gospel, unless the authority of the Catholic Church moved him, Augustine laid down the substance of theological epistemology. It rests on anchoring the intellect in the actual living ecclesial authority which is tied in an uninterrupted chain to the authority Christ gave to the Twelve. And since that authority related to all places and all times, it rightly deserved to be called catholic.[7]

That this was not a reasoning peculiar to Augustine is best seen in what may be the most misinterpreted gem of patristic literature, the *Commonitories* of Vincent of Lerins, written within two decades of Augustine's death. Yet even in its far from felicitous title, meaning "warnings," there is a prophetic quality. For no warning is more needed nowadays than the one which Vincent of Lerins tried to impress on the minds of Christians. What makes the *Commonitories* truly noteworthy is not his incomplete definition—"what has been believed everywhere, always, and by all"—of orthodox doctrine. It is rather his animated and penetrating exposure of the manner in which heresiarchs, big and small, used, or rather abused, the Scriptures for their purposes. The manner was the pitting of learnedness, sophistication, and wilfulness (separately or in combination) against the plainly recognizable authoritative statements of what was to be believed. Moreover, by pointing his finger at Origen (the hero of so many Catholic theologians nowadays), he laid bare the danger which a learnedness, insufficiently tied to authoritative teaching, can pose to the faith of many. The issue at hand seemed all the more crucial to Vincent of Lerins because he

---

[7] This connection of catholicity with an ecclesial authority that alone can guarantee the Bible and its reading came forcefully to the fore again a thousand or so years later. In arguing, in 1515, against Maartin van Dorp, who set up the "critically" established text of the Bible as the supreme standard of faith, Thomas More made much of Augustine's famous phrase (quoted in Latin in note 6 above), which in fact was More's "favorite patristic text." See *The Complete Works of St. Thomas More*. Vol. 15, edited by D. Kinney (New Haven: Yale University Press, 1986), pp. 87 and 528.

saw that even the definite establishment of the Canon of biblical books failed to stem the tide of "private" interpretations.[8]

Vincent of Lerins was, of course, fully aware of the role which Augustine played in firming up that Canon. Augustine's struggle for a Church that had to be catholic or universal if it was the true Church, included his championing, in three African synods, between 393 and 419, the list of 27 books composing the New Testament. He most likely knew that the list had first appeared in the famed *Paschal Epistle* issued by the aged Athanasius in 367. Augustine certainly knew of the fact that in writing to Exuperius in 405, Pope Innocent I gave the list of those 27 books that "are accepted as canonical." In the same breath the Pope also listed a dozen or so books that were "not only to be rejected but positively condemned."[9] This is not to suggest that doubts had not been voiced afterwards about some of the canonical books. Authority, divinely commissioned as it may be, is not supposed to work, in this fallen state, as a panacea. But it gives as much light as that candle, mentioned in the Gospel, that is not hidden under a bushel basket.

So much for the early phase of the determination of the list of canonical books of the New Testament as a manifestation of a relation between organs authoritatively teaching in the Church and the Bible taught within the Church. That phase clearly shows the priority of the Church over the Bible, whose inspired characteristic was, time and again, derived from its being written by those, the Apostles, who started a succession of authoritative preaching. This priority is equally evidenced by the subsequent history of the Canon, and in particular by the problems which the deuterocanonical books of the Old Testament keep posing for Protestants. As the future was to show, the relation between the Bible and science became problematical in the measure in which the priority in question failed to be given its due.

---

[8] See *Vincent of Lerins. The Commonitories*, translated by R. E. Morris in vol. 7 of *The Fathers of the Church* (New York: The Fathers of the Church, 1949), pp. 255-332.
[9] Letter sent on February 20, 405, to Exuperius, bishop of Toulouse. See *Enchiridion Symbolorum*, DS (1965), #213.

But back to Augustine, who also urged the recipient of that great letter of his on reason and grace that "he should greatly love the intellect."[10] Love of reason and respect for logic drew Augustine towards the words of the Book of Wisdom that God "arranged everything in measure, number and weight."[11] The same is true for his celebration of technological and scientific attainments in *De civitate Dei*,[12] a book written against the pagans' claim that the supernaturalism of the Christian message was responsible for the collapse of the Roman empire.

Compared with Augustine's exegesis of Genesis 1, which retained his attention over many years, similar works produced during patristic times should seem insignificant as far as science is concerned. Even some major commentators on Genesis 1, who, like Basil and Ambrose, were also Doctors of the Church, failed to carry out consistently the sound principle that Moses did not want to instruct about matters scientific, but merely recounted what was assumed and seen by the vulgar. For, time and again, they claimed a concordance to be on hand between what Genesis 1 offered about the physical world and what the philosophers (scientists) had demonstrated about it. Still others, like Eusebius, were too eager to claim that Genesis 1 fully corresponded to what Ptolemaic astronomy and Aristotelian physics established about the world. In fact, Eusebius blandly claimed that Plato himself borrowed from Moses all truths about the physical world, including its sphericity.

Medieval Aristotelianism
Such claims, rare even in patristic times, found little echo during the Carolingian renaissance of learning and much less in the School of Chartres. There, respect for reason ran so high as to attribute almost divine wisdom to Plato's *Timaeus*. Plato's idea

---

[10] "Intellectum vero valde ama," *Epist.* 120:13, in *CSEL*, 34: 716. The recipient was a certain Consentius.

[11] See *Confessions*, Bk 2, ch. 1.

[12] For a discussion, see my *The Purpose of it All* (Edinburgh: Scottish Academic Press, 1990), pp. 202-03.

that in making the world the *demiourgos* heavily relied on geometry had a great appeal well beyond Chartres. The fact that among all physical realities light offered itself most readily to being treated geometrically led Grosseteste, bishop of Lincoln, to turn geometrical optics into cosmology. He took all physical reality for a form of light which, with its geometrical properties, supported the conviction that God's creation was fully rational.

But by the time Grosseteste died in 1253, interest in Aristotle's works began to rule supreme. This meant that interest in geometry had to be recognized as not being particularly relevant to broader and deeper questions that could appeal to reason. The breadth was looked for in the sweeping systematization offered in Aristotle's works, largely obtained through Muslim mediation. The depth meant concern for tangible physical reality, including its ontological foundations, and for the respective merits of information that came from reason and revelation.

The logical coherence of Aristotle's philosophy and the apparently full agreement of Aristotelian physics and cosmology with experience inspired Thomas' interpretation of Genesis 1, which would set a pattern for much of subsequent scholastic reading of that chapter. The sequence of the steps in the making of the world as described there was taken to be equivalent to the logical correlation, as argued by Aristotle, of the main parts of the world and of the four elements.

The lure of this concordism can be measured by the relative ease with which the question of the firmament was handled during scholastic times, and in particular the problem of how light could be on hand prior to the creation of the sun. No one took proper note when, around 1180, Abbot Arnold of Bonneval, near Chartres, wondered aloud whether anyone had ever observed non-artificial light as truly independent of the sun. In general, no real effort was made to think through the principle, invariably asserted, and not least by Thomas, that Moses wrote for the uneducated. For if such was the case little justification could be given for the recasting of Genesis 1 in terms of Aristotelian physics.

While the authority of the Bible could seem too heavy in some respects, the medieval Christian mind was fully aware that authoritative teaching alone could guarantee its right reading. That teaching prompted countless commentators (patristic and scholastic) on Genesis 1 to use it as a vehicle to assert basic truths of the Christian creed and theology. Such were the propositions that all was created by God, that He was free to create, that He alone was the Creator, that all He had created was good (at the total exclusion of an evil principle), that He created out of nothing and in time (namely, that the past history of the world was finite), and that He created for a purpose which culminated in man's special status and destiny. Implied in these propositions was a rejection of several notions which in modern times have invariably misguided scientists whenever they fell under their lure. Such notions were the eternity of matter and its necessary existence in the form in which it actually existed. That these notions were no less contrary to the message registered in the Bible than to scientific creativity could, however, be seen only some time after there was a genuinely creative science on hand. The spark that triggered the rise of that science came from Ages to which some myopic centuries grimly fastened the label Dark.

6

The Light of True Science

The Spark from "Dark" Ages

Some of the propositions listed at the end of the preceding chapter could be directly read out from Genesis 1, others could be seen there only in the light of a theology which was shaped by authoritative teaching of the faith. Guided by that light, some Dominicans and Franciscans urged a study of the original Hebrew and Greek texts of the Scriptures.[1] Insistence on the original Hebrew and Greek did not, then or later, necessarily mean genuine enlightenment in exegesis. This is well illustrated by the inability of scholastic exegetes with good command of Hebrew and Greek to break out from the shackles of a concordist interpretation of Genesis 1, an interpretation that had just been initiated in a systematic manner.[2] As will be seen, concordism was not vanquished by further insistence on Greek and Hebrew in the days of the Reformers or by the real growth of expertise in biblical languages during the nineteenth century. The realization that Genesis 1 should be radically separated from scientific considerations postdated even the rise of geology as science during the early nineteenth century.

Within that powerful current of concordism, steeped in Aristotelian physics, no broad attention could be commanded by geometry, even in its connection with the Bible. But such a connection was at least perceived as implicit in the declaration,

---

[1] See on this B. Smalley, *The Study of the Bible in the Middle Ages* (Oxford: Clarendon Press, 1941), pp. 245-55.

[2] Strangely enough, this aspect of the vast medieval interest in the Bible is ignored in *Le Moyen Age et la Bible* (Paris: Beauchesne, 1984), a collection of two dozen essays, edited by P. Riché and G. Lobrichon. A similar neglect characterizes the other, equally vast, volumes in the same series, *Bible de tous les temps*.

already discussed, of the Book of Wisdom that God "arranged everything according to measure and number and weight" (11:20). These words enjoyed enormous popularity during the Middle Ages and were, to quote a prominent Protestant expert on medieval Latin literature, among the biblical phrases most often cited during medieval centuries.[3] Of course, as was already the case with Augustine, fondness for that passage also produced a cavorting in allegorical interpretations. But its plain sense, which could not be uninfluential, is certainly germane to the medieval development of the art of latitudes that dealt with heat, motion, and other physical parameters. The art is a clear anticipation of some basics to which Descartes was to give full form in his analytical geometry. Herein lay also the roots of the working out, during the fourteenth century, of the idea of a "uniformly difform," that is, uniformly accelerated motion. Galileo was fully aware of these medieval ideas as he gave in a geometrical form the distance covered by a falling body in a given number of time units.

But another passage of the Bible inspired an immediately significant scientific breakthrough. The passage was the very first phrase in the Bible: "In the beginning God made the heaven and the earth." To be sure, the passage was not given an authoritative interpretation in Lateran IV in 1215, where it was made a solemn duty for Christians to believe that the world was created in time and had therefore a strictly finite past history. But the decree of Lateran IV could only engrave on minds that the phrase, "In the beginning," meant precisely that.

It was in that sense that the phrase was taken by John Buridan, professor at the Sorbonne, as he produced, around 1350, his commentary on Aristotle's *On the Heavens*. This work of Aristotle, let it be recalled, was until early modern times by far the principal document expounding the contention that the world necessarily existed and that therefore it was eternal. In comment-

---

[3] R. Curtius, *European Literature and the Latin Middle Ages,* tr. R. Trask (London: Routledge and Kegan Paul, 1953), p. 504.

ing on *On the Heavens,* Buridan, a good Catholic, naturally took exception to Aristotle's advocacy of the eternity of the world.

Of course, Buridan was not the first medieval thinker to do so. Others, including Aquinas, had already done this. In fact, Aquinas wrote a special commentary on the Decrees of Lateran IV, or Decretalia as they were called. Aquinas was also the leader of those who held that the doctrine of creation "in time" could not be established by reason but only through revelation, which authoritative ecclesial teaching alone could guarantee. The contrast with Jewish medieval tradition could not have been more marked. The grammatical uncertainties of the expression, *bereshit* (in the beginning), and the absence of a teaching authority gave rise among medieval Jewish scholars to some perplexity as to whether the past time span of the universe was strictly finite.

Yet the Christian disagreement with Aristotle on the eternity of the world was for a while a strictly theological procedure. After all, most scholastics were theologians. A prime example was Aquinas, who reflected on philosophy only insofar as it was required for dealing with this or that theological question. In relation to physical things those theological and philosophical reflections had for their objects the *why* or ontological causation, a chief interest for Aquinas. In relation to the *how* of causation, or distinctly scientific questions, Aquinas showed no enthusiasm. As was noted by more than one modern student of Aquinas, he did not seem to have his heart in the work of commenting on the scientific writings of Aristotle.

In Buridan, however, basic theological training was combined with keen interest in *how* things take place. The result was a spark which for the first time in history enabled man to enter the path of genuine physical science, or the science of things in motion. The spark in itself was not yet a quantitative study of things in motion. But it placed the reality of motion in a perspective in which alone its quantitative study could make sense. For within that perspective there emerged the most fundamental of the three basic laws of motion, the law of inertial motion. What triggered that emergence was the awareness, bolstered by authoritative ecclesial preaching, that if cosmic motion was not eternal, it had to have a beginning.

As was already noted, John Buridan emphatically endorsed the idea of creation in time. And since he did this in his commentary on Aristotle's *On the Heavens,* he had to reject right there and then Aristotle's claim that the motion of the heavens was eternal and face up to the question of *how* that motion got under way. In doing so, Buridan first removed a possible factor, the angels (or celestial intellects), on the ground that "the Bible does not state that appropriate intelligences move the celestial bodies." He then disclosed his own answer to that *how*: "It does not appear necessary to posit intelligences of this kind, because it would be answered that God, when he created the world, . . . impressed in them [heavenly bodies] impetuses which moved them without his having to move them any more except by the method of general influence whereby He concurs as a co-agent in all events which take place." By impetus Buridan meant quantity of motion, which later became known as momentum. In addition, he posited that this momentum was conserved because the celestial motions took place in a region in which there was no friction.[4]

This meant that, to use the modern expression, momentum was conserved. It is this conservation principle on which rests the idea of inertial motion, known nowadays as Newton's first law. That law is the basis of the two other Newtonian laws of motion. The three together are the very foundation of all physics, classical and modern. The one who laid the basic layer of that foundation was Buridan. His insight should seem all the more novel the more strongly one perceives the novelty of the new science with respect to everything that passed for science in ancient times. The novelty meant the final breaking out of the dark circle within which man's scientific efforts had been enclosed until then. If physical science was to be fully science it had to be the science of

---

[4] Buridan's passage first appeared in print in the third volume of Duhem's *Etudes sur Léonard de Vinci* (Paris: Hermann, 1913), p. 52.

motion above all. For in that physical universe which science is meant to interpret and over which science was to gain control, everything is in motion. As it ultimately turned out, the universe itself was subject to an overall motion, known as its expansion.

A novelty and its strange fading

The deepest and most crucial aspect of that novelty is that inertial motion implies a genuine measure of autonomy in any physical process with respect to its ultimate origin. In all ancient cultures that ultimate origin was a pantheistic deity, never truly distinct from anything physical. Thus an instantaneous transfer of momentum is inconceivable for Aristotle. Even more is this the case with the champions of far cruder animistic and pantheistic notions of the universe, such as Porphyry. To be sure, the Prime Mover of Aristotle is not in continual physical contact with the sphere of the fixed stars. But the Prime Mover nevertheless performs much the same function through continually inspiring in that sphere the desire which is the very source of its circular motion. That desire established such a unity between the Prime Mover and the sphere of the fixed stars that Aristotle carefully refrains from presenting the two as essentially different.

One can indeed picture Aristotle's Prime Mover as having a hand that is always in touch with the sphere of the fixed stars and keeps pushing it along its circular path. Such an image can in no way be read into Buridan's statement. The latter is an implicit restatement of the Christian (and therefore biblical) doctrine of the absolute distinctness of the Creator from his creation and also of his ceaseless presence in creation, which thereby remains in existence. This uniquely Christian conviction about a most nuanced rapport between the ultimate cause and all other causes operating through it, made it possible for Buridan to formulate a new idea of motion: the body is put in motion not because it remains a projection, so to speak, of the mover which moves behind it, but because the moved body becomes a true projectile with a motion truly imparted to it, as something which becomes its own possession. Such a transfer of something real is inconceivable in a pantheistic outlook for the very reason that there is no entity there with a real power to give, whereas this is precisely what a true Creator, and only such a Creator, can do.

There can be no more fundamental difference than the one between a world which is in no need of being created and a world that owes its existence to the Creator. That difference lies at the root of the invariable stillbirths of science in all ancient cultures. Although replete with talent and some marvelous technological feats, none of those cultures could spark the idea of inertial motion. The spark needed the support which the Christian dogma of creation out of nothing and in time could alone provide. The reason for this lies with the notion of inertia itself. At a cursory look it suggests the very opposite of something positive. But that apparent negativity presupposes the supreme positivity that can only be had in the infinite ontological richness and power of a true Creator. He alone can give without being diminished thereby. He alone can give autonomy without lessening, however slightly, the utter dependence of the recipient upon Him. This is certainly a biblical doctrine, but a doctrine which only the authoritative catechesis could turn into a tone of thought that certainly animated John Buridan.

About Buridan the Renaissance and the Reformation knew next to nothing, and the Enlightenment merely fantasized. Ill-disposed fantasy produced the eighteenth-century tale about Buridan's ass that dies of hunger between two equal bales of hay placed, at equal distances, to its right and left. Since equal but opposite attractions cancel one another, Buridan's ass is not pulled either to the right or to the left and therefore dies of hunger. So much for a fantastic reasoning wrapped in mere fantasy about Buridan.

The tale originated in that City of Light which, during the century of the Enlightenment, boasted of its ignorance about everything medieval, including the Sorbonne. For this no small price had to be paid at times. In speaking about the world as a clock which, once wound up, ran its course independently of God, Voltaire merely turned inside out a proposition of Buridan, while thinking himself very original. No wonder. Buridan was a believing Christian, whereas Voltaire was a mere deist. Thus, while Voltaire made the Creator appear superfluous following the act of creation, Buridan's Catholic faith demanded a basic role for the Creator even after that very act. Again, it was not this or that particular biblical passage that explicitly motivated Buridan, but his awareness of the dictates of faith.

This is very clear from Buridan's statement, quoted above, where he insists on the action whereby God has to keep things, already created, in existence. It was in this theological perspective that Buridan also called attention to the fact that the inertial motion of the heavens could be viewed as the running of the clock which was let go after it had been wound up.[5] He was not a forerunner of Voltaire, but certainly the initiator of a robust late-medieval tradition about inertial motion and about a mechanical picture of the world as a clockwork. It was precisely this autonomous permanence of a mechanical operation that could not have been inspired by Ockham's writings. They exuded distrust in physical laws and in physical causality to the extent that Ockham had no choice but to claim that God created everything anew on every occasion. Such was a most unbiblical distortion of God's will, a distortion that readily asserts itself whenever the Bible is held high against its authoritative ecclesiastical interpretation.

It was in the same non-Ockhamist spirit that Nicole Oresme, Buridan's successor in the Sorbonne, gave further elaboration to the impetus theory. Not a few among the sixty-thousand or so students of the Sorbonne carried the doctrine of impetus to the four corners of the learned world, that is, throughout the system of universities that invariably rested on the highest level of authorization the Church could provide. Manuscript copies of

---

[5] By Buridan's time clocks operated by falling weights had been on the scene for more than half a century. They were one of the signal evidences of medieval technological creativity. See on this my article, "Medieval Christianity: Its Inventiveness in Technology and Science," in A. M. Melzer *et al.* (eds), *Technology in the Western Political Tradition* (Ithaca: Cornell University Press, 1993), pp. 46-68.

Buridan's and Oresme's commentaries quickly became available from Oxford to Bologna, from Salamanca to Cracow. Copernicus became familiar with Buridan's and Oresme's teaching while studying in Cracow in the 1490s. Decades later he used that doctrine as his chief answer to physical objections against the twofold motion of the earth.

By then, or the 1540s, the impetus theory and its medieval provenance had become so ingrained in the minds of natural philosophers that there was no need for Copernicus to refer to Buridan. More than half a century later Descartes was still aware, if not of Buridan, at least of the medieval origin of inertial motion. He was not, however, willing to give anyone as much as an inkling about his indebtedness to the medievals. He was paid back in kind when Newton spent precious time erasing in his manuscripts all references to Descartes. The world of the learned was never to suspect that a great Englishman had learned a thing or two from a Frenchman, however celebrated.

It may be that Copernicus, who certainly could not find in Buridan's and Oresme's writings the idea of an orbital motion of the earth, was nevertheless inspired by Oresme concerning the earth's rotational motion. Oresme himself proposed that motion as a possibility. He could not offer more on its behalf than its great explanatory power, while he had no answer for the physical problems it created. Last but not least he felt the weight of the words of the Bible about an earth which the Lord fixed firmly in its place. More science was still needed to liberate believers from their fixation on those hallowed biblical words so that their worship could be the truly "reasonable worship" (*logike latreia*) advocated by Paul (Rom 12:1).

The darkness of biblicism

That weight was increased beyond measure when Luther threw the Bible, as if it were a gauntlet, in the face of the authority of the Church. Here only the consequences for science will be considered. In interpreting Genesis 1 Luther insisted that everything there had to be taken in the strictest literal sense. The absurdities that followed for man's rationality he brushed aside with the claim that Genesis 1 was meant to reduce man's mind to an utterly humbling servitude for the reception of revealed truths. If anyone, then Luther certainly preached the non-biblical doctrine of *credo quia absurdum* while trying to appear more biblical than anyone else. He appeared most unscientific as he claimed that, since the firmament was stretched out like a tent, it "could persist in its motion for thousands of years only by a sheer miracle of God."[6]

Calvin, though with a more rational frame of mind than Luther, was also carried by his biblicism into scientific absurdities as he commented on Genesis 1. Certainly absurd was his claim that clouds did not fall on us and crush us only because God kept them aloft. This exercise in physics, very disreputable even around 1560, came two decades after Copernicus refused to agonize over why much heavier bodies than clouds did not crash into the earth. Calvin tried to be original in insisting that Moses had written for the uneducated, an observation that had by then been a commonplace for more than a thousand years. At any rate, Calvin failed to implement that principle consistently. A case in point was his explanation of the relation of the sun and the light. Latter-day creationism owes much to the biblical literalism advocated by Calvin with sweeping diction and apparent rationality. Apparent indeed, because Calvin also stated that the laws of physics did not begin to operate until after the sixth day.

Insofar as the study of the original languages of the Bible was severed from authoritative ecclesiastical preaching as its matrix, it fueled literalism. The day to day and hour to hour correspondence which Archbishop Ussher, with his strong Puritan leanings, set up between the six days of creation and Copernican astronomy set the stage for many similarly self-defeating performances to come. Biblical literalism taken for a source of scientific information is making the rounds even

---

[6] See my *Genesis 1 through the Ages*, p. 158.

nowadays among creationists who would merit Huxley's description of bibliolaters. They merely bring discredit to the Bible as they pile grist upon grist on the mills of latter-day Huxleys, such as Hoyle, Sagan, Gould, and others. The fallacies of creationism go deeper than fallacious reasonings about scientific data.[7] Where creationism is fundamentally at fault is its resting its case on a theological faultline: the biblicism constructed by the Reformers.

Biblicism almost succeeded in bringing irreparable discredit to the Counter-Reformers. This happened as they showed too much readiness to meet Lutherans and Calvinists on their own chosen ground, that is, biblical literalism. Perhaps partly because of this less attention was given to an all-important question about the authoritative ecclesial interpretation of the Bible as offered through the voice of a hierarchy centered on the bishop of Rome. The question was whether that hierarchy had ever put itself on record that geocentrism was a matter of faith. One aspect of the question was whether the Fathers had ever done so with convincing unanimity and, in particular, with explicit reference to Joshua's miracle.

Surprising as it may appear, patristic references to Joshua's miracle are few, and none of them shows the kind of scientific concern that one would expect to be on hand even within Ptolemaic geocentrism.[8] Joshua's miracle was not mentioned when Oresme, bishop of Lisieux, proposed, around 1370, the earth's rotation as a convenient solution to the daily rotation of the heavens. Oresme referred only to the biblical parlance about the fixity of the earth, as a reason for making that proposal only tentatively.[9] Copernicus made no reference at all to Joshua. The

---

[7] A point ignored by W. Young in his *Fallacies of Creationism* (Calgary: Detselig Enterprises Limited, 1985). The same is true of many similar critiques of creationism.

[8] For a collection of those texts, see F. Hummelauer, *Commentarius in Librum Iosue* (Paris: P. Lethielleux, 1903), pp. 238-39.

[9] Nicole Oresme, *Le Livre du ciel et du monde*, edited A. D. Menut and A. J. Denomy; translated by A. D. Menut (Madison: University of Wisconsin Press, 1968), pp. 536-37.

dubious distinction of dragging Joshua into the debates about
Copernicus belongs to Luther who fulminated: "The fool
[Copernicus] will turn upside down all astronomy, but as the
Holy Writ shows, Joshua commanded the sun, and not the earth,
to stand still."[10] Melanchthon followed Luther, if not in tone at
least in substance, in endorsing geocentrism. He did so in a book
on physics that earned him in large part the title, "praeceptor
Germaniae."[11] Kepler, the most scientific of all early Lutherans,
strongly disagreed. He did so with a detailed discussion of
Joshua's miracle, among other things, in the Preface to his epoch-
making book on the orbit of Mars.[12]

Calvin himself claimed that when Joshua gave his command
the sun was already setting and that "Joshua bids it stay and rest
there, in other words, remain above what is called the horizon."
This rendering of the sun's position revealed a cavalier attitude
toward the text, and Calvin displayed much the same in the
remainder of his remarks: "I do not give myself any great anxiety
as to the number of the hours; because it is enough for me that the
day was continued through the whole night." In staking
everything on God's omnipotence (Calvin's chief concern here
too was to insist that it was not Joshua but his faith that let God
produce the miracle, as if any Christian until then or after had
thought it otherwise), Calvin could be nonchalant about history
too: "Were histories of that period extant, they would doubtless
celebrate this great miracle." Calvin then presented the author of
the Book of Joshua as having been agitated by exactly this type
of historical consciousness: "Lest its [the miracle's] credibility,
however, should be questioned, the writer of this book [Joshua's]
mentions that an account of it was given elsewhere, though the
work which he quotes has been lost, and expounders are not well
agreed as to the term Jazar."[13]   While Calvin did not refer to

---

[10] Luther made that remark on June 4, 1539. See *Tischreden*, in the Weimar edition
of *Werke*, vol. I, p. 77.

[11] *Initia doctrinae physicae* (Wittenberg: 1549), p. 60.

[12] J. Kepler *Astronomia . . . de motibus stellae Martis* (1609; in *Werke* [1937], vol. III, p.
30).

[13] J. Calvin, *Commentaries on the Book of Joshua*, translated from the original Latin,

Copernicus, it is difficult to assume that in 1568 he could write this without thinking of the heliocentrism that had already made its grand debut with the publication in 1543 of Copernicus' great book.[14]

Lutheran and Calvinist emphasis on the literal interpretation of the Bible forced their Catholic counterparts to take a literalist interpretation as far as possible. They did this partly because it was demanded by the climate of opinion, and partly because it is always tempting to vanquish one's opponents on the battlefield of their choice. This is, of course, a risky strategy. Wellington won at Waterloo in good part because he had prevented Napoleon from choosing the site of that historic battle. Military history provides many other illustrations of this. In fact, the context of Joshua's command provides one such illustration. He certainly took the Amorites by surprise.

Galileo took the Church by surprise by claiming that he had demonstrative (experimental) proof on behalf of the earth's motion, and that therefore the teaching of the Church had to be adjusted to the new situation. He did not have the proof, nor did he prove that the Church taught geocentrism as something to be believed. He simply took the Bible's parlance for Church dogmatics. It remained hidden to him that he had merely encouraged biblicism within the Catholic camp, where it began to make itself felt, in respect to Copernicus, with the reflections of Clavius, the Jesuit professor of astronomy at the Collegio Romano around 1600. But one wonders whether it was not Galileo, who in 1613 began to wax theological in long letters to trusted friends, hoping that they would serve as his channel to Bellarmine. One of them, Dini, did indeed inform Galileo that Bellarmine held the reference in Psalm 18 (19) to the sun's

and collated with the French edition by H. Beveridge (Grand Rapids, Michigan: Wm. B. Eerdmans, 1949), p. 154. The translator emphasized that this commentary was Calvin's most mature work.

[14] It is rather self-defeating to argue against some anti-Calvinist historians of science, if in so doing one ignores Calvin's commentary in Joshua, as done, for instance, by R. White in his essay, "Calvin and Copernicus: The Problem Reconsidered," *Calvin Theological Journal* 15 (1980), pp. 233-243.

running like a giant on its course to be the most important
scriptural proof of geocentrism. Galileo then took up in a long
letter the interpretation of that passage of which Bellarmine had
already published his own exegesis. In all this, not a word was
said about the truly decisive factor, namely, the biblicism to be
adopted in order to meet the Protestants more than half way.

Worse, the ever bellicose Galileo pressed his cause as the
protector of the Church. In 1615 he addressed a long letter to the
dowager Grand Duchess Christina of the Medicis in whose court
Galileo served as astronomer (and astrologer!) and let it circulate
in manuscript copies. By the time it was published in 1636,
Galileo had been sentenced for a second time. However, very
prominent exegetes are still to take proper note of what should
appear a gem of biblical hermeneutics, as evidenced even in its
typically long title: "The new as well as old teaching of most
holy Fathers and approved theologians about the Holy Scripture's testimony in respect to purely natural conclusions. These
conclusions, though they can be proven by sense experience and
necessary demonstrations, ought not to be recklessly abused."
Unfortunately, only the added words, "gratefully dedicated to
the most serene Christina of Lotharingia," are usually mentioned, which is true even of the excellent modern translation.[15]

Perhaps under the influence of Galileo's letter, which he
must have known, Bellarmine softened somewhat his position,
but not to the point of parting with the biblicist strategy. It is
therefore a bit pointless to muse with Fr. Brodrick, Bellarmine's
modern biographer, as to the course history might have taken

---

[15] The English translation, *Letter to the Grand Duchess Christina* by S. Drake is in his
Discoveries and Opinions of Galileo (Garden City, N.Y.: Doubleday, 1957), pp. 173-216,
with Drake's introduction, pp. 145-171. Since Drake does not give the full translation
of the title, it is reproduced here in Latin: *Nov-antiqua sanctissimorum patrum &
probatorum theologorum doctrina, de sacrae scripturae testimoniis, in conclusionibus mere
naturalibus. Quae sensata experientia, & necessariis demonstra-tionibus evinci possunt,
temere non usurpandis: In gratiam serenissimae Christinae Lotharingiae . . .* (Augustae
Treboc, Impensis Elzeviriorum, 1636). As the title indicates, Galileo discussed
Joshua's command in the widest possible hermeneutical context concerning the
Bible's statements about natural phenomena.

had Bellarmine pondered that now famed letter of Galileo.[16] After all, while Galileo made much in that letter of the difficulties which geocentrism(!) posed to the literal interpretation of the Bible's texts on the fixity of the earth and of Joshua's command, theologically and exegetically he stated nothing that Bellarmine had not known.

Bellarmine was, of course, fully familiar with Galileo's chief source of theological information, the commentaries written around 1450 by Alonzo Tostado, bishop of Avila, on chapter 10 of the Book of Joshua. Yet neither in 1616 nor in 1632 could Galileo make good on his claim that there were experimental proofs on behalf of the earth's twofold motion. In fact he miserably failed with his ace card, the use of the tides, as such a proof. He not only contradicted his earlier statements that there could be no such proofs, but he was found to have committed the elementary error of confusing two coordinate systems: One was pivoted on the center of the earth, the other on the sun, as the center of the earth's orbital motion.[17]

To be sure, from Tostado's book Galileo could gather a number of patristic statements that stressed a basic hermeneutical point. One of them was Jerome's dictum that "it is the custom of the biblical scribes to deliver their judgments in many things according to the commonly received opinion of their times."[18] This principle and Augustine's principle about how to resolve a conflict between something that could be known with certainty by reason and a biblical passage in apparent contradiction with it, should have given enough justification for preventing the bungle of 1616. Coupled with the condemnation, in 1632, of Galileo's book comparing the respective merits of the geocentric and heliocentric systems, that bungle became the hobby-horse of all those who (often without considering whether they them-

---

[16] J. Brodrick, *Robert Bellarmine. Saint and Scholar* (London: Burns, 1961), p. 378.

[17] A point aired in print a mere half a year after the publication of Galileo's *Dialogues*. For details and documentation, see W. R. Shea, *Galileo's Intellectual Revolution: The Middle Period, 1610-1632* (New York: History of Science Publications, 1972).

[18] *Discoveries and Opinions of Galileo*, p. 201.

selves are not living in glass-houses) have made it their pastime to debunk the Bible, miracles, and Rome—taken singly or together.

Yet, in the flood of words produced about the Galileo case, little attention has been given to what in the eyes of a Protestant may be sheer luck or cunning, but in the eyes of a Catholic should appear as the kind of providential assistance which is implied in the dogma of papal infallibility. For in 1616 papal infallibility escaped by the skin of its teeth from proving itself very fallible. The decree condemning the idea of the earth's motion was to be issued by Paul V himself as president of the Sacred Congregation. Being a lawyer by training, he was known to be fond of handing down decrees in a manner nothing short of imperious. Suffice to recall his order that put an end to the mutual vilifications of Dominicans and Jesuits on the relation of grace and free will. Everything indicated that the Pope himself would issue the famed condemnation of two basic propositions of heliocentrism: the removal of the earth from the center and its being put in motion. Yet, for reasons still clouded in mystery, the condemnation was issued not by Paul V, but by Cardinal Bellarmine. This fact, or the difference between a Cardinal, however prominent, and a Pope, was not missed by contemporaries. Descartes, a somewhat timid advocate of heliocentrism, made much of that difference. Later, Leibnitz used that difference to argue that the condemnation was not irrevocable. But while Leibnitz, a Lutheran in Lutheran land, was at a safe remove from the penalties of disobeying that decree, Descartes, the French Catholic, knew that it was wiser to fall silent on the subject and, in fact, to remove himself to Protestant lands, first to Holland, and then to Sweden.

The Catholic Church came to the brink of a disaster after truly auspicious beginnings. While Luther was eager to declare Copernicus a fool, when only rumor had it that he had been working on a heliocentric astronomy, Copernicus was feted in the Vatican gardens as he lectured there on the new theory. Two generations later, with Protestantism on the march in all transalpine countries, the Catholic Church decided upon a new strategy vis-à-vis the Reformers. The strategy implied an insistence on the literal sense of the Bible in as large a measure as possible. Lest new ammunition be given to the Protestant charge that the Catholic Church disregards the Bible, biblical statements about the earth's fixity in the center were given too much weight. Once more it proved true that to meet one's opponents on ground chosen by them is more laden with dangers than with genuine prospects of gaining decisive victories.

The supreme touch of irony in all this was a strange reversal of roles. Galileo's ecclesiastical judges could rightly argue that he had failed in his stated claim, which was to present unassailable experimental or observational proofs on behalf of the twofold motion of the earth.[19] Meanwhile Galileo, with his Letter to the Grand Duchess Christina, bested the finest theologians and exegetes of his Church.

All this shows that the relation of the Bible and science is full of light and shadows. But such has to be the case as long as there is any truth to the parable that the Kingdom of God is like the field into which good seed was sown. As the seed sprouted and grew, plenty of weeds also appeared. Moreover, this result of the enemy's work has to be accepted as a process going on until Judgment Day.

Anyone lured by the spurious light which the wisdom of hindsight provides may take the invoking of that parable for an easy escape from difficult problems. But that light is the folly of utopian expectations. Superficial trust in science has all too often inspired the expectations that utopia is possible on earth. Part of that utopia would be the discrediting of Christianity as well as of the Bible as a concrete expression of its faith. But as science grows older, it reveals much of the far from perfect character of its

---

[19] Only long after Galileo did science muster those really convincing proofs. One was Bessel's observation of stellar parallax in 1837. The other was the pendulum experiment, performed by Foucault in 1851. Less significant were two earlier proofs. They were connected with Roemer's deduction in 1675 of the speed of light from the observation of the motion of Jupiter's moons and with Bradley's observation in 1728 of the aberration of light.

purely conceptual structure, let alone the often questionable application of its increasingly powerful tools.

Nothing of this was suspected until rather recently, partly because reliable historiography of medieval and modern science does not antedate the beginnings of this century. Even more checkered is the history of modern man's understanding of how he has come to possess science. Worthless clichés about that process still abound,[20] although major findings concerning it had been made early in this century. The character and context of those findings are such as to be profoundly revolting to anyone imbued with the spirit of an enlightenment for which the supernatural, especially in its Christian form, is the chief embodiment of darkness. But the findings were also very upsetting even to those who champion the Bible as the primary source and standard of the supernatural. For them too the Middle Ages were to be painted in as dark hues as possible. They could hardly take kindly to the possibility that those Ages played a crucial role in sparking the light, the light of science, which has come to stand for the supreme form of illumination in this age of ours. That those two groups, so different from one another, should agree, for very different reasons, to ignore or slight the very same findings, may appear particularly odd but also very instructive.

---

[20] For details, see my Fremantle Lectures (Balliol College, Oxford), *The Origin of Science and the Science of its Origin* (Edinburgh: Scottish Academic Press, 1978).

7

Light oddly enough

First notices of an oddity
Tellingly, the finding that Christianity had provided the indispensable spark for science was brought to the attention of both groups mentioned above at the same time and through the same medium. The year was 1913. It was still possible to brand as pessimistic anyone forecasting an imminent end to a by then almost hundred years of peace and progress. Much of the credit for progress went to science, partly because of the influence of Comte's positivism, very strong in France and especially in Paris. Within Comtean positivism no less a role was assigned to science than that of the true savior of mankind.

The medium was the biweekly *Revue des Deux Mondes*, one of the most prestigious publications Paris could boast of. In the *Revue* everything, either in the humanities or in the broader interpretation of the sciences, was legislated about in a form called by the French "haute popularisation." Among the readers of the *Revue* there were not only freethinkers but also Protestants and Catholics. Even to most of the latter, to say nothing of those in the two former groups, very odd had to appear an article which the *Revue* carried in its July 15, 1913, issue.

Paris was still two weeks away from its usual August exodus when its literati were told in that article about the origins of modern science in the light of some recent discoveries. The author of the article was Albert Dufourcq, professor of Church History at the University of Bordeaux.[1] The article began with the declaration that "the origins of science are less known than its

---

[1] A. Dufourcq, "Les origines de la science moderne d'après les découvertes récentes," *Revue des Deux Mondes* 16 (1913), pp. 349-78.

discoveries. . . . Yet there is no more interesting study." This claim should have appeared as brazenly impertinent to a readership most of whom were convinced that Condorcet and Comte had already spoken the last word on that subject. Still in that opening paragraph Dufourcq also claimed that, according to those discoveries, the origins of modern science antedate not only Newton, Descartes, and Galileo, but Copernicus and Leonardo as well.

The *lèse majesté* against the received view about the origin of science came as that origin was credited to some fourteenth-century masters of the University of Paris. The University in question was the Sorbonne, a bastion then of Catholic orthodoxy. To quite a few readers of the *Revue* the name of the discoverer, Pierre Duhem, was well known as a philosopher of science, but less so as a theoretical physicist at the University of Bordeaux. Few, of course, could yet be aware of the freshly published third volume of Duhem's *Études sur Léonard de Vinci*, where, already in its long introduction, the world of the learned was informed about Buridan's epoch-making formulation of inertial motion and of its theological context.

Dufourcq, a devout and articulate Catholic, was not reluctant to elaborate on that context, which was known to him through his personal friendship with Duhem. Dufourcq was the kind of sober Catholic who did not expect most readers of the *Revue*, who were so much out of sympathy with Catholicism, to take note of his startling communication, full of data, taken from Duhem's various publications. Much less did Dufourcq expect most of those readers to face up to the broader implications of those consequences, among them a thorough revision of Western cultural history and of the history of science in particular. Dufourcq could at most hope that Catholic intellectuals would sit up and listen. By and large, they are yet to do so.[2]

---

[2] A point which I am in the process of setting forth in great detail. Here let me refer the reader, ready for a shock, to *Christianity and Science* by the Jesuit Jean Abelé (translated from the French by R. F. Trevett; New York: Hawthorn Publishers, 1961), a book widely available as volume 14 of the *Twentieth Century*

Here begins a rather odd development that hardly does credit to twentieth-century academia. For while members of that academia, or scholars in short, are free to hold any view, they are not free at least in one respect. Academic freedom is no licence to ignore important research and findings; it is not even a licence to remain in blissful ignorance of them. It was on this point that Arthur Koestler once rebuked British academics, who claimed that they had no knowledge of what happened to Jews in Hitler's Germany prior to World War II and much less of what happened to Jews during the war years. If academics have no right to plead ignorance about matters well outside their fields of study, then they certainly have no right for entering such pleas about matters closely relating to those fields. Yet prominent academics kept writing about the origin and early history of science as if Duhem's vast scholarly work, produced by first-rate publishers, did not exist.

Alfred North Whitehead was certainly prominent. Moreover, having a cultured French woman for a wife, Whitehead had even less excuse at a time when many academics in the English-speaking world still had a working knowledge of French and considered it obligatory to be *au courant* with what was published in France. It may safely be assumed that the library of White-head's Trinity College (Cambridge) had a standing order for the publications of Hermann and Cie, one of the two chief scientific publishers in Paris and also the publisher of Duhem's researches on medieval scientific history. The same may also be assumed of the Widener Library of Harvard University, where Whitehead settled after the War. But once more it became true about prestigious academic stature that it could serve as a justification for not doing one's homework, indeed, as a licence to get away with the academic equivalent of murder. For nothing short of an intellectual murder was perpetrated in those couple of paragraphs for which Whitehead's famed 1925 Lovell Lectures, *Science and the Modern World*, gained most fame.

Encyclopedia of Catholicism. Abelé jumps from the Greeks to Galileo as if Duhem, a fellow Frenchman and Catholic, never existed.

In those couple of paragraphs Whitehead informed the academic world that modern science owed its birth "to the inexpugnable belief that every detailed occurrence can be correlated with its antecedents in a perfectly definite manner, exemplifying general principles." By the belief in question Whitehead had much more in mind than the faith of a few individuals. He meant a "tone of thought" which had to come "from the medieval insistence on the rationality of God, conceived with the personal energy of Jehovah and with the rationality of a Greek philosopher." Then he described that tone of thought as not the belief of a few individuals but "the impress on the European mind arising from the unquestioned faith of centuries."[3]

This latter statement was undoubtedly true, though certainly in need of clarification. The faith, in line with a by then thousand-year-old tradition, was a response to an authoritative preaching of propositions included in the credal formulas. Even from the viewpoint of sheer practicality it could not have been otherwise. Although printed sheets of biblical texts became available early in the fifteenth century, only a small segment of the faithful could read them. Illiteracy remained dominant in Western society until the first half of the nineteenth century, that is, half a millennium after complete bibles began to be printed. For a long time even bibles far less sumptuously produced than the two hundred or so copies printed by Gutenberg[4] had remained very costly, as did all books of comparable thickness. At any rate, the ready acceptance of an authoritative preaching of the main articles of the Creed made it possible for the contents

---

[3] A. N. Whitehead, *Science and the Modern World* (1926; New York: New American Library, 1948), p. 19.

[4] Incidentally, Gutenberg's contribution to the art of printing may not exceed the the designing of large, highly decorated letters put at the head of chapters. In fact, P. Butler, in his still authoritative *The Origin of Printing in Europe* (Chicago: University of Chicago Press, 1940), states nothing less than that "from the archeological evidence alone one would therefore conclude that printing from movable type must have begun several decades before 1450 at the very latest" (p. 83); see also p. 143.

of the Bible to be presented with emphasis on their applicability to devotional life. This characteristic of the use of the Bible during the Middle Ages,[5] was very much in line with its use throughout patristic times. Indeed it was in this vein that much of the New Testament itself came to be written.

Whitehead's endorsement of the rationality typical of "a Greek philosopher" cannot be reconciled with the emphasis which all Greek philosophers put on the partial irrationality of the sublunary world. Whitehead's failure to speak of Arius and Athanasius is of a piece with his putting Jehovah in a context where the Incarnate Son of God should have figured prominently. This slighting of Christ flew in the face of medieval theological history. A quick look at any index of the *Summa theologiae* of Aquinas could have taught Whitehead some basics as to the central place of Christ there.[6]

It is difficult to assume that Whitehead, who perhaps never opened the *Summa*, had not seen, at least in reproductions, the mosaics of Christ the Pantokrator that grace the apses of some famed romanesque cathedrals. Possibly, Whitehead, the son of an Anglican parson, tried to justify his loss of faith in Christ by eliminating Him from Western cultural history. At any rate, Whitehead lived for another twenty years without ever uttering a word about Buridan, Oresme, or Duhem, although their names did not fail to be mentioned at Harvard, though never too noticeably. And perhaps from Harvard unimportant could appear Columbia University, where Thorndike was writing his multivolume history of science and magic during the Middle Ages, in which enough references were made to Duhem to alert any perceptive mind.

Whitehead was still holding court at Harvard when the next major step was taken in the production of that "oddity of the twentieth century." That Whitehead did not seem to take note of

---

[5] See Smalley, *The Study of the Bible in the Middle Ages*.

[6] Even more instructive in this respect are the thirty-odd folio volumes of the IBM computer printout, produced in the 1960s, of all the cross references in all the works of Aquinas.

that step is rather strange. The step consisted of three articles that saw print in 1934 and 1935 in *Mind*, the leading British philosophical quarterly.[7] Their author, Michael Foster, of Christ Church, Oxford, did not claim expertise in the history of science and he certainly had none. He was the kind of Kantian philosopher who confidently dictated to reality, physical and historical, what it ought to be. He was also the kind of Christian who retained from his Protestantism only a slightly disguised distaste for anything Christian between Constantine and the Reformation. To justify that distaste Foster had to rely on the odd tactic of placing trust in clichés that made little sense by 1934 or so. But he could safely assume that those clichés were still dear to many in academia in spite of extensive researches that had been going on for decades concerning the true history of philosophy during the Middle Ages.

So much in way of a background for the negative part of Foster's main claim, or his dismissal of medieval science. Without considering the vast array of facts, widely available in Duhem's monumental investigations, Foster argued that, by yielding to the aprioristic features of Aristotle's pantheistic cosmology and theory of matter, medieval scholastics derived all particular sensory properties of things from an a priori definition of their substances. Had they done so, they would have certainly guided into a blind alley whatever scientific interests they might have had. But the scholastics never forgot that sensory evidence was the basis of Aristotle's realist epistemology. Otherwise, neither would Aristotle have excelled as an observational biologist, nor would medieval times (one should think of Albertus Magnus), have shown a keen interest in gathering empirical data.

Nor did Foster establish a factual basis on behalf of the positive side of his main claim. According to Foster the Reformers made it possible for the mind to become really aware of the

---

[7] For a detailed analysis of Foster's three articles, see my essay, "Telltale Remarks and a Tale Untold," in *Creation, Nature, and Political Order in the Philosophy of Michael Foster (1903 - 1959)*, ed. C. Wybrow (Lewiston: The Edwin Mellen Press, 1992), pp. 269-96.

biblical notion of the freedom of God's will to create. This awareness provided the matrix, so Foster argued, for the formulation, in the late 16th and early 17th centuries, of the empirical method needed by science. Foster did not seem to suspect that, apart from voicing slogans and clichés about that method, Francis Bacon and his Puritan cohorts promoted a bibliolatry that had little to do with the rise of science in general and with the nascent Royal Society in particular. There the only ones swearing by Lord Verulam were those who instead of doing serious science merely dabbled in it. Newton's icy silence on Bacon is the proof that he did not go by Bacon's inept dicta on how to do science. Newton did thereby ironic justice to the Baconian motto, *nullius in verba*, of the Royal Society.[8] A generation after Foster's articles saw print, the history of science during the 17th century was avidly searched on behalf of his claim about the Reformers. The search, done by one whose Calvinist respect for the Bible was certainly vigorous, failed to unearth anything substantive even in the writings of second-rate scientists of those times.[9]

Odd reactions to an oddity

Foster's articles quickly established themselves as the authoritative Protestant/anglophone interpretation of the role of Christian faith, with emphasis on the Bible as its source, in the rise of modern science. Nothing was said on the Protestant side about Foster's rank disregard of Duhem's work, fully available in Oxford and Cambridge libraries. Nor was anything offered in reply from the Catholic side. Apparently, Christopher Dawson, the most widely read Catholic cultural historian in the 1930s and beyond, remained unaware of Foster's articles. Unfortunately, Dawson did not see through the hollowness of Whitehead's

---

[8] See on this the chapter on Bacon, "Empirical Scouting," in my *The Road of Science and the Ways to God* (Chicago: University of Chicago Press, 1978).

[9] I mean R. Hooykaas, *Religion and the Rise of Modern Science* (Edinburgh: Scottish Academic Press, 1972).

statements either.[10] Catholic academics, both in France and in the English speaking countries, failed to mount concerted action to press for the publication of the last five volumes of Duhem's *Système du monde*, already twenty years behind schedule by the mid-1930s. Albert Dufourcq was the sole support of Hélène Duhem, Duhem's only child, during much of her heroic struggle over three decades to have those volumes published at long last in the 1950s.[11]

The inertia of French Catholic intellectuals vis-à-vis Duhem's great researches should seem all the more reprehensible as it was a French scholar, Victor Monod, with the best Calvinist credentials, who called attention to Duhem, the historian of medieval science, in 1933. Monod did this in a book in which he surveyed the influence of Platonist and Aristotelian cosmology on Christian thinking and on Newtonian and modern science.[12] Monod would not have done his Calvinist best had he not overemphasized the role which Duhem assigned to the Franciscan movement, markedly voluntarist, in opposing Aristotelian Thomism. Protestant readers of Monod's book could be lead into thinking that Duhem merely discovered the Reformation to have been at work centuries before Luther and Calvin. This, of course, would have meant by implication that the Bible, or at least its Protestant reading, had something to do with the rise of science.

Catholics by then should have seen in Duhem's work a godsend that provided them with the only reliable standpoint concerning science and the Church. Duhem elaborated that standpoint both in the philosophical and in the historical perspective. About the former, here it should only be noted that he brilliantly articulated the nature of physical theory, this most exact form of the scientific method. While the method of physical theory was positivist, its raw material, or sensory data coming

[10] See ch. 8, "The Scientific Development of Medieval Culture," in C. Dawson, *Medieval Essays* (Garden City, N.Y.: Doubleday, 1954), especially p. 123.

[11] See my book, *Reluctant Heroine: The Life and Work of Hélène Duhem* (Edinburgh: Scottish Academic Press, 1992).

[12] V. Monod, *Dieu dans l'univers* (Paris: Fischbacher, 1933).

from the immediate knowledge of external reality, could only be justified by a metaphysics about which physics had no competence at all. Just as Duhem defended thereby the autonomy of physics, he also held high, by the same stroke, the full legitimacy of metaphysics. If anything was alien to his precise thinking, it was Hegel's illusion about a direct conceptual transition from quantities to qualities (ontological considerations and ethical values) and back again. Putting this in the facetious form that what God has put in separate conceptual domains no one should fuse together, lest confusion arise, would be very Duhemian indeed.

But to return to the historical perspective opened up by Duhem. Before him Catholics or Christians arguing the harmony of science and faith were reduced to counting the number of scientists who were believers. At a time, the turn of the century, when skillful propaganda created the belief that most scientists were agnostics or even atheists, such a count could actually be very effective.[13] But Duhem put the question about that harmony (and indeed the relation of the Bible and science) on an entirely different and, at the same time, very safe level, where the force of that count could not be weakened by the count of non-believing scientists, whose number, it should be recognized, kept increasing as the twentieth century kept progressing. Since Duhem showed that science owed its very birth to a Christian creed which assures belief in the Bible, any opposition between science and religion had to appear as a mere misunderstanding between a father and his son. Although the son could act with a chip on his shoulder vis-à-vis his father, he remained nonetheless a chip from the old block. In driving home this point, Duhem pulled the carpet from under the feet of the academic

---

[13] The best of such counts was produced by Karl A. Kneller, a German Jesuit, whose *Das Christentum und die Vertreter der neueren Naturwissenschaft* went through four editions between 1903 and 1911. An English translation, by T. M. Kettle, of the second edition appeared in 1911 under the title, *Christianity and the Leaders of Modern Science* (London and St. Louis: B. Herder), 403pp. This translation has been reprinted, with my introduction, by Real-View-Books (Fraser, MI) in 1995.

brand of village atheists who worship science in order to ward off the specter of true worship.

Seen against this fundamental unity between science and Christian faith, all other issues appear relatively unimportant. Clearly, Catholics should have rejoiced for having been given a liberating perspective about the objection, of which their opponents invariably made much, namely, that the Church was the enemy of science. But not even the publication in 1936 of what may perhaps be Duhem's most spirited letter stirred Catholic intellectuals in France. The one who published that letter was none other than Hélène Duhem, in a priceless biography of her father.[14] The letter was Duhem's reply, written in 1911, to Père Bulliot, dean of the philosophy Faculty of the Institut Catholique in Paris. Duhem branded as a craven lie the contention that the Catholic faith and science are in opposition and referred to that very faith as the cradle that nursed the birth of modern science in the fourteenth century.

The book and the letter did not fail to impress George Sarton, by then for twenty years the editor of *Isis,* which has remained up to now the most influential quarterly for historians of science. That influence has never been lacking in a thrust which conforms to the interpretation of Western cultural history as demanded by Sarton's unabashed freemasonic predilections. Thus Sarton merely mentioned the letter to Bulliot, without giving specifics about it.[15] Ten years later and in a prominent context in Paris, Sarton gave shocking evidence of his resolve to say as little as possible about Duhem's achievements.[16]

To keep under cover data inconveniencing one's secularist ideology proved to be one effective way of blunting the thrust of Duhem's findings. Another was a questioning of Duhem's interpretation of Buridan's idea of inertial motion. What could

---

[14] H. Duhem, *Un savant français. Pierre Duhem* (Paris: Plon, 1936), pp. 158-69. The English translation of that letter is given in my *Scientist and Catholic: Pierre Duhem* (Front Royal, Va.: Christendom Press, 1991), pp. 235-40.

[15] For details, see *Reluctant Heroine,* pp. 140-41.

[16] See ibid., pp. 214-18.

not be questioned was the crucial importance of inertial motion for the Newtonian science of motion. Inertial motion is the basis of the law that gives force as the product of mass and acceleration. In terms of that law it is possible to have the kind of science which is a quantitative study of the quantitative aspects of things that move. Such a science is physics, all of whose branches deal with one or another class of things in motion. Whatever is not moving is not an object of physics, be it the physics of Newton or of Einstein or even of "God's quantum mechanics," to recall a phrase of Schrödinger.

Disputing the main notice

But before all Newtonian and modern physics there came Galileo. He quickly became the symbol of the break with Aristotelian science, about which it could rightly be said that hardly a single proposition of it was correct. What, then, if one could show that Galileo's inertial motion was essentially different from the one articulated by Buridan? Could not one thereby dissipate Duhem's perspective, so liberating for a Catholic but so stifling for anyone who could not stomach the supernatural as embodied in Christian revelation?

To formulate a positive answer to these questions was the task which Alexandre Koyré, whose ideology was a mixture of pantheism, German idealism, and French illuminism, set for himself. He did so by writing in the late 1930s a tripartite work, *Études galiléennes*, a series of studies on the late medieval and early Renaissance background of Galileo's idea of inertial motion. Koyré was already in his forties when he engaged in this first major venture of his into the history of science. Previously, his major interest related to the influence of German idealists on some Russian thinkers of the mid-nineteenth century and to Jacob Boehme's and Spinoza's philosophy. All these topics had strongly pantheistic connotations for which Koyré, a secularized Jew, had great sympathy.

There was nothing in the *Études galiléennes* that would have directly given away Koyré's secularistic pantheism. But something of his real motivations might have become visible had he provided his work with a name index. A quick compilation of the names of modern authors most often mentioned by Koyré reveals that his fifty or so references in the *Études* to Duhem far outnumber references there to any other modern author. In almost all cases Duhem is made to appear as having misconstrued or misinterpreted the record. His merits therefore could not be more than those of a heroic yeoman who gathered up a great many data, often very interesting and novel, but beside the essential point. Thus was Duhem damned with faint praise in order that the "liberating" vistas of the Enlightenment might be saved from their scholarly indictment by Duhem.

Nobody took issue with the central contention of Koyré, namely, that Buridan's idea of inertial motion was still intimately connected with Aristotelian concepts. True enough, for Buridan the celestial bodies had to move in circular orbits because they had no inclination for any other motion. Necessarily circular was the motion of those bodies also for Galileo, though with a difference. Galileo spoke of no inclination (appetite), only of geometrical forms. It is in this difference that Koyré saw the great dividing line between the old (Aristotelian) and the new (Cartesian and Newtonian) physics. He argued that this difference was motivated solely by the revival of Archimedes' admiration for geometry from the mid-sixteenth century on. The bearing of this on theology was too obvious to be spelled out bluntly: Since Archimedes took the place of Buridan, purely humanist insights, and not the impress made by Christ on the medieval mind, were to be credited for the rise of science. For a secularized Western culture, this conclusion had to appear outright liberating.

Indeed, as Koyré began to tour American universities in the 1950s, his message was found liberating by not a few of those who subsequently dominated the study of the history of science in the 1960s and 1970s. It appeared to them that once more one could confidently write histories of science by starting with Galileo. It was enough, though not really necessary any longer, to give lip-service to the facts unearthed by Duhem about pre-

Galilean science.[17] It even became possible to talk of the study of the history of science during the Middle Ages as being equivalent to proving and disproving propositions formulated by Duhem, and thus slight him indirectly.[18] For, owing to the enthusiastic reception given to Koyré's *Études*, it became scholarly to take lightly the weight of Duhem's primary proposition about that history.

In fact even those who did not come under Koyré's direct influence failed to take Duhem's principal contention in its true weight. A case in point is A. C. Crombie's *From Augustine to Galileo*, first published in 1951. Once it was republished as a two-volume paperback under the title, *Medieval and Early Modern Science*, in 1959, it quickly established itself as the best general survey of the topic. The book, well written and bursting with data, certainly helped in creating a broad consciousness about the reality of medieval science, but could provide little if any stimulus for perceiving the Christian dogma of creation as lying behind Buridan's great breakthough.[19] The reader was left to speculate that since the Middle Ages were dominated by the Church, there must have been a role for the Bible and for its being read in a Catholic way, that is, in the light of an authoritative catechesis. Meanwhile, non-Catholics could react to Crombie's book with the scornful remark that it takes a Catholic to be interested in medieval science.[20]

[17] For example, C. C. Gillispie in his *The Edge of Objectivity* (Princeton: Princeton University Press, 1959), which begins with Galileo's geometrical demonstration of the time-squared law of free fall.

[18] See M. Clagett's reviews of Volumes VI-IX of the *Système du monde* in *Isis* 49 (1958), pp. 359-62 and 53 (1962), pp. 251-52.

[19] As can be seen from a glance at pp. 60-70 in the Image Books edition (Garden City: Doubleday, 1959). Even more perplexing is Crombie's cursory treatment (a mere two pages) of Buridan, impetus, and creation (with Duhem not even being mentioned!) in his *Styles of Scientific Thinking in the European Tradition* (London: Duckworth, 1994, see pp. 1091-92). Clearly, in a perspective where the conceptual parameters of "argument and explanation" rule supreme, the question of *real* motion, as the very central issue of physical science, can but fade into the background.

[20] I have in mind the utterance which a prominent non-Catholic historian of science made in my presence in 1961.

A further indirect, and important, slighting of the notice served by Duhem came with H. Butterfield's *The Origins of Modern Science 1300-1800*, first published in 1959. By then Butterfield had made a name for himself with his critique of the Whig (or liberal-secularist) interpretation of history. He was not, however, predisposed for a conservative (Tory) interpretation of Western intellectual history to the point of being attracted to the deeper layers of Duhem's findings. This is all too evident in his book's first chapter, "The Historical Importance of a Theory of Impetus." There is no trace there of the drama for which the monumental failure of all great ancient cultures to make the breakthrough toward the impetus theory, and ultimately toward science, forms the backdrop.

Butterfield did not find it worthwhile to focus on Aristotle's pantheism, nor did he make any effort to point out the historical uniqueness of the biblical doctrine of creation. About Buridan's reference to creation he reported only the advantage that the new way of looking at the origin of motion would dispense with angelic intelligences in charge of the motion of the planets. Butterfield showed indeed a condescending attitude as he spoke of the stricture which the bishop of Paris issued in 1277 against those who resisted such non-Aristotelian doctrines as empty space, infinite universe, and plurality of worlds: "A religious taboo operated for once in favour of freedom for scientific hypothesis."[21] Curiously, Butterfield did not mention that the decision of 1277 was rooted in the age-old Christian conviction that God was free to create, or not to create, or to create any kind of universe provided it was rational. Aquinas fully shared that conviction. He merely did not find convincing the "scientific" reasons which the champions of those non-Aristotelian doctrines offered in support of them. And Aquinas was far from wrong in this respect.

Butterfield could have rightly taken Duhem to task for not emphasizing that the bishop of Paris was not the first to voice

---

[21] H. Butterfield, *The Origins of Modern Science: 1300-1800* (New York: Macmillan 1960), p. 9.

that Christian conviction. But one could just as well take Butterfield to task for not pointing out that some interpreters of Duhem disregarded the qualification, "in a sense," of his singling out that decision as being the beginning of modern science, in addition to taking his statement out of context. Duhem, a champion of continuity in intellectual development, knew fully well the significance of that qualifying phrase. Butterfield rather restricted the merit of Duhem's researches as being instrumental in effecting "a great change . . . in the attitude of the historians of science to the middle ages."[22] But this change merely meant that some, and not too many, were willing to see the development of modern European scientific thought as a continuum from the twelfth century on, a continuum not broken by the Renaissance. Since nothing during the twelfth century was similar in importance to Buridan's great breakthrough, the continuum in question could not therefore have really disturbing aspects for the secularist mind. After all, those in Chartres, singing the encomiums of geometry, could be mistaken for the avantgardes of an Archimedes to be rediscovered.

In fact, one could even speak of the medieval antecedents of the Copernican revolution in such a way as to undercut the stated purpose of a book with the title, *Christian Theology and Natural Science* and with "Some Questions on Their Relation" for its subtitle. About its author, Eric Mascall, it is difficult to assume that he would have found unpalatable the medieval roots of that relation. After all, he was a Thomist Anglican with High Church sympathies. But his citing of Duhem's *Système du monde* in his bibliography is eye opening, to say the least. For in the entire book there is not a single reference to Buridan or to Duhem. Of course, since Mascall's book was printed in 1956, he could not have included in his treatment of the subject what Duhem set forth on Buridan in the sixth and seventh volumes of the *Système*. But much of the material there on Buridan had

[22] Ibid.

already been available in the third volume of Duhem's Leonardo Studies, first published in 1913 and reprinted in 1954.

Still, Mascall's perspective did not have room for history. He failed to realize that one could say a great many worthwhile things about the relation of science and Christian theology, and yet not touch on a pivotal issue. It is surely useful to articulate essentially philosophical propositions that are equally basic to Christian faith in creation and to a truly creative method in science. But unless one proves that in the historical genesis of science those propositions played an indispensable and demonstrable role, the parallel thus drawn will lack effectiveness.

Christianity in the dock

Not being a historian, Mascall's oversight of Buridan's historical as well as historic role may be understandable. The same consideration cannot be invoked to exculpate professional historians of the technology of the Middle Ages, especially when they set great store by possible ideological motivations behind mechanical inventiveness. Such a historian was Lynn White, Jr., whose writings spread far and wide novel information about the startling creativity of Latin medievals in the technical arts. But about those ideological motivations he had appreciation for only one. It was the resolve to subdue nature, which those Latin medievals derived from Genesis 1, where the first parents are given the command: "Be fertile and multiply; fill the earth and subdue it. Have dominion over the fish of the sea, the birds of the air, and all the living things that move on the earth" (Gen 1:28).

In White's eyes, the resolve quickly became dominated by irresponsible selfishness. White memorably made that charge in his lecture delivered before the plenary meeting of the American Association for the Advancement of Science shortly after Christmas 1966 and carried worldwide in the pages of *Science*.[23] The sermon-like character of the lecture contrasted sharply with

[23] L. White, Jr., "The Historical Roots of our Ecological Crisis," *Science* 155 (March 10, 1967), pp. 1203-07.

White's *Medieval Technology and Social Change*, published in 1962 and bursting with data and references.[24]

To anyone, except a rabid Marxist, the wealth of data unearthed by White had to suggest forcefully the role of an ideological framework much broader than a mere resolve to dominate nature. That ideological framework was never considered by White in its breadth even in publications whose title indicated the contrary. Such was his address, "What Accelerated Technological Progress in the Western Middle Ages?" delivered at a major conference in Oxford in 1961 and published two years later in its proceedings.[25] For there too White had an eye only for the biblically motivated trend to dominate nature.

As a medieval historian, it was White's duty to be familiar with Duhem's works, especially with the vast documentary evidence Duhem made available about Buridan. White's silence on Duhem and Buridan must have had therefore a very strong motivation. The latter can readily be found in White's increasingly hostile attitude toward Christianity, medieval or not.

Behind that hostility there lay a reverence for nature smacking of pantheism. White therefore could but frown on a Christian ethic anchored in eternal life where alone the horrid injustices, not only moral but also physical, of human life can be equalized. Christian saints have always been fully aware of this, whatever the overflowing measure of their compassion for the suffering. White, however, had a different theology of compassion, which he set forth in 1978. The compassion was more pantheistic than Christian. Only a pantheist could extol, as White did, Albert Schweitzer as "the greatest modern Christian saint,"[26] and see in Saint Francis of Assisi only his love of nature, befitting a Buddhist in disguise. Only a pantheist could put, as White did, concern for animals, plants, and landscape on the same level as

---

[24] Oxford University Press.

[25] In *Scientific Change*, ed. A. C. Crombie (New York: Basic Books, 1963), pp. 272-91.

[26] L. White, Jr., "The Future of Compassion," *Ecumenical Review*, 30 (1978), pp. 99-109; for quotation, see p. 103.

concern for man. Dominating that level is a "nebulous respect for life" for which, curiously enough, White strictured Albert Schweitzer himself. On that nebulous level alone can it be claimed that faith is not "belief in religious propositions but rather is total surrender of one's being to Divine Being."[27] For on that nebulous level the sentence structure, "not only but also" will invariably look equivalent to "but rather." On that level the clarity of an ever complex truth is bartered for emotionally fueled simplism. On that level one fails to perceive a rank inconsistency. It consists in blaming Christianity for the threat of science to nature and in refusing, at the same time, to credit Christianity with having played a crucial role in making possible a science without which man cannot liberate himself from a fearful servitude to nature.

This is not the place to outline the breadth of the threat which admiration for nature, as espoused by White and the many admirers of his ecologism,[28] poses to Christian faith *and* love. One particular aspect of that threat should, however, be pointed out, because it very much relates to the present study. White's treatment of medieval technology necessarily keeps in the dark intellectual insights such as the ones that propelled Buridan's thinking. There is nothing odd in all this. That so many who claim to be Christians (and even Christian theologians) have fallen victim to that threat will appear odd only to those who continually mistake Nature for its Author, as they set the very goal of their lives.

[27] Ibid., p. 99.
[28] A point developed in my paper, "Ecology or Ecologism," in *Man and His Environment. Tropical Forests and the Conservation of Species* (Vatican City: Pontifical Academy of Sciences, 1994), pp. 271-93; reprinted in my *Patterns or Principles and Other Essays* (Bryn Mawr, Pa.: Intercollegiate Studies Institute, 1995).

8

Three Perspectives

Creed and Science

To counter the threat of an ecologism, which is often little more than nature-worship, much more is needed than a patently unrealistic reinterpretation of the famed injunction in Genesis 1 that man should subdue nature. The injunction may perhaps be interpreted as a quasi-liturgical role for man to voice Nature's submission to its Creator,[1] though not in disregard of an elementary fact: The author of Genesis 1 and all its readers, until very recently, enjoyed nothing of the comforts of modern technology. These comforts effectively distract from the deadly threats which untamed environment poses to man even apart from major natural catastrophes. The threat of a very hostile nature, to be faced daily, cannot be subdued by meditations (let alone by dreams) about a quasi-liturgical role. What is needed is plain realism, which is not forthcoming when one's thinking is dominated either by a sentimentalist approach to the environment, or by the view that mankind is just another species.

There is nothing to apologize for in man's domination of nature as long as it is not an unconscionable exploitation, which, on a large scale, only came with modern industrial society.[2] In

---

[1] As done by J. Barr in his "Man and Nature—The Ecological Controversy and the Old Testament," *Bulletin of the John Rylands Library* 9 (1972), pp. 9-32; especially, pp. 20-24.

[2] Among earlier examples that have nothing to do either with industrial society or with Christianity is the extermination of about a dozen species of moas, the famed giant birds of New Zealand. The method of extermination included the corralling of those birds within rings of forest and brushwood, set afire by the Polynesians, who reached New Zealand in the fourteenth century. None of those birds was smaller than three feet, and the tallest, with its neck stretched, stood at almost ten feet. Any visitor to New Zealand can quickly find out that it has

that society, as is well known, Christianity was given a cold shoulder, if not not met with outright hostility. Christianity is not to be blamed for the raping of the environment by captains of industry who took their inspiration from social Darwinism while paying occasional lip service to the Bible. Nor should Christianity be blamed for the colossal exploitation of the environment which has been the rule whenever and wherever dialectical materialism established itself as a political regime, handling ruthlessly man as well as nature.

To counter White's charges, which involve much more than the proper reading of Genesis 1, it is not enough to add some dabbling in the history and philosophy of science to exegetical expertise.[3] The latter may be counterproductive if it does not include categorical assertions of basic philosophical and theological truths. Theologians who reduce their métier to commitment and imagination, because scientists also find these indispensable, merely disarm themselves vis-à-vis science.

For whatever loose garbs have been thrown around science by psychologists and sociologists parading as philosophers of science, science retains a strictly tailored garment, which is also

become, in recent years, a tabu to dwell on the fate which the moas suffered at the hands of the aborigines. One wonders whether that tabu would be in force if the perpetrators had been Christians, let alone Catholics.

[3] As displayed by Barr who, in his article quoted above, disputed the existence of science in the Middle Ages by invoking a single historian of science, H. Butterfield, who in fact granted much more science to the Middle Ages than Barr suggested. Two decades later, in his Gifford Lectures, *The Bible and Natural Theology* (Oxford: Oxford University Press, 1993), Barr dismissed the idea that the Bible had much to do with the rise of science. In doing so he took for a guide W. M. O'Neil's far from standard work, *Early Astronomy from Babylon to Copernicus* (Sydney: Sydney University Press, 1986), in which ancient Babylonian astronomy is accorded "an almost scientific" status. The fact is that the ancient Babylonians were much farther away from a true science of astronomy than was Ptolemy himself, in spite of his success in predicting planetary positions with as much accuracy as afforded in the original form of Copernicus' system, which, in a sense, made science possible. Yet it was not until Newton that there was on hand that full-fledged science which could cope with the dynamics of bodies, whether celestial or terrestrial. But as Butterfield noted, though far from giving full credit to Duhem, it was in the Middle Ages that the crucial step was taken toward what three centuries later became known as Newtonian dynamics.

uniquely resistant to scepticism and fuzzy-mindedness. The garment is the precision which goes with quantities, that supreme target of scientific investigations. Therefore any theologian, who thinks that "commitment" is a dispensation from coming clean on truth, destroys the very means whereby he can show that quantitative precision is not the whole truth even in science. The *reality* of an instrument cannot be rendered in mere numbers precisely because it is far more than all the measurable properties of that instrument. Even in the most abstract science, mathematics, quantities alone do not explain the operations to be done with them. Only non-quantitative words can explain what is, say, a sign of multiplication.

This leads to the wholeness of truth in the Bible. Within Catholicism that wholeness rests on an authoritative teaching of Christ's message handed down through a very visible, self-perpetuating body, the hierarchy. Such a way of teaching implies, to repeat an old truth that bears repeating nowadays even in Catholic theological circles, a realist epistemology or, rather, metaphysics. Such a metaphysics finds its logical crowning in natural theology. The latter is not a sophisticated talk about something vaguely called God. Natural theology is the highest and deepest form of the exercise of a mind which, precisely because it knows truth, can be known to reflect, however modestly, the infinite rationality of an absolutely truthful God. Nothing is therefore more natural for a Catholic than to find genuine natural theology in the Bible.

A Catholic guided by genuine ecumenism should therefore sigh with relief whenever the expertise of a Protestant exegete leads him to recognize natural theology in the Bible. The Catholic can, however, hardly take heart when the recognition is weakened in the same breath. The old Protestant longing for certainty as something vividly felt can mislead one into thinking that since the demonstrations of natural theology, either within the Bible or without, do not necessarily generate conviction, they are merely half-truths. Today, this halving, if not quartering and decimating, of truth is couched in the distinction between "strong" and "weak" forms of a proposition.

The trick is fashionably contagious because it is widely practiced by scientists whenever they face the task of going beyond a mere quantitative result to its philosophical underpinnings and ramifications. Of course, scientists find no help in that respect in their general education, which, if it included a course or two in philosophy, imbued them with the idea that philosophy is just mere talk about talk. When faced with scientists talking philosophy—and they never cease philosophizing—*caveat* the theological *emptor*, who is still conscious of truth as his only ware to sell.

For the relation of the Bible and science rests no less on truth than any relation worth exploring. This is best instanced by the highest of all relations, the one standing for each of the Three Persons in One God. The idea of such a relation had to be worked out lest that highest of all mysteries of Christian (and biblical) faith should appear a contradiction in terms. The work involved a specification of what the words person and relation may basically mean. In the same way, before the relation between the Bible and science is specified, some basic truths should be stated about the Bible as well as about science. Otherwise discourse about that relation will turn into an exercise in insufficiently defined terms or in terms artfully left undefined.

The most basic truth in the New Testament perspective about the Bible is that it rests on preaching with authority. More specifically, the Bible rests on those who do that preaching with authority in the Church, insofar as the Church is the carrier of a supernatural dispensation and sets thereby the norm of faith, which is the Creed. That Church had existed before any of the books of the New Testament came to be written and had already a three-generation-long existence before the writing of all those books had been completed. That Church alone could guarantee which of the many Gospels, Acts, Letters, and Apocalypses were to be taken for genuine expressions of that preaching. That Church alone guarantees the proper reading of any and all biblical passages, and in particular those that, as Peter warned, could, although written by no less an authority than Paul, easily be used for spiritual self-destruction.[4] That Church alone could defend the Bible from its being abused by a great many who claimed to have a superior kind of knowledge or inspiration. Their line stretches from the Gnostics of old to the champions of Higher Criticism, and beyond these to some latter-day students of literary forms. Differ as they may, they all attribute primacy to the letter, forgetting that in both Covenants (and especially in the New) the authoritatively spoken word assured meaning and validity to what became written down. The reversal of that order has invariably put in motion that logic whereby the letter "killeth."

Instead of the relation of the Bible and Science one should therefore speak of the relation of the Creed and Science. In doing so, one would also do justice to the historical reality of the former relation. Whatever concern some Church Fathers had for science, it was the Creed ultimately that they wanted to vindicate whenever scientific knowledge appeared to contradict this or that biblical passage. Owing to the strength and steadiness of that authoritative Creed, the medieval Christian confrontation with Aristotelian science did not become a replay of the Muslim debacle with respect to reason. Through the Galileo case the authoritative Church tasted the danger of defending the literal meaning of some biblical utterances, although it could be seen right there and then that their truth was ultimately the matter of empirical (scientific) investigation.

Some dangers of science

The danger is on hand even when the literal meaning of a biblical passage seems to anticipate some recent scientific discovery. A chief example is the parallel that offers itself between the divine utterance, "Let there be light!" of Genesis 1

---

[4] "There are certain passages in them hard to understand. The ignorant and the unstable destroy them (just as they do the rest of Scriptures) to their own ruin" (2 Pt 3:16).

and the burst of radiation that dominated in that most distant moment in the past to which the expansion of the universe can be traced back today by science. Of course, Pius XII did not give an official interpretation of that utterance as he told the Pontifical Academy of Sciences on November 22, 1951, that "it would seem that present-day science, with one sweeping step back across millions of centuries, has succeeded in bearing witness to that primordial `Fiat lux' uttered at the moment when, along with matter, there burst forth from nothing a sea of light and radiation, while the particles of chemical elements split and formed into millions of galaxies."[5] Could the Pope mean that the author of Genesis 1 had received revelation about electromagnetic radiation? Yet such a revelation had to be at work if, by speaking of visible light, the author of Genesis 1 also meant, however implicitly, the 2.7°K cosmic background radiation. Perhaps in order to rule out such bizarre speculations, the Pope, in addressing the International Astronomical Union a year later, refrained from referring to Genesis 1.

Almost half a century later, it took a mere week or so for George Smoot, leader of the group that in April 1992 discovered discontinuities in that radiation, to beat a similar retreat from tieing Genesis 1 to science. While in the Pope's case some theologian-scientists voiced their concern,[6] Smoot beat a retreat because many of his colleagues felt upset by seeing theology (or the Bible) brought in on the coattails of science. In both cases the disentangling of the 2.7°K radiation from Genesis 1 could have been done by simply recalling what the discovery, as a step in science, was really about.

The discovery by itself brought further verification to the Big Bang insofar as such discontinuities were among its consequences. They in turn could be used as possible causes of the forma-

---

[5] See par. 44 in the address, printed as a pamphlet with the title, "The Proofs for the Existence of God in the Light of Modern Science" (Washington D.C.: National Catholic Welfare Conference, n.d.), p. 15.

[6] In particular, the Abbé George Lemaître, then president of the Pontifical Academy of Sciences.

tion of very large protogalaxies. There was therefore some truth to Smoot's statement that the discovery "is really a breakthrough, a revolution, in our understanding of the early universe." But the meaning of the discovery was very much stretched as Smoot claimed in the same breath that "what we have found is evidence for the birth of the universe and its evolution."[7] For if by birth the creation of the universe was meant, a meaning was grafted on science which it could not bear. And Smoot merely played the amateur theologian by adding: "If you're religious, it's like looking at God."[8] The kind of God that could be spotted in that way was less than a pale image. Only a blunt No! was to be said in reply to Smoot's musing: "It really is like finding the driving mechanism for the universe, and isn't that what God is?"[9] He should have said right away what he said ten days later: "What matters is the science. I want to leave the religious implications to theologians and to each person, and let them see how the findings fit into their idea of the universe."[10]

The theological fit, if it is to work, is, of course, very simple. Smoot's discovery merely added another telling detail to an already long process that forms the backbone of modern scientific cosmology, this hottest field of research in twentieth-century science. The process is best appreciated against the background of Laplace's cosmogenesis that held sway during much of the nineteenth century. It consisted in an effort to derive the actual high degree of specificity everywhere in the universe from an infinite and apparently homogeneous erstwhile nebula. Little attention was paid to the fact that knowledge about that nebula was very nebulous, to say the least. Worse, precisely because of its apparent homogeneity, it was readily taken for an entity that explained itself. Quite the contrary situation emerges from twentieth-century cosmology that began with the publication in

---

[7] *The New York Times*, April 24, 1992, p. 1.
[8] *The New York Times*, May 5, 1992, p. C1.
[9] Ibid., p. C1.
[10] Ibid., p. C9.

1917 of Einstein's fifth memoir on general relativity, a memoir on its cosmological consequences.

In that memoir the universe appeared to have a specifically limited total mass with a maximum radius of curvature. Ten or so years later another overall specificity was learned about that universe, namely, its expansion at a specific rate. This in turn invited an increasingly intense investigation of the early phases of the expanding universe. The results have been unanimous in one sense that went counter to the Laplacian theory of origins: The farther in the past is the universe traced, the more specific it appears. It is that specificity which justifies the raising of the question about the universe: Why such and not something else?

The question is distinctly philosophical and is the only question that can be fitted onto the science of cosmology so that it may serve as a jumping board for theology. For being a question about the universe, or the strict totality of physical things, the question, "Why such and not something else?" carries one beyond the Universe. The answer therefore conjures up the reality of the only conceivable being beyond the totality of things which is the Universe. That being is the very Creator who alone can choose, by his creative power, a very specific cosmic set out of a conceivably infinite number of such sets.[11]

A painstaking review of the history of modern scientific cosmology is, of course, needed to see what it is truly about. Disregarding such a review would invite an impatient rush to exploit dubious offerings of that cosmology. The most popular among these has been cosmology's alleged ability to establish the moment of creation, which it plainly cannot do. No science can ever spot or describe creation out of nothing and establish thereby the first moment and, on that basis, compute the age of the universe, simply because science cannot observe the "nothing." Science can merely show that the universe has an age which

---

[11] For futher details, see my *God and the Cosmologists* (Edinburgh: Scottish Academic Press, 1989) and my *Is there a Universe?* (Liverpool: Liverpool University Press, 1993), the expanded text of my Forwood Lectures given at that university in 1991.

is it least a dozen or so billion years old, a proposition very different from the claim that since it was created so many years ago, its age has to be such and such.

About the evolution of the universe, from very specific earlier states to a very specific present state, nothing is, of course, as much as intimated in Genesis 1. Much less should one try to find there the idea of a biological evolution and certainly not the idea that every species was separately created by God. Of course, the real threat of Darwinism to the Bible has never been its evolutionary perspective. The latter merely brought into sharper focus the fact (presumably dear to all theists) that the universe is thoroughly correlated in all its parts, and that therefore one species should be assumed to be instrumental in the emergence of another species.

That Darwin failed to explain what that instrumentality consisted of was obvious to any clear-sighted reader of *The Origin of Species*. What obscured clarity was the materialistic propaganda machine that hailed Darwin's book as the ultimate weapon to vanquish the supernatural. Clearly, there was no need to worry about God in a universe in which life processes allegedly went on for no purpose whatever. Not that Darwin's science could ever establish competence about purpose or even about the lack of it.[12] But this was a philosophical point which could not be conveyed in an atmosphere that increasingly wanted scientific answers to philosophical questions. Such a myopia could not, however, dispel the ever greater scientific problems to be faced by Darwinism in its scientific context. Today those problems loom large, partly because findings about the sudden extinction of dinosaurs turned out to be but one of a long set of similar large-scale extinctions that occurred periodically in the geological past. In other words, nothing can any longer gloss over the fact that the fossil record defies the mechanism of evolution proposed by Darwin.

---

[12] See on this my *The Purpose of it All* (Edinburgh: Scottish Academic Press; Lanham Md.: Regnery Gateway, 1990).

All this proved the wisdom of letting science slowly clarify itself, instead of forcing theology to come to terms with patently provisional scientific conclusions. Possibly by learning from its near comeuppance in the Galileo case, the official Catholic reaction was a wait-and-see attitude toward Darwinism. Not all Catholic theologians (at times also scientists) heeded the wisdom of waiting with patience so that Darwinist research may gradually unfold both its lasting and its highly revisable aspects. Some of them rushed to endorse Darwinian perspectives by giving them a dubious theological twist. Teilhard de Chardin, for instance, would have done much more good if at any time during his scientific career he would have courageously called attention to a crucial point that leading Darwinists now readily admit: The paleontological record was never known to have contained clear transitional forms, let alone a series of gentle gradations leading up to man, and much less to an Omega point.

Not that the absence of those forms would demand the specific creation of each and every species, in terms of the phrase, "according to its kind," of Genesis 1. The only solid ground for holding evolution is belief in the createdness of the universe, and therefore in the strict interconnectedness of all its parts, a feature demanded by the infinite rationality of the Creator. This is what many Protestants fail to understand, prisoners as they often are of biblicism. They are therefore bound to look askance at the idea of creation out of nothing insofar as they claim that it is not "clearly" in the Bible. Conversely, they are forced to stick with a separate creation of all species because, according to Genesis 1, God created each of them "according to its kind." Hence the conflict between Darwinism and the Bible has been a conflict mainly for Protestants.

But the idea of creation in the beginning would stand Darwinists themselves in good stead to an extent far greater than they dare imagine. After all, they still have to produce one single empirically verified case of a species transforming itself into another (to say nothing of the steps between ever higher units, such as genera, families, classes, etc.). Transformation all across the board can be argued only on the basis of generalizations and bold extrapolations that are so philosophical, and indeed metaphysical, as to border at times on theology proper. While the often materialistic presuppositions of most Darwinists are incapable of securing that basis, it is readily provided by belief in creation out of nothing.

That belief, as theological history fully attests, flourished only within Catholicism, precisely because there the Bible, unlike in Protestantism, was never placed on the pedestal which only the living voice of a Church authorized by Christ can occupy. The flourishing of that belief is an aspect of the intellectual confidence of the Church, which is not necessarily the confidence or patience of individual Catholics. It is the confidence of a "living authority," to recall a recent momentous utterance of Rome about its consciousness of the standards of its own operations.[13] The endurance of that consciousness, together with the confidence it generates, can hardly be the work of cunning or luck. Considerations of probability would prohibit that such a luck be assumed to work for too long a time. As to cunning, it would readily give itself away under the manifold pressures within which the teaching authority of Rome has to operate.

Herein lies the chief failure of accounting for the endurance of the papacy by such prominent historians of it as Ranke, and of such notable readers of him as Macaulay, the author of the celebrated review of Ranke's *History of the Papacy*. Not that Macaulay had not been impressed by that endurance. Witness his memorable portrayal of a distant future that would find the papacy still alive but the London Bridge already in ruins, taken for the eventual demise of the British Empire.[14]

---

[13] I have in mind the reference in the Apostolic Letter of May 22, 1994, of John Paul II to precisely those words in the letter which Pope Paul VI sent in 1975 to Dr. Coggan, Archbishop of Canterbury, to inform him that the Church has no authority to ordain women.

[14] Among the many non-Catholic admirerers of that passage was Winston Churchill. Lord Moran, his personal physician from 1940 on, recorded that Churchill recited by heart that passage to him at least three times. One of those occasions followed Churchill's audience with Pius XII on August 23, 1944. After mentioning

A historian of science does not even have to conjure up a perhaps not too distant future (scientific theories have relatively short survival values) when graphic portrayals might be sketched about some scientific ruins. Already today one can be amused by seeing the ruins of bridges which certain Darwinists, more ideologues than scientists, had busily drawn as arching across vast gaps in the world of the living. They had claimed for well over a century that they had seen the transitional forms (the segments of those bridges) whose non-existence is now ruefully recognized. Some of them even admit that they have been lying all along.[15] They are still to face up to the fact that those bridges collapsed because they were purported to be strictly scientific. Actually what alone could have given them reality was the metaphysical cement of generalization and vast extrapolation. But of metaphysics they want no part ever since Darwin had banished it twenty full years before the publication of *The Origin of Species*.[16] He did so (and his disciples do so) in full awareness of the fact that if metaphysics is allowed, man's origin and the origin of all will immediately appear to demand much more than science to make sense at all. What will appear to be needed is a philosophy and theology steeped in the doctrine of creation out of nothing as the basis of all.

To recognize the creation of all out of nothing is the first step in thinking that miracles are possible. Creation out of nothing is indeed the basis of all miracles. Not that creation out of nothing in the beginning had been a miracle. That creation made nature whereas miracles merely changes nature, though at times in such a way that creation out of nothing is at work. Of

to Lord Moran the substance of his conversation with the Pope, Churchill recited that passage "as his eyes dilated" and voiced his feeling that "there must be something in a faith that could survive so many centuries and had held captive so many men." *Churchill. Taken from the Diaries of Lord Moran* (Boston: Houghton Mifflin Company, 1966), p. 186.

[15] For instance, N. Eldridge, curator of the Natural History Museum of the City of New York.

[16] In his early Notebooks. See my *Angels, Apes and Man* (La Salle, IL.: Sherwood Sugden, 1983), pp. 52-53.

course, to create out of nothing remains the exclusive privilege of God. In fact, this is so much God's privilege that even He, for all his omnipotence, cannot delegate it to a mere creature, however eminent. Thomas Aquinas made that point with his customarily succinct lucidity. It should indeed be elementary to perceive that only the One who is Existence itself can give existence to any and all. This is why the notion of God and of Creator are so intimately connected.

Wise words from a physicist

This connection is vividly on hand in what may be the finest concise statement which a prominent man of science has ever made about miracles. The scientist in question was Sir George Gabriel Stokes, who held for over fifty years (1849-1903) the prestigious Lucasian Chair of Mathematics at Cambridge, which in our times entered public consciousness through the name of its present holder, Stephen Hawking. Unlike Hawking, Stokes had serious interest in theological and philosophical questions relating to science, as shown by the two series of Gifford Lectures he gave between 1891 and 1893 at the University of Edinburgh. In the very first of those lectures (a total of twenty) Stokes stated: "Admit the existence of a God, of a personal God, and the possibility of miracle follows at once." In justification of this, Stokes added that "if the laws of nature are carried on in accordance with His [God's] will, He who willed them may will their suspension."[17]

But Stokes had a deeper view of a personal Creator than to stop at stating a mere possibility on God's part to interfere in his creation. After all, Stokes meant by creation not a mere fashioning from something that had already existed, but creation out of nothing. That creation has never been connected with Laplace's Superior Spirit, whose intellect, being in full knowledge of all physical parameters at a given moment, could see all future and past events. But it could not see the creation itself, and much less

[17] G. G. Stokes, *Natural Theology* (London and Edinburgh: Adam and Charles Black 1891), p. 24. The second series was published two years later.

could it perform it. Unfortunately, during the hundred years that have gone by since Stokes, the expression "creation out of nothing" has lost much of its force in the eyes of many. We now have prominent physicists (Hawking among them) who claim that the presumed perfection of their physical theories makes the Creator unnecessary. There are even some who claim nothing less than that quantum cosmology enables the physicist, in theory at least, to create entire universes "literally" out of nothing.[18] Indeed, by being exposed to the teaching of some Nobel-laureate physicists, younger physicists have imbibed the notion that modern physics has proved that the nothing is also something and that the something is nothing as well.

The disastrous consequences which such claims have for reasoned discourse should seem obvious, though all too often they are not. No effort will be made in these pages to belabor the infinite distance between something and nothing. For the effort would be largely wasted in this age of ours for which the infinite distance exists only quantitatively but not in that ontological sense which is implied in the difference between something and nothing. No wonder that in this age of ours the idea of God has turned into a mere cultural parameter of value judgments all of which are, of course, relative. Within such a perspective nothing can be seen about the infinite power needed to bridge the distance between nothing and something, that is, between non-existence and existence.

But a hundred years ago, Stokes and a great number of prominent physicists were not yet plagued with blindness for that ontological distance. They therefore perceived something of the unimaginably infinite power needed for bridging it. Indeed, as Stokes' case shows, one needed only elementary reflections in order to draw from the consideration of that distance and power appropriate consequences for the interpretation of miracles as far as physics is concerned. In speaking as he did about the suspension by God of the laws He had ordered, Stokes hastened to

---

[18] A. H. Guth, of M.I.T. For further details, see my *God and the Cosmologists*, p. 138.

explain what that suspension can mean when considered from the side of God's Almighty power: "And if any difficulty should be felt as to their suspension, we are not even obliged to suppose that they have been suspended; it may be that the event which we call a miracle was brought about, not by any suspension of the laws in ordinary operation, but by the superaddition of something not ordinarily in operation, or if in operation, of such a nature that its operation is not perceived."[19]

In other words, once the power of the Creator is truly recognized as infinite, it is inane to restrict its operation to within the relatively narrow confines of science, let alone the always very narrow confines of the science of the day. But Stokes would have been the last to equate God with a superior physicist who is in command of all physics of all times. For in that case God would not be infinitely more than Laplace's Superior Spirit, whose intellect is merely in full possession of all initial parameters. God is God and not merely a superior calculator.

Worse, most interpreters of quantum mechanics would nowadays deny to God even that relatively lowly status. The reason for this is tied to their grafting a mistaken epistemology onto an excellent statistical physics which has for its nerve center Heisenberg's uncertainty principle. The very fact that, almost from its very formulation in 1927, Heisenberg's principle was also called the principle of indeterminacy, foreshadowed an orgy in equivocation. It mattered not that already in late 1930 that abuse of logic was pointed out by a noted philosopher and in, of all places, the pages of *Nature*. The scientific community, and then the body of philosophers too, continued believing that there was nothing wrong with the inference that an interaction that could not be measured "exactly," could not have taken place "exactly." The illegitimacy of that inference lay in taking the same word "exactly" first in an operational, and then in an ontological sense,[20] as if the former necessarily implied the latter.

---

[19] Stokes, *Natural Theology*, pp. 24-25.
[20] For a full discussion, see my essay, "Determinism and Reality," *Great Ideas Today* (Chicago: Encyclopedia Britannica, 1990), pp. 277-302.

To crown this cultural comedy, theologians, who should have known better, took that equivocation for a liberation from the shackles of mechanistic determinism, as if ontological causality was dependent on the idea of perfectly accurate measurements as allowed in Newtonian physics. Thus began the farcical justification of miracles on the basis of Heisenberg's principle, as if it had secured for God convenient scientifically approved loopholes within which to perform miracles without coming into conflict with science.[21]

Miracles will, of course, remain a scandal to reason as long as one fails to dissipate the thick halo that has grown around Hume's attack on miracles. An attack it certainly was but not a proof of the impossibility and factuality of miracles. Hume merely declared that Newton's physics, about which he knew precious little, amounts to the absolute supremacy of the laws of nature. As to the factuality of miracles, his diatribe against them boiled down to his assertion that no report about them satisfied him. Since, in an increasingly unbelieving age, he soon acquired the reputation of a sound reasoner, his attack on the miracles was quickly taken for a rout of all who believed in them. Moreover it has become a culturally respectable tacit assumption that in order to perform a miracle God has to obtain the prior permission from Academies of Science (and today from major TV channels), who in turn will specify the date and the time to suit their convenience.

Far more important than Hume's attack on miracles are some considerations about the kind of God who performs miracles, precisely because, being the Creator, he has full sovereignty over nature. Such a God is infinitely perfect and therefore infinitely rational and purposeful as well. It would therefore be most unreasonable to assume that, by performing a miracle, God would flout, if this were at all possible even for him, the principle of contradiction and identity. In other words, even for God it is not possible to let something exist and not exist

---

[21] See my *Miracles and Physics* (Front Royal, Va.: Christendom Press, 1989), pp. 49-52.

at the same time. Therefore, in reference to his performing a miracle, God cannot be assumed to force people to believe that something took place, although it did not. In performing his miracles, God does not practice make-believe. He can, of course, produce a mental vision (in a dream, for instance) that carries an indication which is valid, regardless of whether something physically real corresponded literally to what was "seen."

God's purpose in performing miracles concerns the promotion of a salvation history which is a supernatural matter. Being the creator of both the natural and the supernatural orders, God will, when performing a miracle, take into consideration the natural order as much as possible. Therefore, although a miracle will in principle break the natural flow of events, it will not make a theatrical mockery of nature. The Christian theological principle that grace was not meant to destroy nature but to elevate it governs miracles as well. This is why all major biblical miracles, especially God's "great acts" (*gedoloth*, or *magnalia*) in the Old Testament, or his large-scale interventions in nature, have always been so many enhancements (subtly miraculous to be sure) of natural forces or conditions already at work.

There is still another consideration, possibly the most important of them all. Having created man with genuine freedom, including the ability to resist plain evidence, God will not engage in theatricality so as to mesmerize man. The flash of light that threw Paul off his high horse did not reveal to him immediately the One who was at work. There too—as in all great acts of God, to say nothing of his innumerable small acts—God remained almost invisible. In none of them did God leave his signature in the sand, or on the rock, let alone on the waters. For all of them stands the remark in Psalm 77 concerning the crossing of the Red Sea: Although no one saw the Lord's footprints, the Lord himself passed through.

9

God's Great Interventions

The Flood

As was noted, God's great interventions in nature (*gedoloth*) served the purpose of a supernatural salvation history, a series of special covenants of God with man. The first of those covenants was the installment of Adam and Eve in the Garden of Eden as God's stewards in the midst of a nature that appeared to them, and still does appear to the naked eye, as a huge tent, with the sky as its canopy. Whatever its primitive details, that tent-like nature stood for a whole about which it was clearly realized that it could be much more than what it appeared to be. Even today, after almost a century of a truly scientific cosmology that deals in terms of supergalaxies, it is well to recall that the true totality of things, or universe, remains more than science can ever convincingly grasp with its conceptual and observational tools.[1] Part of that first covenant was man's duty to make the seventh day holy, by following a pattern set by the Maker of the universe himself. Had Genesis 1 been seen in this light, no flood of words would have been wasted on efforts that aimed at reconciling its primitive world picture with the ever vaster details science has unveiled about the world at large. But no sooner had the Bible been read within a non-biblical ambience, such as Hellenistic Alexandria, than the temptation was on hand to make Genesis 1 culturally respectable, that is, concordant with the science of the day. This trend of concordism—started by Philo and the Church Fathers, eagerly continued by the Scolastics, Reformers, Counter-

---

[1] The inability of modern scientific cosmology to deal with the strict totality of material things (or the universe) is discussed in my Forwood Lectures, given at the University of Liverpool in 1992, *Is there a Universe?* (Liverpool: University of Liverpool Press; New York: Wethersfield Institute, 1993).

reformers, and cultivated up to this very day—has only sown seeds of apparent discordance between reason and revelation.[2]

Insofar as the making of the universe in Genesis 1 means, at least implicitly, a creation out of nothing, science has nothing to say. Science, which should shudder whenever infinite quantities float within its ken,[3] should simply withdraw from the scene in face of an infinitely superior kind of infinity: the truly divine force that alone can bridge the infinite gap between non-existence and existence. Nor can science object to the infinitely large number of ways in which God can produce a physical phenomenon or delete its effects, for that matter. The latter kind of divine power should have indeed been at play if Chapters 6-8 of Genesis impose the view that the Flood covered the whole earth. For such a Flood should have left sediments all over the globe, geological evidences of which are, however, sorely missing. Should one then assume that God had obliterated the traces of a global Flood? Possibly, but what are the biblical proofs of this?

One may be tempted to appeal to the fact that in some deeper layers of the Mesopotamian soil it is possible to find sediments characteristic of flooding. For such sediments to exist, vast amounts of floodwaters had to be on hand. Natural rainfall would have had to be enhanced enormously, and far beyond a mere forty days' worth, if the sea level was to be raised by the three miles necessary to carry Noah's ark to the top slopes of Ararat. In that case, the Flood would have expanded far beyond the general region known as Ararat, or a part of northwestern Mesopotamia. It would have been a global event that would have spared only the upper portions of the Himalayas.

But if heights much lower than the three-mile high peaks of Ararat were meant by the phrase, "the ark came to rest on the

---

[2] For further discussion, see my article, "The Sabbath-Rest of the Maker of All," *The Asbury Theological Journal* 50 (Spring 1995), pp. 37-49.

[3] It is not without reason that the infinite quantity which the classical treatment of black-body radiation yielded a hundred years ago was called infinity catastrophe. Eddington had this in mind when he coined his memorable phrase: "Infinity is the mischief and science must have nothing to do with it." A. S. Eddington, *New Pathways in Science* (Cambridge: University Press, 1934), p. 217.

mountains of Ararat," the Flood would not have been so extensive as to destroy all mankind with the exception of a couple
dozen men and women (Noah and "his sons, his wife and his
sons' wives"). Nor would all animals on earth have been
destroyed save those which Noah entered in the Ark. At any rate,
an ark, about 450 feet long, 75 feet wide, and 45 feet tall (the
Mayflower was about one-fourth as long), could not accommodate
samples of the entire bestiary of the Middle East, nor even a
significant portion of it. There was also the logistics of providing
all those animals with food for at least forty days, assuming that
this number was not a symbol of a very long period. The argument that those animals became comatose while in the Ark works
only if one lets one's intellect fall asleep. Reports about traces of
Noah's ark still lying on the highest slopes of Ararat are best
ignored.[4]

One should therefore settle with a fairly localized flood, a
flood limited to the Mesopotamian basin, the memory of which
survived in Sumerian and Babylonian lore (the Gilgamesh and
the Athrasis Epics), as well as among Iranians and Hindus, a
consensus that must not be taken lightly. (Yet, curiously missing
is a clear tradition of a deluge in ancient Egyptian lore.) Physically, the biblical Flood implies the enhancement of natural
forces for a purpose which puts Noah's story in a class apart from
other Flood legends. The narrator of Noah's story stresses God's
mercy together with the assurance that God's plan of salvation
would prevail, physical and moral catastrophes notwithstanding.
This spiritual side to the story is also subtly intimated by the
symbolism of the dimensions of the ark given in close multiples
(or fractions) of 60, the Babylonian base of counting. Such an ark
successfully rides out the Flood, whose devastating power is
symbolized by its duration of forty days. As to the rainbow, it is

---

[4] Partly because it is not so much over dangerous crevasses as through the pitfalls
of tortuous equivocations and dubious insinuations that certain authors lead their
readers to some half-visible protrusions of the ark, buried under heavy layers of ice
near the top of Ararat. A notorious example is *In Search of Noah's Ark* by D. Balsiger
and C. E. Sellier, Jr. (Los Angeles: Sun Classic Books, 1976), printed by then in more
than a million copies.

not stated that it had not been seen prior to the Flood. Rather, the rainbow, which in other cultures often was taken, because of its resemblance to a huge bow, for a sign of divine punishment, is now presented as a token of the permanence of God's mercy.

The Ten Plagues

Among the events that mark the establishment of a covenant between God and Abraham, there are several miraculous ones, but none of them involve nature at large, the kind of miracles that constitute the biblical *magnalia Dei*. Among these are, however, the ten plagues unleashed on the Egyptians. To take them for historic events has for some time become a mark of backwardness in trend-setting exegetical circles. An uncanny evidence of this is the ill-concealed uneasiness that transpires from the footnote which the editor of the *Zeitschrift für die alttestamentliche Wissenschaft* appended (in German) to the very beginning of an article by Greta Hort, "The Plagues of Egypt," published there in the late 1950s.[5] "We publish this article, *so different* from the prevailing views on the matter, in spite of the repeated imprecision of references in it to sources that would give us assurance from the scientific side that the geological and microbiological data are correct" (Italics added).

The difference derives from Hort's giving the full benefit of the doubt to the veracity of the biblical account of the ten plagues (Exodus 7:14-11:10) and from her showing how the details of the plagues form a coherent whole from the physical, biological, and geological viewpoint. Indeed, once the first plague is taken for real in its specificity, the other plagues almost necessarily follow even in respect to those details on which rationalist critics usually seized in order to show that the biblical account is too specific in places to be taken seriously. According to some such specifics, not all the plagues ceased suddenly, not all extended all over Egypt, and only some of them spared the Goshen area where the Israelites resided.

[5] 69 (1957), pp. 84-103 and 70 (1958), pp. 48-59.

Naturally, science demands that such specific physical parameters be taken in their strict coherence. Yet, in a surprising witness to the oneness of truth (natural and supernatural), this approach casts a most favorable light on the biblical account of the plagues insofar as it is a composition of at least three sources, J (Yahwist), E (Elohist), and P (Priestly). Only the first and the tenth plagues are found in common in those three sources. While J gives eight plagues (1-2, 4-5, 7-10), E gives only five (1 and 7-10), and so does P (1-3, 6, 10). Coherence in the final form would, however, be found wanting, if J and P, because of their much more recent date, were not trustworthy records. Ingenious as their insertion into the original narrative may have been, the result would most likely contain details irreconcilable with one another and, most importantly, with physical reality. But, as shown by Hort's exegesis (which contains sufficiently precise references to geological and microbiological data), the physical details of the plagues constitute a marvelously coherent whole.[6] A narrative with such a coherence is not the fruit of story-telling.

In the first plague the Nile rose to unusual heights and the color of its water took on the hue of red as if full of blood. In the river and in the canals all fish died, producing a an oppressive stench. Only such water remained drinkable that was filtered through the soil. This is why the Egyptians had to dig for water. Taking the red-blood hue literally, Hort had to look for a physical cause other than excess mud and sand, which can produce but a brownish hue. In fact, unless one takes that hue to have been as intense as stated in the Bible, one would not have on hand the kind of unusual event that can pass for a portent.

That the Nile could, on occasion, take on that hue may seem to be indicated in Egyptian prophetic texts where such a hue is a characteristic of an evil eon to come. It is therefore quite possible that the Egyptians, who were most careful observers of the sundry variations of the Nile, had seen that phenomenon before.

---

[6] There is far more indeed to the coherence of those parts than a heightening of the dramatic effect, as put in *The Jerome Biblical Commentary,* one of the very few places where Hort's article is referred to.

They could not, of course, know its cause: various purple bacteria and flagellates that thrive in high mountain lakes, such as Lake Tana in Ethiopia. The heavier the precipitation, the more effectively does Lake Tana spill its water into what subsequently becomes the Blue Nile, or the main source of the yearly flood in Egypt proper, that is, north of Khartoum.

An unusually high flood posed a far greater threat than an unusually low flood. While a low flood could also cause stench, it could not be biologically lethal for the fish, because of the practical absence in that case of those bacteria and flagellates. The death of fish forces one therefore to connect the first plague with an unusually high flooding of the Nile. The inundation as part of the first plague must have therefore started in July-August and subsided in October-November. But its biological effects were far from over then.

The primary biological effect, or the dying of fish, was caused by the presence of flagellates. They absorb much oxygen during the night and emit it during the day, disturbing thereby the steady level of oxygen vital for the fish. The dying fish, in turn, infected the frogs, always plentiful in the Nile, which therefore left the river and sought places that were still sufficiently moist and also protected from the sun. Hence the invasion of houses and courtyards by frogs. Their sudden death there can be traced to the *bacillus anthracis,* which is found on the banks of the Nile and which is transported by insects. The second plague therefore must be placed within a short time of the rise of the Nile, that is, in August. It was a plague, and not a typical invasion of the land by frogs in November, when, instead of dying, they perform their noisy mating. What happened was therefore a portent that, like the unusual rise of the Nile, did not break the laws of nature.

The same is true of the third plague, an unusually heavy appearance of mosquitos when the unusually high flood receded in November. Goshen, where the Israelites lived, is not said to have been exempted from the effects of this plague, or the first two plagues either. This is in complete harmony with the physical parameters of all three plagues. That the fourth plague, the sudden muliplication of flies, did not affect Goshen, can be explained from the fact that such swarms of flies move under the impact of the prevailing climate, which in Goshen, unlike in the rest of Egypt, is governed by Mediterranean air masses.

The fifth plague was a disease that killed all the cattle in the field, although not one head of cattle of the Israelites died. This strange disparity can be explained by the fact that in the low-lying Goshen area, where the Israelites lived, the flood did not recede so quickly as elsewhere and therefore the cattle had to remain stabled for a longer time. Thus they were spared of eating grass grown in fields infected by the heaps of frogs that succumbed to *bacillus anthracis*.

The sixth plague, or "boil with blains" upon men and animals, especially on their legs and feet, could be skin anthrax, originating with bacilli that caused the death of frogs in the first place. Skin anthrax first produces a big swelling of the affected part of the skin, then a bluish-red pustule with a central depression in it. The skin then swells into blains as if burnt, and finally peels off. The biblical diagnosis, "boil with blains," is therefore remarkably accurate. But there is more to that accuracy. While skin anthrax can be carried by wasps of the family Tabanidae, they are attracted mostly by the ears of men and animals. It is the fly, *Stomoxys calcitrans*, that spreads skin anthrax by seeking out the legs and the feet. Moreover, because that fly has a relatively short flight range, "boil with blains" did not appear on those living in Goshen.

A most remarkable feature in all these connections is that they can be established only, as Hort aptly notes, when certain phrases, dismissed by critics as belonging to the "late" J (Yahwist) tradition, are taken as seriously as are phrases ascribed to the "early" E (Elohist) tradition. Criticism can indeed easily boomerang on its devotees. While critics may argue that the actual accounts of the plagues are very different from the original version, "that difference," as Hort pointedly noted, "has been obtained by elaboration of a given material and its rearrangement, not by tampering with it or by additions of new features."[7]

By the time of the sixth plague it was early January, just a month or so before the seventh plague, a hail- and thunderstorm of unusual violence hit the land, with the exception of Goshen. There such storms never come between November and March. The timing of that plague is accurately brought out by the identification of four crops: The two (flax and barley) that were devastated were indeed ripe in February, but not the wheat and the spelt. Although the flax should have bloomed already in January, the unusually high flood delayed its sowing by three or four weeks. It was a plague that came and went suddenly as stated in the Bible.

The eighth plague, or a mass invasion of locusts, can readily be tied to the first plague. The vast inundation triggered an excessive breeding of locusts in the Nile delta, very different from their ordinary annual quantities. Their huge swarms could then be swept southward through all Egypt by strong winds that blow from the Mediterranean all winter, on occasion even as late as April. Here the only difficulty relates to the statement that the swarms of locusts were driven by a westerly wind into the Red Sea. The difficulty disappears if one assumes that two final Hebrew letters, extremely similar to one another, were mistaken for one another by a scribe at a time when even words were not yet separated from one another in Hebrew scripts.

The ninth plague was a darkening of the air, though something much darker than the effect of a typical sandstorm. What happened was that by March the land, covered with extra layers

---

[7] Ibid., p. 95. The importance of this remark will be readily grasped on recalling that J contains ten plagues, E and P five each. The three sources cite in common only the first and last plagues. The combination of the three sources into a whole, that turns out to have a physical coherence, as rightly emphasized by Hort, is bordering on a literary miracle. From what had already been said about the awareness in the Bible of a lawful, coherent nature, no comments should be made on the downplaying of the partly miraculous character of the plagues on the ground that anything extraordinary could be a "sign" for the Israelites, or for the Egyptians for that matter.

of the reddish deposits of the Nile, was extremely dry and barren, owing partly to the action of locusts. Such a dry red soil could be easily whipped up by strong winds. The Israelites, however, enjoyed normal daylight. This may be explained by the fact that the Wadi Tumilath in Goshen, which housed many of the Israelites, runs east-west, and therefore posed a barrier to the north-south wind that carried with it clouds of dark dust.

In all this, there is only a natural chain of cause and effect, the phases of which could not, of course, have been foreseen by Moses and Aaron as they appeared and reappeared before the pharaoh with their threats. A telling instance of this disparity between what Moses and Aaron knew and the way in which things happened was the dust they were commanded to throw into the air prior to the eighth plague, or the rise of vast swarms of locusts, swept southward. Of course, even today no combination of meteorological, biological, and ecological lore would suffice to predict that plague, natural as it could be in all its aspects. Much the same applies to the other plagues as well and especially for their entire chain. This is why all this emphasis of natural factors behind the plagues should not amount to even the vaguest suggestion that a similar chain had already occurred previous to the biblical plagues or might occur again. Still, however miraculous in ultimate analysis, those plagues were not a rape of nature's forces. The latter were merely given a prompting here and there by the One who in the first place gave them a reality.

As to the last plague, it is not possible to go along with Hort's suggestion that its target was the "first fruits" (*becharim*) of the wheat harvest, or rather what was left of it after the passing of the locusts, and not the death of the "first born" (*bachar*) of men and animals, save those of the Israelites. While the two words are very similar in form, their respective meanings greatly differ. Hort did not even suggest how that shift from "first fruits" to "first born" might have occurred in the living memory of the people that, as recorded in the Bible, shows no references to a mere destruction of the harvest, but many emphatic references to the destruction of the first born of the pharaoh and of the Egyptians.

In fact, a mere destruction of the harvest might not have broken at all the pharaoh's resistance to the demand of Moses and Aaron, repeated before each plague, that they may lead the people into the desert to pray. Undoubtedly, if the tenth plague had been the destruction of the wheat harvest, the situation would have become very critical. The prospect of famine could have, however, been allayed by plans of wheat purchase from neighboring countries. But, as Hort rightly emphasized, the pharaoh would have undermined his own divine status by yielding on that point. The real threat did not even consist in the possibility that the demand was a camouflaged step toward an ultimate escape. The point at issue was that the demand was made in the name of another god. Yielding to the demand would have amounted to the recognition that the God of the Israelites was more powerful than the gods of the Egyptians. Only the sudden death of the first-born throughout Egypt, or at least in its part fairly close to the pharaoh, served a sufficiently effective notice that the other god was not something to be taken lightly. For the time being nothing in the magical lore of the Egyptian priesthood appeared useful in countering a god who could be so selectively destructive among the children of the Egyptians. But that lore was expected to prevail, after all. Such and similar considerations may have been in the mind of Moses as he led the Israelites into the desert. He knew he had to take them quickly beyond the desert, even beyond the Sea of Reeds with its various fords, well into the Sinai, where they would be out of the pharaoh's immediate reach.

Into the Sea of Reeds, the Desert, and the Promised Land
The Sea of Reeds, at the northwestern extremities of the Gulf of Suez, resembled a chain of lakes and marshes. A strong and steady southeasterly wind could push the waters towards the

Bitter Lakes and make several fords especially usable.[8] Those
among them close to Moses knew, of course, that it was through
his prayers that the wind suddenly took on an unusual force.
Thus the possibly no more than ten thousand or so Israelites[9]
could make a somewhat safe crossing under such circumstances.
But the leaders of the 600 select and other kinds of Egyptian
chariots (a force strong but not unusually so) assumed that such
a strong wind would would not die out suddenly. Therefore they
rushed after the Israelites. The sudden dying out of the wind
caught them by surprise and led to their drowning in waves that
unexpectedly rushed on them. The impression which all this
made on the Israelites could then be recorded, with poetical
license, as if the waters formed a vertical wall (Ex 14:22) and as
if they could see the bodies of all the Egyptian army scattered
along the shore. Certainly dramatic is the reconstruction of the
event in Psalm 77 which refers to heavy lightning and earthquakes as well, as two other natural forces also playing a part.
But in a subtle indication of the fact that God merely enhanced
such forces, it is added: "The waters saw you, O God, the waters
saw you and trembled; . . . when your way led through the sea,
your path through the mighty waters and *no one saw your
footprints*" (Ps 77:17-20). In other words, what had to be taken by
the Israelites for God's intervention, to the Egyptians could
appear an unexpectedly disastrous fluke in a natural process,
acting with unusual intensity.

That the ten plagues, let alone the drowning of the pharaoh's army, was not recorded by the Egyptian scribes is easy to
understand. Insofar as the pharaoh was believed to be divinity

[8] A recurrence of this fact was observed even half a century ago. See the report of
the Egyptian engineer, A. N. Shafei, "Historical Notes on the Pelusiac Branch, the
Red Sea channel and the Route of Exodus," *Bulletin de la Société Royale de Géographie
d'Égypte* 21 (1946), pp. 231-87. After having driven with his automobile across a lake
bed, he got stuck when the wind stopped and the waters returned.
[9] This number is based on taking the word *elef* not for a thousand but for a family
or clan and assigning ten or so men (not counting women and children) to each of
the families or clans (*elef*) that participated in the Exodus. Such an additional
meaning is strongly supported in Judges 6:15.

incarnate, he had to be considered immune to defeats on the battlefield. The historical records of ancient Egyptians—or of other ancient peoples for that matter—are very short on defeats and exceedingly long on victories. And if mentions of defeat are long, they aim at justifying the policy of one of the factions within the defeated. Josephus would not have been so prolific on the devastating defeat of the Jews in 70 A.D., had he not wanted to vindicate his own political course. Therefore he had to portray in great detail as insane the policy of those of his compatriots, the Zealots, who felt that, by God's dispensation, they would resist successfully Titus and his legions. But as Josephus argued, the Zealots had merely brought about the destruction of the Second Temple and Jerusalem.

The forty or so thousand (or possibly less than ten thousand) could be sufficiently isolated during their sojourn of several decades in the desert to prevent word from spreading about their daily manna which is stated to have been a chief constituent of their daily provisions. Here too the miracle may have been the extraordinary enhancement of the naturally occurring sweet juice of the *Tarfa*, a species of Tamarisk. As has been known for a long time, "it exudes in summer by night from the trunk and branches, and forms small round white grains, which partly adhere to the twigs of the trees, and partly drop to the ground: In the early morning it is of the consistency of wax, but the sun's rays soon melt it, and later in the day it disappears, being absorbed in the earth."[10] That no one could gather more of it than necessary for a day, except on the day before the sabbath, was, of course, miraculous, a factor unacceptable for those who fail to consider not only theology but also what the physicist, Stokes, had set forth about God's power over the laws of nature created by Him.

The miraculous damming up of the waters of the Jordan (Josh 3:9-13) is stated in a strikingly matter-of-fact way, which is also noteworthy for an almost scientific detail: it is the gradual

---

[10] See S. R. Driver, *The Book of Exodus* (rev. ed.: Cambridge: University Press, 1953), p. 153.

rising of the level of the Jordan to the north from the point where
the priests held the Ark of the Covenant and the comparatively
rapid disappearance of the water downstream. As to the rise of
the water level upstream, the high banks of the Jordan and its
long course up to Lake Gennesareth could provide enough room
for containing the water that accumulated in a day. That amount
of time would have been more than enough for the people to
take good advantage of the availability of a bare riverbed and
make the crossing.

As to the crumbling of Jericho's walls, the text (Josh 6:20-21)
does not impose the view that it was effected physically by the
blowing of trumpets by the Israelites, at the exclusion of a
coincident earthquake. Excavations at Jericho indicate that
earthquakes at least once played havoc with its walls. There
remains therefore plenty of room for a divine intervention that
ordered an earthquake, with appropriate force, at the right place
and the right time. Viewing matters in such a perspective leaves
the miracle intact and, even more importantly, leaves God subtly
invisible behind the cloak of nature.

And if one objects that nothing similar to the *magnalia Dei* so
far reviewed are known to have occurred either before or after,
one should merely recall points that cannot be pondered long
and deeply enough. The bodily (or ethnic and geographic)
establishment of the Old Covenant is unique in religious history,
because it had unique consequences on subsequent religious,
cultural, and even scientific history. It first implanted in men's
minds a linear view of all history, human and cosmic. And
insofar as that view extended into eternity, the freedom of
individual moral choices was emphasized, lest their eternal
bearing should appear a cruel tyranny decreed from above.[11]
Finally, in the dramatic consummation of that Covenant, the
unspeakably vast domain of human suffering obtained a
convincingly redeeming value. In considering the great physical

---

[11] The fumbling of Greek philosophers with the question of free will can best be
understood against the background of their insensitivity to eternal personal
prospects. See ch. 7 in my *The Purpose of it All.*

miracles of the Bible, it would be a mistake to center narrowly on physics and not on that reach which it allows beyond things physical. Those who treat biblical religion with ill-concealed disdain are no more competent in regard to its physical miracles than those who try to do modern physics while showing contempt for advanced mathematics.

Joshua and the sun

Mathematics, as part of celestial mechanics, would, of course, have a competence if, at Joshua's command, the sun and the moon had really stopped in their course for a day. Of course, not even the most literal interpreters of the Bible (unless they are flat-earth fanatics) would nowadays take the outcome of Joshua's prayer for a divine seal on geocentrism. But no less serious problems remain if one assumes that the earth stopped rotating for 24 hours or even for 12 hours, or even for a split second.

Worse, exegetes still are not in agreement as to what was really meant by Joshua's miracle. Everything is, of course, clear in what immediately precedes and follows Joshua's command to the sun and the moon. There is nothing mysterious in the fact that the inhabitants of Gibeon, a large city seven miles slightly to the northwest of Jerusalem, made peace with Joshua upon learning of the latter's merciless handling of the inhabitants of Ai who resisted him. Just as understandable was the resolve of the five Amorite kings, led by Adonizedek, king of Jerusalem, to teach a lesson to the Gibeonites and other possible deserters. Thus we read in the verses (Josh 10:7-11) that, upon receiving an urgent call from Gibeon, Joshua marched with his picked troops during the night from Gilgal, near the Jordan, to Gibeon (on a plateau about 700 meters higher), forced the armies of the five Amorite kings to flee westward and downslope, who during that flight were decimated by a terrible hailstorm: "Many more died because of the hailstone than the Israelites had put to the sword" (verse 11). Equally clear is the narrative (verses 16-27) about the punishment which Joshua dealt to the five kings who hid themselves in a cave. But following that verse 11 about the destructive effect of the hailstone we are told that

> [12]Then Joshua appealed to Yahweh, on the day God gave the Westerners [Amorites] into the hand of the Israelites. When he attacked them at Gibeon, they were smitten before the Israelites.
>
> > He said in the sight of Israel
> > "Sun, over Gibeon, be still,
> > Moon too, over Aijalon Valley."
> > [13]Sun was stilled,
> > And Moon stood fixed
> > Until he defeated his enemies' force!
>
> Is this not recorded in The Book of Yashar? The sun stayed in the center of the heavens and did not hurry to set for almost a whole day! [14]Never has there been a day like that before or since—God's heeding of a human voice! Surely Yahweh fought for Israel![12]

In this passage verses 12b-13a are clearly a song, one among many about Israel's heroes in a collection of songs, now lost, known as the Book of Yashar, composed in early post-Davidic times. The same book is also the source of David's lament for Saul and Jonathan in 2 Sam 1:19-27. Apart from another brief reference to the Book of Yashar, the foregoing two passages are its only presence in the Bible. Obviously, if much more had survived from the Book of Yashar, it would be easy to evaluate on purely literary grounds the kind of proposition contained in the song, verses 12b-13a. In that case it might be easy to cope also with verses 12a and 13b-14, most likely a commentary by the redactor of the Book of Joshua on the song itself.

This is not the place to take up the question about the theological authority of a borrowing from a non-canonical book in general, let alone from a non-canonical collection of songs, however edifying, in particular. At any rate, the tone of the

---

[12] *Joshua.* A New Translation with Notes and Commentary by R. C. Boling. Introduction by G. E. Wright (Garden City, N. Y.: Doubleday & Company, 1982), p. 274. I have written simply "Israelites," instead of "Bene Israel," literally, children of Israel.

commentator is very realistic. But does that realist tone imply a report about an observation, made by hundreds of Israelites, that the sun and the moon had stopped for so long as to make a day last two days? For nothing would have been more obvious to plain observers than that the sun stood fixed for hours on end. Let us not forget that an immediate plain grasp of external reality is an essential factor in establishing the credibility of biblical narratives, miraculous or not. Such a realist tradition is clearly witnessed by the author of the Book of Sirach. There the event is remembered in the form of a question: "Did he [Joshua] not by his power stop the sun, so that one day became two?" To be sure, due mention is also made of "hailstones of tremendous power," which "rained down upon the hostile army till on the slope he [Joshua] destroyed the foe" (Sir 46:4-6).

It is in part this realistic tradition that weakens the purely semantic consideration that the Hebrew *dmm* (stop) can readily mean "stop from shining" in the context at least.[13] But even if the sun did not stop in its track but merely stopped shining, the possibility that it ceased shining for twenty-four hours still would pose a problem that has a scientifically meaningful component. Did sunshine cease along vast stretches of the globe on both sides of the longitude of Gibeon? This problem would cease if one should understand that the cloudstorms blocked the sun's rays for eight or twenty-four hours. But this is not what the text states, although it speaks of an unusually heavy storm of hail.[14]

Here it is assumed that the sun (and the moon) did not stop in their courses for any amount of time. The chief reason for this is the weight of Augustine's principle, namely, that if something is known about the physical world with reasonable certainty, any phrase of the Bible which is in apparent contradiction with that certainty should be reinterpreted accordingly. Now it is certainly

---

[13] See *The Jerome Biblical Commentary* (Englewood Cliffs, N.J.: Prentice Hall, 1968), p. 135.

[14] Neither the Bible nor science would benefit from the suggestion, as proposed by J. Bosler on May 3, 1943, before the Académie des Sciences in Paris, that the storm was that of aerolites and meteors, that, by producing a northern light, would have offset the ordinary darkness of the night.

known that (*pace* Einstein's relativity) the earth orbits around the sun and not the other way around.

The consequences of this for the famed verses in Joshua are enormous. They cannot be evaded by assuming that the earth stopped rotating on its axis "for a whole day." Nor would it help if the earth had stopped rotating for only seven hours, that is, doubling the daylight between noon and sunset, and not for twenty-four hours, as demanded by the strictly literal meaning of "the whole day." For even those extra seven hours (that had to be global if caused by the stopping of the earth's rotation) could hardly have passed unnoticed, say in China and in Babylon, where careful records were kept on astronomical phenomena. And even today there would be a trace of that extra span of time in respect to the computation of the spots on earth where solar and lunar eclipses should occur. In his omnipotence, God could have, of course, eliminated a most serious dynamic consequence had the earth's rotation come to a sudden halt. The resulting inertial effect on anything on the earth's surface in the middle latitudes would have dwarfed the launching velocity of the fastest space rocket. Only some polar bears on the North Pole and some penguins on the South Pole would have been left at ease.

At any rate, since even divine omnipotence is not above the principle of contradiction, it cannot be assumed that for a day the earth both rotated and did not, at Gibeon. And this also holds of Gilgal too, the main camp of the Israelites, to which Joshua returned after he had dealt with the Amorite kings. Did the people at Gilgal complain of an unusually long day that would have made everybody very sleepy? And what about cows that even in modern times refuse to cooperate with the shift from standard time to daylight saving time, a difference of a mere hour? It is indeed fraught with great dangers to say, as did a modern interpreter of the Book of Joshua, that "it is more prudent to regard the phenomenon [of the stopping of the sun and the moon] as one of the numerous miracles of the Bible" and leave it at that.[15] Nor would legitimate questions about the command of Joshua go away by the declaration that "it is profitless to rationalize this and many other miracles of the Bible."[16]

For, in order to believe in a miracle, one is entitled to be given a clear idea as to what was the miracle. But precisely this point is evaded when, for instance, it is simply stated that, while the Bible does not teach about astronomy, "Yahweh worked a great and unique nature miracle for his people at Joshua's request."[17] Worse, the same point is at times simply ignored in prominent exegetical contexts, such as the *Jerome Biblical Commentary*, although it is at least shown that Josh 10:11-14 is far from being clear.[18] And even if it were clear, and no less clear than the Bible's statements about the earth's fixity, the passage should be reconciled with reason. After all, man's reason, however finite, is a chief ingredient in man's being made in the image of an infinitely rational God.

Now, reason can readily establish that the miracle could not have been caused by an eclipse. More than a total eclipse would have been necessary, as such an eclipse lasts only a few minutes. It is impossible to coordinate eclipses with the respective positions which the sun and the moon had at noon of the day of the battle. Those positions can, however, be used to suggest that the battle could very well have taken place around the 21st of the fourth Jewish month, or the middle of our July. The astronomer who made that suggestion was E. Walter Maunder, Fellow of the Royal Astronomical Society, who devoted dozens of pages to Joshua's miracle in his *The Astronomy of the Bible*, which he modestly subtitled, "An Elementary Commentary on the Astronomical References of Holy Scriptures."[19] But Maunder over-stated his

---

[15] J. A. Soggin, *Joshua* (London: SCM Press, 1970), p. 123.

[16] *The Interpreter's Bible* (Nashville: Abingdon Press, 1989), vol. 2, p. 605.

[17] *A Catholic Commentary on Holy Scripture* (London: Thomas Nelson, 1951), p. 285.

[18] *Jerome Biblical Commentary*, pp. 135-36.

[19] I am referring to the third edition (London: Hodder and Stoughton, 1910). It came out in three editions within two years. A fourth, slightly enlarged, edition was published in 1922, or six years before Maunder's death.

case in arguing that "the real difficulty to the understanding of this narrative has lain in the failure of commentators to put themselves back into the conditions of the Israelites."[20]

One did not have to be an astronomer, or a student of the best maps of the terrain, in order to realize what the Book of Joshua makes all too obvious. By the morning of the day of the battle Joshua's forces had already completed a difficult night-long march from Gilgal, near Jericho, to Gibeon, on a plateau 700 meters higher. In the pre-noon hours they had won there a battle over the Amorites and cut off their escape route to the south toward Jerusalem. The enemy had to begin to flee first toward Aijalon, to the northwest, and then make a left turn to the southwest toward Azekah. As they started fleeing, Joshua begged God not to let his troops' exertion be in vain. The result was an unusually destructive hailstorm that miraculously skirted the Israelites.

Maunder assumed that the storm blocked the sun's rays for several hours. He also assumed, very plausibly, that while the storm devastated the Amorites, it refreshed the Israelites. The latter could then march twice the typical distance that troops normally covered in a day. By nightfall they reached Azekah, some twenty miles away, but mostly downslope, over the scattered bodies of their enemies. In other words, the length of the afternoon was psychologically doubled for the Israelites. Only the measuring device was not a chronometer, not even a sundial or a clepsydra, either of which was hardly carried into a surprise attack. The device was the one which the Babylonians themselves used, or the typical distance troops walked in a day.

Most importantly, in the case of Joshua's miracle Stokes' principle is better not invoked, because it may prompt one to assume that something (the earth's rotation) happened and did not happen at the same time. There would also remain the task of explaining how the sun resumed its normal course. Assuming that the sun stood still in the middle of the sky for seven hours,

[20] Ibid., p. 381.

how did it set in the evening of the day? By suddenly jumping seven times fifteen, or about 100 degrees across the sky? That would have been a spectacle incomparably more conspicuous than its standing in the middle of the sky for seven hours. But the passage from the Book of Yashar suggests nothing of the sort.

One therefore has to apply not so much Stokes' principle, but rather the principle which Saint Augustine formulated as he grappled with the biblical references to the earth's flatness. Since such a flatness contradicted something (the earth's sphericity) that could be clearly known by the light of reason, it was the Bible's interpretation that had to be tailored, Augustine insisted, to well known facts, and not the other way around. Such a procedure is further supported by the fact that the Book of Yashar was never considered as having been divinely inspired. It remains for theologians to decide therefore the value of those famed verses. They may, eventually, be blessed by the lucky discovery of a scrap of papyrus that might clear up the passage from the Book of Yashar.[21] But they would make an unnecessary hermeneutical mistake, if they took the view that at Joshua's prayer either the sun and the moon, or the earth, or all of them together stopped doing for hours something they had been doing for many millions of years and with stunning regularity. In any case, theologians should always be on guard against setting themselves for no good reasons at loggerheads with the quantitative exactness of astronomical observations and predictions.

What then was the miracle of Joshua? To answer this question, one has to recall that the passage quoted from the Book of Yashar is neither clear, nor authoritative. Further, one must not

---

[21] One may think of the support which the Qumram texts brought to the reliability of the Masoretic version of Isaiah. One may also recall the scrap of papyrus, published in 1935, which contains parts of the dialogue between Jesus and Pilate (Jn 18:31-33 and 18:37-38). It refuted the once "highly respected" claim that John's Gospel could not have been written by John himself, who died around 96 A. D. (For details and documentation, see G. Ricciotti, *The Life of Christ*, tr. A. I. Zizzamia [Milwaukee: Bruce Publishing Company, 1947], p. 142). Still another such item is a marble epitaph from Egypt, first aired in 1922, to be discussed in the next chapter, in connection with Jesus' birth.

involve God in performing a miracle that cannot be specified and, whenever specified, implies consequences that will not be disposed of by falling back on studiedly vague expressions. Therefore, one is left with a hailstorm, by itself a rarity in that area, that rained down only on the fleeing Amorites, but not on the Israelites in hot pursuit of them. It is difficult to escape the conclusion that the storm's timing, intensity, and route was decided from above. To the "rationalists" among the Amorites, if there were such among them, this could merely appear a terribly bad bit of luck. To Joshua and his troops, God himself passed through, though carefully cloaked in an unusually severe storm cloud that, in addition, kept a most curious path without contravening nature. The natural was merely enhanced, without being denatured.

The sign given by Isaiah to Hezekiah directly involved at least the rays of the sun (Is 38:7) as they fell, on a late afternoon, on the staircase that led eastward from the royal palace toward the Temple.[22] Had not Hezekiah seen day after day the shadows advance on the staircase, he would not have asked the prophet to move the shadows backward. For even a cloud, suitably placed, could push the shadows forward. At the prophet's command the shadows moved backward by the easily observable stretch of ten steps. It was enough for God to produce a purely local optical effect that did not involve any change in the motion of the earth. A late afternoon setting is particularly significant because then a relatively large change in the position of the shadow would involve only a minor change in the apparent position of the sun, a change not observable by the naked eye. So much for the possibility that only a purely local optical effect was achieved miraculously. However that may be, it is well to recall Stokes' remark, quoted above, about "the superaddition of something not ordinarily in operation, or if in operation, of such a nature that its operation is not perceived." But as long as it is a superaddition, it is a miracle.

---

[22] Here I follow Maunder who gives a detailed reconstruction of the situation.

10

God's Greatest Intervention

Conceived by the Holy Spirit
In the very moment when the maiden in Nazareth heard the words that the Holy Spirit would come upon her and the power of the Most High would "overshadow" her, she could at first be but "deeply disturbed." The phrase, "to be overshadowed," was a euphemism for the act whereby man makes woman pregnant. But since she "knew no man," a euphemistic declaration on her part that she was to remain a virgin, she had to be assured that the child was not to be conceived in a human way. The child was to be a "holy offspring," indeed the Son of the Most High himself. Once she assented by saying, "Let it be done according to thy will," God's greatest conceivable intervention in history, human and cosmic, was accomplished: Jesus was conceived in the womb of "the virgin called Mary."

Search as one may human history, no greater and holier figure can be found in its pages than the fruit of that womb, described in the four Gospels. There have been many efforts to cut Jesus down to human size. Some of these efforts were rude, such as the claim in the Talmud that Jesus was the illegitimate son of Mary, a hairdresser, by a certain Panthera. A hundred or so years after his death, Jesus, the crucified, was pictured with the head of an ass in a Roman graffito. Still another two hundred years later, Julian the Apostate contended to show that Jesus was inferior to Jupiter and the rest in the Greco-Roman pantheon.

Julian's was a desperate rear-guard defense. Paganism soon became what the name itself suggests, a feature of remote rural areas. For fourteen hundred years afterwards no one within the Christian *oikumene* could challenge, without being roundly rebuked, Christ's status as the very divine intervention in human history. True to logic, in the measure in which that *oikumene* began to lose its uniformly Christian character, efforts to "humanize" Christ became more and more frequent. Soon it became a sign of scholarship to describe Christ's demotion from that unique status of his in a tone which, however poignant, claimed that his death on the cross was indeed his very end. Needless to say, in all such efforts gentle scorn was poured on the belief that he was conceived by the Holy Spirit and born of the Virgin Mary.

Still, Christ remains the greatest puzzle for all who, though they do not look at him as the Son of God and mankind's Savior, have retained their ability to pause and ponder. Not all of these have put their puzzlement about Jesus in equally memorable phrases. Certainly worth recalling is an appraisal of Christ given by the American psychoanalist, G. Stanley Hall, whose chief claim to fame is the role he played in bringing Freud, Jung, and others to the United States in 1909. Sizing up Jesus with the eyes of a psychologist, Hall spoke of the personality of Christ as an undiminished source of inspiration that gives man "some incentive to reapproximate his unfallen self."[1]

Christ could also be rediscovered in a far more dramatic way and in a drastic rebuttal of "received" wisdom, be it the wisdom of those liberals who, half a century ago, celebrated Leninist and Stalinist revolutionaries as so many saints of a new and radically materialistic dispensation. They prefer to forget the words, "Jésus, vous êtes le seul qui ne m'a pas déçu," which a French Communist, just before his execution by the Nazis, wrote on the wall of his prison cell, using his own blood for ink and his finger for a pen. Now that Communism is mere history and the Capitalist western world is visibly afraid of basing its prosperity on open-ended borrowing, one should recall Simone Weil, who extricated herself of the illusions of both by experiencing Christ. She spoke about "this sudden possession of me by Christ," or "a

---

[1] *Jesus, the Christ, in the Light of Psychology* (New York: D. Appleton, 1923), p. 244.

presence more personal, more certain, more real than a human being."[2]

For those uneasy about even a whiff of mysticism there is Bernard Levin, a regular columnist in *The Times*. On having read the advance report about another condescending biography of Christ (by A. N. Wilson), Levin had this to write, after having stated for the "fourteen thousandth time" that he was not a Christian: "I suppose the pamphlet was a herald of the forthcoming book, which will knock down Christianity and bury it. Well, its founder was very thoroughly knocked down and ever so buried, and whether he rose from the grave or whether he was playing possum, he still looms over the world, his message clear, his pity still infinite, his consolation still effective, his words still full of glory, wisdom, and love."[3]

Levin merely restated what had been said many times before and in most elaborate ways as well, namely, that Christ was a psychological miracle. It already breaks the frames of psychology that in Christ's comportment one finds a harmonious unity of qualities that in others are mutually exclusive. Indeed, were anyone else to make the claim Christ made about himself, it would be taken for a sign of insanity. Not only his disciples, but also his antagonists realized that he claimed himself to be equal to God in some mysterious way. As C. S. Lewis remarked, Christ did not leave us with the option to come to Him with "patronising nonsense" as if He had looked upon himself as a mere moral teacher, however eminent.[4] If his claim, words, and deeds were the mere invention of some of his disciples, then the miracle becomes even greater, if this is possible at all.

The miracle in question has another aspect, which is much more scientific than psychology can ever be. In an age that probes deep into the range of what genes are responsible for, the biological origin of Jesus gives a startling twist to the psycho-

---

[2] Quoted from S. Pétrement, *Simone Weil: A Life*, tr. R. Rosenthal (New York: Pantheon Books, 1976), p. 340.
[3] B. Levin, "The Ultimate Unauthorised Life," *The Times* (London), June 6, 1991.
[4] C. S. Lewis, *The Case for Christianity* (New York: Macmillan, 1948), p. 45.

logical miracle he still is, which, of course, never bothered most of those who took him for the natural son of Joseph. Most of those who were impressed by that miracle held on to the faith, held by the Church from the earliest times, that Jesus was conceived by the Holy Spirit and born of the Virgin Mary. They had no use for talking around this and other biblical miracles by taking any unusual event for a "sign" and justifying this as the Hebrew way of disinterest in miracles, properly so-called. For already Justin Martyr, a convert from Judaism, warned his antagonist Trypho, a Jew, that if a "sign" is worthy of a prophet, it has to be more than an unusual event, it strictly has to transcend nature. Great events were not to be inferred "if a woman should beget from sexual intercouse, which indeed all young women, with the exception of the barren, do; but even these, God, if He wills, is able to cause [to bear]."[5] This remark Justin Martyr is far more than a rebuttal of Trypho's contention that he was reading into the Bible some pagan myths about virgins giving birth. The miracle of Mary having conceived by the Holy Spirit had to be admitted, so argued Justin Martyr, if the Bible was to remain a sensible text about what constitutes a sign in the Bible.[6]

This argument has not weakened just because science disclosed more and more details about the physiology of human conception. Prior to the discovery of the ovum and ovaries, about three hundred years ago, one had to think that the Holy Spirit

---

[5] *Dialogue with Trypho*, chap. lxxxiv. Justin had already devoted chapters xliii and lxvi to the same prophecy of Isaiah. In Justin's view Jesus' divinity was inseparable from his having been conceived by the Holy Spirit.

[6] Justin's remark sharply contrasts with many a modern exegete's declaration that in the Bible a miracle is both a "work" accomplished by God and a "sign" of something spiritually accomplished in man. But can this mean that the "work" does not stand for God's intervention in nature and that man need not notice it as such in order to let it biblically act for him as a "sign" to his spiritual benefit? That this question is very biblical will be seen shortly in connection with Christ's repeated references to the regularities of nature. Therefore it should seem very unbiblical to leave this question to apologetics, while dismissing its biblical relevance, as done, for instance, by R. Brown, in his "The Gospel Miracles," reprinted in his *New Testament Essays* (Milwaukee: The Bruce Publishing Company, 1965), pp. 168-91; see, especially, p. 186.

created some male sperm (at times taken for a homunculus) in Mary's womb. The discovery of the role of the ovum revealed that the mother too played a significant role in the procreation of a human being. It was not until this century that the difference between the respective roles of the father and of the mother diminished to that between two X chromosomes in the mother, and an X and Y chromosome in the father. The miracle of the physical conception of Christ, who was to become the greatest intervention of God in history, human and cosmic, may be, physically speaking, nothing more than the creation of a haploid male cell, with its set of chromosomes, to fertilize a female haploid cell (ovum) in Mary's womb.

If such was the case, God once more achieved the greatest effect with the smallest means, in a totally unobtrusive way. Geneticists and biochemists know, of course, that a chromosome is a vast complexity. Each of the two thousand or so genes that compose one chromosome is a convoluted world of double helices of DNA and RNA strands. Within these the individual molecules consist of atoms, these of electrons and nuclei, the latter of protons and neutrons, arranged in intricate shells. Protons and neutrons are in turn made up of quarks, themselves of considerable variety, though hardly the final stage of the search for the truly fundamental particles.

But a haploid male cell, for all its complexity, is simplicity itself compared with a galaxy, with its billions of stars. Thus, insofar as one ascribes the existence of the universe of all galaxies to God who created it out of nothing, the miraculous introduction of that haploid male cell into Mary's womb should pose problems only for those who have lost their sense of proportion. What should one then think of that biochemist who found it difficult to accept that Jesus had no human father, while he, as a Catholic, did not find it difficult to admit the creation of the universe? One should indeed be puzzled, to say the least. On further probing that difficulty, it turned out that he was willing to admit only a creation that was not a creation out of nothing. According to him creation was but a total dependence of the universe on God. But why would a well-trained individual think that one can have total dependence without creation out of nothing? Is this merely the case of a poorly articulated philosophy, so often in evidence in scientists, or of something else, equally frequent among them? That something else seems to be a tacit option for pantheism, which, of course, is a case of naturalism. Once more a miracle is resisted, because acceptance of miracles, and it alone, puts one unequivocally in the camp of the supernatural. The entire history of Christianity is a proof that only as long as Christ is taken to be the supernatural salvation is He believed to have been conceived by the Holy Spirit in the womb of the virgin, called Mary.

Born of the Virgin Mary

Without that faith even the most splendid displays of liturgical paraphernalia have turned into a hollow show of mere nature, and a very fallen nature indeed. Such a nature finds nothing noteworthy in Luke's narrative of the Nativity, so full of tactfulness that shows him to be far more than a mere physician, however sensitive about that special right to privacy which is the particular prerogative of a woman. If anyone, then Luke, the physician, could have gone, under the cover of medical reporting, into clinical details, such as the various discharges concomitant with giving birth to a child. No trace in Luke's account of that morbid curiosity which one confronts time and again in the apocryphal accounts of Jesus' birth.

Luke is taciturn, though eloquently so. After stating in a lapidary style that following Mary's arrival with Joseph in Bethlehem, "the days of her confinement were completed" and that "she gave birth to her first-born son," Luke makes a statement that should startle any perceptive woman (or man) even in these days of "painless births" and of almost rudely quick dismissals from maternity wards. Even fifty, let alone two thousand years ago, one would have considered it very risky on the part of a woman to give birth with no assistance from other women, or to get up immediately after birth to take care of her infant child. But this is precisely what Luke states: "She wrapped him in swaddling clothes and laid him in a manger, because there was no room for them in the place where the travelers lodged" (Lk 2:6-7).

Concerning this last statement Christians have for some time fastened on secondary details, like the manger and the heartless locality that had no room for a young woman ready to give birth to her first child. Even the swaddling clothes became part of a romanticism, however well-intentioned. Yet in more realistic times it was still seen that something miraculous was conveyed by Luke's notice about Mary herself doing all that, an activity hardly to be expected from a woman who had just given birth. Moreover, no one was more conscious of the absence of anything "clinical" in Luke's narrative than was Jerome, still the greatest of Christian biblical exegetes: "Should the woman giving birth be overtaken by pain, midwives pick up the crying infant and the husband will hold the exhausted wife. . . . But in no way should this be thought of the Savior's mother and of that just man, Joseph. Here is no midwife; no need here for women to be fussing about. His mother herself wrapped Him in the swaddling clothes, herself mother and midwife."[7] Such was one of Jerome's arguments against Helvidius, who went down in theological history as the only one in Patristic times who denied Mary's virginity in giving birth. Jerome also held that Luke was somehow made privy to Mary's most cherished experiences. If not from Mary herself, Luke might have gained priceless information from John who was enjoined by Jesus on the cross to take Mary in his care.

The view that Mary kept her virginity as she gave birth to Jesus is, of course, a solemnly defined dogma for Catholics,[8] and a particularly stinging one in these times when Catholic theo-

---

[7] *Adversus Helvidium*, cap, 8, in Migne PL 23:201. Jerome, like other Church fathers, refers also to the absence of references on Luke's part to those discharges, or *sordes* as they call them.

[8] The classic declaration was made at the Council of Trent in 1555 against the Unitarians.

logians are engaged in all sorts of verbal acrobatics to raise the natural to the pedestal of the supernatural. To that skill nothing can contribute so much than a falling back on the art of mystification by words as developed mainly by the champions of critical philosophy. They tried to be critical by parting with the real.

A revealing illustration of this is the manner in which Karl Rahner put the dogma of Mary's virginity *in partu* through the wringers of his progressivist theology.[9] Rahner thought that, in order to state his acceptance of that dogma, it was enough to endorse its essence, that is, its *noumenon*. Such was a telling maneuver on the part of a chief champion of transcendental Thomism, or a Thomism infused with Kant's critical philosophy so as to make it palatable to the modern mind. Actually, only Kant's inconsistencies were thereby grafted onto Thomas's always straight thinking. For just as Kant ignored the objection, raised already by one of his students, that by having declared the *noumenon* unknowable, he had forfeited his right to talk about it, Rahner failed to heed that still valid point. But Rahner was so much taken up by what he seemed to know about that unknowable *noumenon* that he dismissed all the phenomena that could be specified about that virginity *in partu*. Thus he slighted the Patristic references to the absence of *sordes*. He poured gentle scorn on the specific detail that Mary's hymen remained intact as the infant left her body. Rahner was equally dismissive of the fact that Patristic and Scholastic theologians compared the birth of Jesus to the risen Christ's passing through the door.

It may indeed be due largely to Rahner's overweening influence among Catholic theologians that so far no proper rebuttal has come forth against H. von Campenhausen's monograph, *The Virgin Birth and the Theology of the Ancient Church*.[10] There Mary's virginity *in partu* is credited to the ascetical influence of monks, to Augustine's "hostility" to sex, and to the

---

[9] "Virginitas in partu," in K. Rahner, *Theological Investigations*, Vol. IV, tr. K. Smyth (Baltimore: Helicon, 1966), pp. 134-62.

[10] This English translation by F. Clarke, appeared as Nr. 2 in the series, *Studies in Historical Theology* (Naperville: IL.: A. R. Allenson, 1964).

Church's insistence on priestly celibacy. A far cry indeed from the splendor with which Blake, painter-poet-mystic rolled in one, portrayed the virgin birth. Nothing surprising in this for anyone ready to recall that in old age Blake, according to the reminiscences of a friend of his, "quite held forth one day on the Roman Catholic Church being the only one which taught the forgiveness of sin."[11]

The theological poverty that generates resistance to the belief in Mary's virginity *in partu* is a piece with the gradual parting, within liberal Protestantism, with genuine belief in sin, in fallen human nature, and, of all things, in properly supernatural grace. Such is a further illustration of the logic which sensitive leading Protestant theologians dare only whisper in private but never in the broad daylight of academic publicity. The logic, as one of them put it squarely, is that Protestantism is a logical road to naturalism.[12] To expose that logic for what it is, one cannot count on some felicitous archeological find, such as that marble epitaph from Egypt, first discussed in 1922. There a Jewish bride, who died in childbirth in 5 B.C., or very close to Jesus' birth, bemoans: "Destiny had led me to the end of my life in the birthpangs for my first-born (*prototokon*) son."[13] Yet the suggestion, indeed the brazen assertion, continues popping up that Jesus had siblings.

The Star of Bethlehem

By far the most widely discussed among the *magnalia Dei* is the star that led the Magi to Bethlehem.[14] It is not the purpose of this book to debate the question whether the visit of the Magi is but

[11] See my booklet, *The Virgin Birth and the Birth of Science* (Front Royal, VA.: Christendom Press, 1990), p. 23, which contains three reproductions in color of Blake's various renderings of Jesus's leaping forth from Mary's womb.

[12] I am quoting the remark made to me by a prominent Calvinist theologian in the 1970s.

[13] See G. Ricciotti, *The Life of Christ*, tr. A. I. Zizzamia (Milwaukee: Bruce Publishing Company, 1947), p. 242.

[14] The list of publications on that star published by Ruth Freitag of the Library of Congress in 1979 under the title, *The Star of Bethlehem*, runs to 44 pages. For a shorter list, see K. Boa and W. Proctor, *The Return of the Star of Bethlehem* (Garden City, N.Y.: Doubleday, 1980).

a "naive" narrative, amounting to a "Christian midrash," patterned on midrashic stories about Moses, with no factual basis to it. If such be the case, the story raises no legitimate scientific questions. But it can be rightfully asked whether it is scientifically compelling to see Matthew's star as a "zig-zagging" star, one "that rose in the East, appeared over Jerusalem, turned south to Bethlehem, and then came to rest over a house."[15] Undoubtedly, such a star would have constituted a celestial phenomenon unparalleled in astronomical history, in fact, in the history of all star gazing, scientific or not. In *that* case the exegete might be entitled to marshall against that "zig-zagging" star's factuality the fact that "it received no notice in the records of the times."[16]

As will be discussed shortly, the absence of contemporary records about a spectacular (though not a theatrical) event is not necessarily a strong argument against its factuality. Further, had the Magi (quite possibly some sages from Persia[17]) seen a "zig-zagging" star, they would have hardly taken it for a good omen. Much less would they have set out to the court of Herod, proverbial for his zig-zagging politics steeped in ruthless cruelty. Their motivation for undertaking an arduous journey that could have trapped them in trying situations must have therefore been very strong. Most importantly, the fact, that upon arriving in Jerusalem they startled its leaders with their report, indicates that nothing novel or spectacular in the sky had been noticed in Jerusalem during the previous year or so.

Clearly, then, the Magi had to see something very different from a great conjunction of Jupiter and Saturn. It is a conjunction in which they appear close to one another three times within one year, such a year occurring every 250 or so years. One such

[15] Thus R. E. Brown, *The Birth of the Messiah: A Commentary on the Infancy Narratives in the Gospels of Matthew and Luke* (Garden City, N.Y.: Doubleday, 1977), pp. 188-190. The same pages occur without any change in the new updated edition (1993).

[16] Ibid. p. 188.

[17] Much important research was done in the 1930's on the Magi's likely provenance from Persia. A good summary of details is in G. Ricciotti, *The Life of Christ*, pp. 249-252.

conjunction occurred in 7 B.C., a very likely date for Christ's birth. In that year Jupiter and Saturn were in conjunction on May 27th, October 5th, and December 1st, owing to their retrograde motions. There is no evidence that at that time astrological lore had taken the constellation Pisces, in which that conjunction occurred, for a symbol of the Jews. Nor is there contemporary evidence on behalf of the belief that Saturn controlled Jewish destiny.[18]

Assuming then that the Magi had trustworthy eyes and were trustworthy in reporting that they had seen a star, it may be best assumed that what they had first seen was a nova. The apparent brightness of novae varies greatly and very few of them are noticeable to the naked eye. The supernova of 1054 was recorded in China, but not by the Muslim stargazers whom certain modern interpeters of scientific history love to extol over their Christian counterparts. Yet some medieval monks, often held high as the epitome of obscurantism, noted an exceedingly brief eruption of huge flames from the moon's surface in 1178.[19] Most importantly, there is nothing unscientific (unless it be "scientific" to deny the possibility of the supernatural) in supposing that the Magi were alerted by God's grace to the appearance of a nova. Or should one dismiss the dreams that guided Joseph, that "good and just

---

[18] In Ptolemy's *Tetrabiblos*, written a century and a half later, Jews are not mentioned. There Judaea is lumped with various surrounding countries. About the inhabitants of Coelosyria, Idumæa, and Judæa it is stated that they are "principally influenced by Aries and Mars, and are generally audacious, atheistical, and treacherous." See Book II, ch. 3 in *Ptolemy's Tetrabiblos* (reprint of J. M. Ashmand's translation from 1823; North Hollywood: Symbols and Signs, 1976), pp. 46-47.

[19] Those monks were five in number and testified under oath about about their observation. They were interviewed by Gervase of Canterbury who reported in his Chronicle that those five monks saw, on the evening of June 25, 1178, the upper horn of the New Moon split in two and "from the midpoint of the division a flaming torch sprang up, spewing out fire, hot coals, and sparks." The indicated place of the impact closely coincides with the crater Giordano Bruno. The analysis which the astronomers D. Mulholland and O. Calame made of a wobbling of the moon also points to the same spot and time. Their study also indicates that the celestial body which caused that impact would have hit the earth had the moon not been in that position at the right time.

man," through the perplexities and dangers surrounding Christ's birth, just because they were supernatural in origin?

Of course, if Matthew's story of the Magi is taken for a Christian midrash, then one is not bound to take his words, "they saw the star at its rising," for a physical fact, let alone for a series of astronomical observations. But Matthew's story does not cease to be a real story even if one does not see in it traces of science. It is worth noting that Matthew does not say that the Magi kept seeing that star throughout their journey to Jerusalem. Moreover, the realism of Matthew's story is supported by the fact that there was a distinct awareness in Persia about Jewish Messianic expectations. There is therefore nothing implausible in the Magi's decision that they should go to Jerusalem.

While in Jerusalem, the Magi were told about Bethlehem as the place where the Messiah was to be born. In heading toward Bethlehem, they most naturally started out in the early morning before the sun's blaze had come down too strong. It was from that point on that they once more saw a star and saw it against the sky of daylight. But in seeing such a star, they did not see it against the mental background of moderns, who are fully aware of the immense distances and sizes of stars.[20] Few and far between were those in antiquity who guessed the immense distances of stars, and hardly anyone cared to take up the problem of their sizes. For most of the learned (to say nothing of the uneducated) stars were small concentrations of very luminous matter (usually called the ether). Let us not forget that even about the sun and the moon it was possible to claim (Democritus is an example) that stars were not larger than what they appeared to be to the naked eye. Nor did Lucretius expect ridicule when he claimed that the sun and the moon were no bigger than a foot in diameter. On the contrary, Aristarchus brought upon himself a hale of reproofs when he spoke of the sun as being as large as the Peloponnesus.

---

[20] It is well to recall that Kepler still thought that all stars were confined within an imaginary spherical shell whose width was only 2000 German leagues!

The minds and senses of the Magi would not therefore have been "fooled" if, on their journey to Bethlehem, they would have been led by a miraculously produced optical appearance, closely resembling the image of a star they had noticed earlier. Such an image, miraculously produced and only for the Magi (as miracles are never produced for the public satisfaction of Academies of Science), could readily descend on a house. And since the Magi had no inkling of modern conceptions about the size of stars, they would not have been bothered by the smallness of that bright point in mid-air. Nor could Mary and Joseph be puzzled as they were obviously made privy to what the Magi had seen. And the same holds true of Matthew, who had access to far better sources on what happened than all old and new exegetes taken together. Thoroughly believable is his report that the Magi saw the star going "ahead of them, until it came to a standstill over the place in which the child was" (Mt 2:9).

Such a sight left intact all the laws of astronomy and all the data of its history. Therefore it is unnecessary to give attention, however fleetingly, to a well in Bethlehem. The legend was still alive during the nineteenth century among the inhabitants of Bethlehem that, once the Magi arrived there, they looked for lodgings and found one with a well attached to it. Looking into that well they could see in its water the reflected image of their star (nova?) that by noon may have appeared directly overhead.[21] That stars can be seen during daylight, as reflected in the bottom of a well, is a fact too well known by professional and amateur astronomers to require explanation or documentation.

Far more importantly, the star as a miraculously produced visual image could have perfectly served the real purpose of the infancy narrative of Matthew, which was steeped no less in respect for the reality of God's supernatural entry into human and physical reality than was Luke's narrative of Christ's birth. Such an entry was resplendent in miracles, spiritual as well as physical. Acceptance of such an entry demands much more than

---

[21] The legend was reported by Maunder as a mere curiosity (*op. cit.* pp. 399-400).

the fleeting dismissal of the unscientific character of the claim that miracles are impossible. It demands mental courage to rally in support of the physical reality of specific miracles, biblical and other, even though this does not demand credulity about any and all "miraculous" stories.

At any rate, once more, as in other cases of the *magnalia Dei*, here too one is merely asked to combine what is clearly natural with what is obviously supernatural, though unobtrusively so. The former could be a nova, extremely rare and fortuitous though it was. The latter was a miraculous fact, a specially produced optical phenomenon in the air, looking like a star and moving ahead at a pace matching that of the Magi. Those who refuse to admit even an unobtrusive presence of the strictly miraculous have inevitably found the Bible narrative to lose not only its supernatural but also its natural credibility.

The supernatural reality of faith may also be threatened when it is reduced to a mental act severed from its object. To speak of belief as not being an act whereby one believes in somebody or in something is a sign of philosophical and theological poverty, if not perversity. It is present when the literary forms, in which biblical miracles are reported, are taken for an excuse to take lightly the content of what was reported. But it is a howler when theologians, such as Bultmann and his many admirers, claim that the modern science of electricity makes the idea of physical miracles untenable. In doing so they merely surrender to a fashionable as well as shallow philosophy of science, whose protagonists ignore the fact that science is not a set of propositions with an *a priori* necessity. Hollow references to science are, therefore, in the case of Bultmann and his followers, so many concealments of a faith in miracles which is mere subjectivity about events that, according to them, did not take place at all.

Christ's interventions in nature

The New Testament is full of Christ's various miracles, so many interventions of his in nature. Most of them were sudden healings of grave defects of human bodies, small matter in themselves, although they were the ones that triggered a showdown between him and the leaders of his own people. The reason for this was that Jesus used those healings as so many proofs that he was commissioned by God to perform the kind of spiritual healing which consists in forgiving sin. Since his antagonists knew that no Prophet, not even Moses, has ever made such a claim, they recognized that Jesus claimed to be infinitely more than a prophet. He claimed himself to be equal to that God who alone can heal in the sense of redeeming man from his sins and restoring him to a life which no hunger, thirst, or death can ever touch.

As he momentously interfered with nature, Christ wanted above all that the Twelve be persuaded about that claim of his about himself. He was fully aware of the fact that the Twelve and all the others knew enough about nature as to perceive a genuine interference to be on hand. Otherwise, he would not have reminded the crowds of their ability to predict future physical events and do so accurately: "When you see a cloud rising in the west, you say immediately that rain is coming—and so it does. When wind blows from the south, you say it is going to be hot—and so it is" (Lk 12:54-55). In fact, Christ could assume such a keen knowledge on the crowds' part about the regularities of nature as to take them to task, on that very ground, for their unwillingness to recognize the thrust of his interventions in those regularities. He indeed called them hypocrites for their failure to do so. One wonders how he would brand today so many theologians who boast of their familiarity with science in order to talk away his miracles.

He could remind them of how he recalled to the Twelve their ability to know that eagles would gather around any dead body (Mt 24:28 and Lk 17:37) and that summer was near once the fig tree sprouted its leaves (Mt 24:32, Mk 13:28, Lk 21:29-30). But he could also safely assume that none of the Twelve had ever assumed that mere words of command were enough to make a fig tree wither up right away (Mt 21:19 and Mk 11:14) and to have stormy waters suddenly calm down. Even today science has not come even remotely close to controlling a stormy sea. Thus no "scientific" explanation should interfere with moving straight to Christ's purpose in performing that miracle, which was to prompt the Twelve to ask themselves: "Who can this be that the wind and the sea obey him?" (Mk 4:41). Any reference to antigravity (and antimatter thrown in for good measure) would be counterscientific in dealing with Christ's walking on the waters and making Peter do likewise. Most importantly, it is altogether beyond physics what the Twelve suddenly realized after Christ climbed into the boat: "Beyond doubt you are the Son of God!" (Mt 14:33).

It was in order to reveal himself in that capacity that he performed his very first miracle, the transformation of six large jars of water into choice wine. The miracle had to appear very material to John, otherwise he would not have specified the amount, equivalent to over a hundred gallons. Such was indeed the quantity needed to satisfy the gusto of the several hundred guests attending a typical country wedding in Palestine in Jesus' time. The first as well as the second multiplication of the loaves and fishes left no less vivid memories about the quantities involved. In the first, five loaves and two fishes (Mt 14:17, Mk 6:38, Lk 9:16, Jn 6:9) formed the starting point for the feeding of five thousand (Mt 14:21, Mk 6:44, Lk 9:14, Jn 6:10). All four evangelists specify that twelve baskets were filled with what was left over (Mt 14:20, Mk 6:43, Lk 9:17, Jn 6:13).

That such data are the same in all four Gospels has not ceased to inconvenience rationalist critics of the Bible who take the Evangelists' agreements for proof of their having copied one another and their differences for independently inventing the same story. Their professed bent on scientific exactness gives itself away as they decline to take for real an event presented with such exact figures, just because it was miraculous. There is further the detail, again with numerical exactness, that two hundred denarii would not have been enough to provide the quantity of bread needed. In reporting this, Mark (6:37) and John

(6:7) further witness the concreteness of a factual event. This is also brought out by Mark's (6:40) and Luke's (9:14) reporting about the manner in which the headcount could easily be achieved: the people were made to sit down in groups of hundreds and fifties. Last but not least, Matthew mentions the grass (14:19), Mark the "green grass" (6:39), and John "the abundance of grass in the place" (6:10). Only those familiar with the scarcity of grass in much of Palestine could be impressed by that fact.

These references to the plentiful grass at the spot where that miracle took place receive further credibility from the fact that Matthew (15:33) and Mark (8:4) specify as a desert the place of the second multiplication of bread. Once again further specifics are not missing. No wonder. Such a feat must have been graphically engraved in the memory of those who witnessed it. Thus Matthew (15:32) reports Jesus' observation that the crowds had already followed him for three days, and so does Mark (8:2). They also specify as seven (Mt 15:34, Mk 8:5) the loaves that were multiplied. They are in agreement concerning the number of baskets, seven, filled with leftovers. Finally, both report as four thousand (Mt 15:38, Mk 8:9) the number of men who were the beneficiaries. In both cases Matthew adds that those numbers, five and four thousand, do not include "women and children" (14:21 and 15:38). What is taken nowadays for a misogynistic touch, was, in saner days, taken for another touch of authenticity on behalf of a stunning miracle.

Those who benefited were certainly startled. Otherwise they would not have tried to make Christ a king after the first multiplication of bread (Jn 6:15). Their design would not have made any sense if (as some champions of a "new" theology keep proclaiming, repeating an old delusion) Christ merely persuaded those in the crowd with provisions to share these with those who failed to bring some along. There could be on hand a similar commotion even after the second multiplication of bread, otherwise Jesus would not have gotten immediately into the boat and gone to the district of Dalmanutha (Mk 8:10). In all appearance, by multiplying the loaves and the fish, Christ did not noticeably increase the effusion of brotherly love. He also failed to persuade not only the thousands, but also the wide group of his disciples, that what they had to crave for was a bread which he equated with his very flesh and blood. For even the twelve seemed to be wavering. But once more Peter stepped in the breach on behalf of them by crying out: "Lord, to whom shall we go? You have the words of everlasting life!" (Jn 7:68).

But long before John jotted down this satement of Jesus in which the spiritual effect of a miracle as "sign" obtains its crowning, Matthew and Mark had already registered another aspect of Jesus' own view of his miracles. For long before the rise of Christian apologetics Jesus emphasized the "work" aspect of his miracles. He did so by excoriating two attitudes vis-à-vis his miracles. One was that of the Pharisees and the Sadducees who were determined not to absorb as a spiritual "sign" his miracles (Mt 16:1-4 and Mk 8:11-13). The other was that of the Twelve who had to be reminded that they indeed *saw* with their very eyes the twelve large baskets full of fragments after the multiplication of five loaves for the five thousand and again that they *saw* the seven large baskets full of leftovers after the multiplication of seven loaves for the four thousand. Only after he obtained their answers about the "work," did Christ take up the "sign" by asking them: "How is it that you do not yet understand?" (Mk 8:21).

But to turn to the physics of the "work." Almost a century after the atomic structure of matter has been discovered, one can at least make that miracle "scientifically respectable," if this is important at all. It is certainly unimportant to do the impossible, namely, to coordinate the Aristotelian doctrine on substance with some modern physicists' inept remarks that their skills do not bring us any closer to the true nature of material reality.[22] Scientists have, of course, made it abundantly clear that all atoms

---

[22] One such effort appeared in 1955 in the pages of the *Osservatore Romano*. Lengthy excerpts from its English translation reappeared in *The Book of Miracles* by Z. Aradi (New York: Farrar, Strauss and Cudahy, 1956), pp. 272-75.

and molecules are different configurations and numbers of protons, neutrons, and electrons. One may therefore speculate that Christ merely rearranged the atomic constituents of a large number of air molecules into a dough.

With his divine power Christ could have easily let the energy radiated or absorbed during that instantaneous process become insensible to those around. One need not, however, cast Christ into the role of a super-physicist, who did with mere mental command what it would now take for scientists an incredibly complex instrumental apparatus, if they were to succeed at all. Speculation along these lines is best left to those whose faith in miracles cannot rest until their mind finds some "scientific" understanding. They usually fall prey to a very inept way of "legitimizing" miracles with an eye on modern physics by thinking that Heisenberg's uncertainty principle leaves God with loopholes to interfere with nature without disturbing it. In doing so they would simply oerlook the enormous difference between what is operational and what is ontological.[23]

It is not easy to enlighten theologians and exegetes who try to legitimize Jesus' miraculous interventions in nature by invoking the uncertainty principle. One can but pity those of them who have fallen prey to Bultmann's remarks about the unchangeability of the laws of physics. One wonders whether they would ever extricate themselves from the snares of studiedly sophisticated considerations that are not worth the ink with which they are printed. Nothing, of course, can help those who in the name of advanced exegesis merely rely on misguided imagination which cannot even cope with the fleeting nature of human enthusiasm. The crowds grew tired of Jesus no sooner had they realized that he would not make bread a miraculously effected daily dispensation.

Very likely there must have been some who expected many corpses to rise once they saw that Christ called back to life the young man from Naim. Some, infatuated with science, may now

[23] See p. 151 above.

speculate that Christ relied on some still unknown force of biophysics. If he did, he merely piled a miracle upon a miracle and, *horribile dictu*, defied Ockham's razor, according to which miracles are not to be multiplied without necessity. At any rate, by unnecessarily multiplying miracles, he would have caused his miracles to go as unappreciated as do all frequent events.

Lack of appreciation for a miracle may have more serious sources as well. One wonders whether the enthusiasm of those many Jews who came to see Lazarus walk out from the tomb prompted any of them to send reports about it everywhere in the Diaspora. In fact, those who were deeply resentful of Christ did not tire of giving the silent treatment to what happened after Lazarus came forth from a tomb already filled with the stench of his decomposing body. They certainly tried to give the silent treatment to that greatest spectacle ever, Christ hanging on the cross. It remains a greatness which is a laughing matter for pagans and a scandal for the Jews—but in both cases a sort of disturbing factor to be ignored as much as possible or to be downgraded by "higher" criticism.

Critics are hardly ever consistent. Those who evicted Mary, Joseph, and the Child from Bethlehem are still to replace Jerusalem with some other locality as the place of Jesus' death. After all, since none of the contemporary scribes cared to jot down that Jesus had died in Jerusalem, it would follow that he did not die there. By admitting that absurd consequence, it might dawn on them that at times they promote darkness at noon, as they try to shed the best "scientific" light on their subject matter.

Christ's death and resurrection

While Christ was hanging on the cross, "darkness fell over the whole countryside" (Mk 15:33). That only the larger Jerusalem area was affected by the darkness is perfectly consonant with the Greek expression (*eph holen ten gen*) that need not be literally translated as "over the whole earth." The context lacks the specifics that would impose a meaning with greater geographical reach than the area of greater Jerusalem or at most Judea proper. The darkness, whatever it was physically, was not an event for astronomers. Occurring as it did the day before Passover—a time of full moon—it could not be caused by a solar eclipse. But even taken by itself, Luke's reference to the "sun's failing" (*tou heliou ekleipontos* Lk 23:45) is not a technically astronomical expression, meaning eclipse. It means no more than that the sun's light was not on hand. At any rate, an eclipse could not last for three hours. The three-hour-long duration of darkness was, of course, remarkable, even if it was caused by a dust storm, not unusual in Palestine in springtime. The darkness itself does not mean that there was pitch dark during that period of time. The coming of a storm with such an intensity at a given time could very well constitute the miracle, once more in line with the precept that, although God passed through, no one saw his footprints. Unusual features as that darkness might have had, it was not a fantastic show.

Fantastic or not, the last thing Pilate wished to do was to report that darkness to his superiors in Rome. Only in the wholly unreliable apocryphal *Acts of Pilate* is he said to have made a report. (And only in the equally unreliable *Gospel of Peter* is it stated that people went about with torches.) It was not in the interest of the Sanhedrin to keep that darkness a subject of conversation. Josephus, though an opponent of the nationalist party, was too much of an opportunist to have sympathy for a Messiah who sternly warned against the casting of one's lot with the opportunities of this life, among them the leisure of writing history books.

The darkness was, of course, a notice served on the officialdom of Jerusalem and a reminder of the fact that all true prophets were destined to die there. Only those taking certain literati of Pilate's Jerusalem for objective and disinterested registrants of all facts would find it strange that they did not leave an account of those three hours. Much less was it in their interest to register the fact that "the veil of the Temple was torn in two from top to bottom" (Mt 27:51 and Mk 15:38). To assign this to a storm of unusual intensity is conjectural, even though such storms can certainly bring down tents. At any rate, here too, a natural factor, whatever it may have been, could readily serve as an excuse for disregarding the supernatural at work.

Undue uneasiness about a miraculous fact, be it very plainly stated, such as the tearing of that veil in two, can land one in an almost ridiculous predicament. A case in point is that prominent Catholic exegete who wrote: "this event is not to be taken *too* literally either"[24] (Italics added). Such an expression is not a whit more enlightening than the assertion that a woman can be "*almost* pregnant." But unfortunately, such expressions have lately gained wide currency among learned exegetes. Perhaps they take their cue from scientists, who, when faced with far-reaching philosophical implications of some of their theories, propose them in two versions: one is *weak*, the other is *strong*. They merely display their utter debility to face up to the strength of logic in using plain words.

Such exegetes would delight Gibbon, that arch-critic of the historical grounds of Christianity, who seized on the fact that the darkness in question was not recorded by contemporary pagan historians. (Gibbon did not display the evenhandedness appropriate to historians as he ignored Jewish historians). The definitive judgment on Gibbon, the historian, when dealing with that darkness, had already been passed by John Henry Newman. He held up Gibbon, on that very account, as the signal example of "the not unfrequent perversion which occurs of antiquarian and historical research, to the prejudice of Theology." Newman did this in a section of his lectures on the idea of a university that really embraced the universe of what can be known. There he deals with the intellectual harm done whenever a particular science tries to set the standard for all other fields of learning. Historiography does that harm whenever it accepts for facts only entries in its documents: "I suppose on this score one ought to deny . . . that any individual came from Adam who cannot

---

[24] An evasion by P. Benoit, in his *The Passion and Resurrection of Jesus Christ*, tr. by B. Wheatherhead (New York: Herder and Herder, 1969), p. 201.

produce the table of his ancestry. Yet Gibbon argues against the darkness at the Passion, from the accident that it is not mentioned by Pagan historians:—as well might he argue against the existence of Christianity itself in the first century, because Seneca, Pliny, Plutarch, the Jewish Mishna, and other authorities are silent about it."[25] Newman's words are, of course, appropriate also concerning the Star of Bethlehem and other *magnalia Dei* unattested by "independent" sources, and, above all, concerning that other of God's *magnalia* in the New Testament, indeed the greatest of all great acts of God, the resurrection of Christ.

This is not the place to recall the verbal and mental contortions which are needed to turn Christ's bodily resurrection into a result of the faith of the disciples. A theologian-exegete who heavily relies on myths, without caring to specify what he means by that word, will trap himself (or herself) in a diction intellectually as worthless as Renan's reconstruction of how the wishful thinking of the disciples let Christ rise from the dead. They all fail to ponder the fact that the Sanhedrinists did not find at all unbelievable the report which the guards gave them about the tomb. The guards themselves would have been the last to put themselves in a double jeopardy by saying that, while they were sleeping, they also witnessed the disciples come and run away with Jesus' body. The question, which Saint Augustine figuratively addressed to the Sanhedrin, can still validly be raised: "How come? Do you call on witnesses who were asleep?"

In noting that the most incredible thing about miracles is that they happen, Chesterton merely gave, and unwittingly so, a nutshell formulation of a famous passage toward the end of Augustine's *City of God*, a book which more than any other book besides the Bible shaped Western cultural consciousness. The passage is worth repeating in these days when so many well-meaning theologians and exegetes deliver "liberating" messages about biblical miracles, without first honing their intellects on insights that not long ago were still the stock of streetcorner

---

[25] J. H. Newman, *The Idea of a University* (London: Longmans Green and Co, 1898), p.95.

defenders of Christian orthodoxy. These also knew what some modern exegetes readily overlook as they emphasize the "spiritual" nature of Christ's risen body. They remembered that the risen Christ accepted from the apostles "a piece of broiled fish and a honeycomb," and gave them to eat what was left over. In speaking about the resurrection of the body, Augustine makes much of three incredible features involved in Christ's resurrection by stating that, "yet they happened. It is incredible that Christ rose in the flesh and with his flesh ascended into heaven. It is incredible that the world believed so incredible an event; and it is incredible that men of no birth, no standing, no learning, and so few of them, should have been able to persuade, so effectively, the whole world, including the learned men." The force of these three incredibilities is then expanded by Augustine in a brilliant dialectic, which is, however, anchored in the assertion that the apostles preached what they had seen: "What I mean is that those who persuaded men of this truth did so by utterances which on their lips were turned into miracles, rather than mere words. For those who had not witnessed Christ's resurrection in the flesh, and his ascension into heaven in that same flesh, believed the report of those who told what they had seen, who not only spoke of it, but displayed miraculous signs."[26]

No trace here of deriving Christ's resurrection from the faith of the primitive community. For the Twelve it was the other way around. And for the apostle Paul, it was the same logic. First the fact, then the recognition that it is a miracle. Otherwise nothing makes sense in the Christian dispensation. For as Paul warned the faithful in Corinth, and through them all Christian communities everywhere and forever: "If Christ was not raised, your faith is worthless" (1 Cor 15:17). He did not berate them for not energizing their faith enough to let Christ thereby rise from the dead. He berated them for soft-pedaling Christ's crucifixion. But this is what all do who take the faith of the community for the source of Christ's resurrection.

[26] Augustine, *City of God*, tr. H. Bettenson, with an introduction by D. Knowles (Harmondsworth: Penguin Book, 1976), p. 1028 (Bk XXII, ch. 5).

11

Why a Bible? Why Science?

The crux of miracles

The crucifixion of Christ has remained what it was called by St Paul, a scandal, a stumbling block, and the most monumental of them all. This has important ramifications for the understanding of the Bible as well as of Science, which ought to be kept in mind if satisfactory answers are to be found to the questions: Why a Bible? Why Science? The answers may in turn serve as so many replies to the objection: Why bother at all to correlate the Bible with Science?

The question—Why a Bible?—cannot, of course, be asked, unless one first asks: Why a Church? This in turn presupposes the question: Why a Revelation? Why should God bother to speak to man in a way far superior to what mere Nature can reveal about Him and about His intentions with man? The latently aprioristic ring of this question should be carefully noted, lest it sound the deathknell of sanity. Those who started with the idea (their idea) of an infinitely perfect and good God, could not get (Spinoza is a memorable example) even to finite real things, let alone to some understanding of moral evil and physical suffering. The idea of a perfect God can mesmerize the mind into thinking that it was meaningless for God to create a universe, let alone one riddled with physical and moral miseries.

Yet it is precisely the very limitation of things, or their *such*ness, that grounds the possibility of science as well as of natural theology.[1] Within science itself any *such*ness is traced to

[1] This epistemological similarity between those two enterprises is the theme of my Gifford Lectures, given at the University of Edinburgh in 1974-75 and 1975-

another. But when the *such*ness of the totality of things, or the universe, is being confronted, explanation of it cannot be looked for in another universe without demeaning that very word. Consistent rationality then demands that the *such*ness of the universe be sought in recognizing the existence of a Creator. As the source of all being, the Creator also has to be the source of all goodness, including that most mysterious, yet very luminous human good, the freedom of the human will. Then, it is possible to argue that man's misery must be the result of an erstwhile calamity (original sin) and that an infinitely good God would not have left man to his own devices. Hence the answer to the question: Why a Revelation? Once a Revelation was given, it then had to be protected. Hence a Church, with an authority to teach, which has to be infallible, unless God's very plan is to fail. Such is an old train of thought. One of its most graphic and gripping articulators was John Henry Newman, in the closing chapter of his *Grammar of Assent*.

So much in the way of a classic argument on behalf of the starting point that God indeed spoke to man in two Covenants and that in both there developed a set of canonical scriptures. But in both, well before their respective Scriptures had reached their full growth, indeed before there had been any authoritative written documents at all, there had been miracles, some of them so great as to be called *magnalia Dei*. Therefore, the questions—Why a Bible? Why Covenants? Why a Church?—can be reduced in a sense to the question: Why miracles? Far from being separate from the scandal of the cross, this question has a close connection with it, indeed so close as to eliminate any triviality from raising the point about the *crux* of miracles.

In fact, it was just after overcoming his death on the cross that Christ spoke of the blessedness of those who believed, without having seen his risen body, the greatest of the *magnalia Dei*. But already in the early phase of his ministry, he declared those who did the will of God to be his mother, brothers, and

76, *The Road of Science and the Ways to God* (Chicago: University of Chicago Press, 1978).

sisters (Mk 3:35). Yet the more that will demanded, the more ready he was to support the acceptance of it with miracles. His own mother, who carried the greatest burden of that will, was the beneficiary of a miracle right at the outset, when without any prompting, any suggestion, any hint on her part Elizabeth greeted her as "the mother of my savior" and added: "Blessed is she who believed that there would be a fullfillment of what was spoken to her from the Lord." By then the child in Elizabeth's womb had already signaled his own joy. Saint Ambrose began his commentary on all this with a pithy phrase: "The moral is that those who demand faith, should give support to that faith."[2] So was Mary's faith, the greatest faith ever, given support when Christ performed, at her suggestion, his very first miracle by turning the water filling six large jars into wine. But he saw to it that most of the wedding guests, several hundred of them, would not notice anything. For his purposes it was enough to strengthen the faith of a chosen few.

Miracles are never made for the entertainment either of simple folks or of scholars. Miracles are not for the benefit of scientists as such or of Academies of Science. If they were, they would be the tricks of the devil, who in turn would not fail to make appear plain fools all those who had fallen in his trap. Cartoonists have at times grasped this far more effectively than sharp apologists. One such cartoon, now a hundred years old, was resurrected not long ago in the pages of one of the world's leading dailies, *Le Monde*. The occasion was the review of a book on Jesus, whose author contended, among other things—and in the name of advanced scholarship, of course—that Jesus was the natural son of Mary, one of her several children. The cartoon—indeed, quite an elaborate drawing—showed Christ walking on raging waves, not too far from the shore of a lake, while from the shore a photographer tried to catch the event on his glass plate, and a scientist, in swallowtails, observed Him through a huge magnifying glass.[3] A hundred years later, one

---

[2] St. Ambrose, *Commentary to Luke*, Lib. 2, cap 19.
[3] *Le Monde*, Dec. 23, 1994, p. IV.

need only replace the old box-camera with a Nikkormat, the magnifying glass with a satellite antenna, and the swallowtails with blue jeans. The modern artist need not worry about the mental attitude of those to be portrayed: it has remained unchanged.

Miracles, whether of Christ or of others, still retain their *crux*. Those particularly stung by them usually claim that no event qualifying for a miracle has ever been observed. Carl Sagan has lately tried to explain away the miracles of Lourdes as so many cases similar to remissions that occur once out of ten thousand cases of cancer.[4] He, of course, failed to note that in Lourdes such remissions occur with remarkable speed, and festering wounds, not at all cancerous, have also healed at a rate that no clinician in his right mind would qualify as a mere "remission." Sagan should have noted that a conclusion quite different from his was reached by the foremost surgeon of this century, who, unlike him, studied matters on the spot. Alexis Carrel, the surgeon in question, who received the Nobel Prize in medicine in 1912, had received a very informative portrayal in *Scientific American* shortly before Sagan came out with that disreputable piece of his on Lourdes. In that portrayal, Carrel's work, done during the first decade of this century, is presented as the very basis of all the spectacular breakthroughs that for the last three decades or so have become household words, such as coronary bypass, cardiac valve repairs, organ transplants, etc.[5]

Carrel himself left a most moving as well as very instructive account of what had taken place, under his searching eyes, within less than an hour, in the early afternoon of May 28, 1902. Only an hour or so earlier, he had made a most foolish vow. He assured several other doctors that he would become a monk, if Marie Bailly, a woman of twenty-three, dying of tubercular peritonitis, would survive the time, a mere fifteen minutes,

---

[4] C. Sagan, "Channeling or Faith Healing—Scam or Miracle?" *Parade Magazine*, Dec. 4, 1994, pp. 14-15.

[5] V. E. Friedewald, Jr., and C. Crossen, "Vascular Anastomosis," *Scientific American* (Science and Medicine), September/October 1994, pp. 68-77.

needed to be pushed on a gurney from a hospital in Lourdes to the Grotto itself. Between 2:20pm and 3:10pm, Marie Bailly was relieved, as if by magic, of a huge abdominal protrusion, although nothing left her body either then or in the next twelve hours. By the evening Carrel too had to register that her cure was complete.[6] He resisted the wider bearing of the evidence for the next four decades or so. Carrel did so because he too had fallen victim to a favorite delusion of modern times, namely, that truth is limited to scientific truths,[7] and therefore miracles as supernatural interventions in nature are impossible.

Consequently, interventions of extraordinary magnitudes are being shrugged off, even though advance warnings have been given in truly extraordinary forms. Otherwise the media of Lisbon, still the capital of a colonial empire, would not have shown up on November 13, 1917, in the vicinity of the backwater village of Fatima. They went there in the firm expectation that nothing would be seen at all in the sky, let alone in the sun, as specifically predicted a month earlier by three peasant children. As those media people stood there, in the midst of a crowd swelling by noon to fifty thousand or so, they must have taken perverse delight in the steadily pouring rain, as good a cover as can be against seeing anything in the sky. But suddenly, around 1 pm, the rain stopped and the lead-gray clouds broke just where the sun stood. The sun itself began to act as if it were a whirling dervish, filling the large crowd with sudden fright. Some merely saw a yellowish hue that covered people, foliage, and the muddy ground. But many others, of most different persuasions and predispositions, refused to disbelieve their very eyes about what the sun showed them. On the next day, Sunday, the leading newspapers of Lisbon let the world know that as far as man could

---

[6] Carrel's own account of those extraordinary days was published posthumously, in 1949. The English translation, *Voyage to Lourdes*, was recently reprinted with my introduction (which contains all the archival evidence) by Real-View-Books (Clinton, Michigan, 1994).

[7] Carrel made this clear in his runaway bestseller, *Man the Unknown* (1935), where he postulated still hidden forces of nature to explain miraculous cures.

trust his very eyes, the sun indeed performed as had been predicted.[8]

The world of the learned, always professing interest only in facts and in nothing but facts, could not lose interest in Fatima, because it took no interest in the first place. That world included the world of science as well. It was not with an awareness of that prediction that an observatory on the Canary Islands reported at that time some unusual solar activity. The world of science did not care to correlate the two events, because most in that world had been victimized by a further delusion of modernity. Therefore that world set up, against the Creator, whose very being is the source of the oneness of Truth, as a rival principle to it the illusion that scientific truth alone counts. Illusory indeed is the view that second-order propositions, or the quantitative assertions of science, can function as first steps in knowing reality. For unless a thing is recognized to exist, no assertion can be made about its quantitative properties, the sole business of science. No less illusory should seem the claim that nothing can be reliably known except quantitative propositions. Still, such illusions have gained wide currency, because they are packaged in copious references to science, which, tragically enough, has become one of the three most effective wrappings that assure runaway sales. The two others are sex and sport. It is difficult to debase science lower than to the level of recycled wrapping paper.

This is still to be realized both by propagandists of science and the non-scientists bewildered by them. The latter, especially if they are theologians and exegetes, should hang their heads in shame for their misplaced efforts to meet the objections which those propagandists, whose number today is vastly greater than in the days of T. H. Huxley, posed to the Bible in general and to Genesis 1 in particular. After all, Huxley was all too clear as to what the primary issue was about. Of particular significance is the fact that he explained himself in this respect to a prominent clergyman of his time, the Rev. Charles Kingsley. For the import

---

[8] Many books on Fatima carry long quotations from those reports, which are at times given in facsimiles.

of Huxley's words was not diminished by the fact that the distinguished clergyman, like other liberal confrères of his, then as now, did not seem to care whether Genesis 1 agreed or conflicted with the findings of astronomy, or whether the biblical narrative as a whole had any historical credibility. These were secondary issues for Huxley. For him the decisive issue was that persons were central to the Bible, whereas, since they were irrelevant for science, they had no real validity.[9]

To his credit, Huxley admitted in the same context that others, no less intelligent than he, may not see an unbridgeable gap between the strictly impersonal world of science and a broader world about which science could not legislate. He was also right in sensing about that broader world that it culminated in religious realities, with the human person in their focus. But he failed to see that, well before one came to the realm of religion, one's intellect demanded an account of countless experiences about reality that were neither scientific nor religious. Nor could he see that the scientific world itself could not be handled unless one had a handle, a very philosophical one, on that broader world of real experience. Huxley at least perceived that his vision might be a matter of self-imposed myopia that severed him from most of his fellow men: "I don't like this state of things for myself—least of all do I see how it will work out for my children. But as my mind is constituted, there is no way out of it, and I can only envy you if you can see things differently."[10]

Huxley's envy was not so much about seeing things differently, as about an intellectual justification of that different vision. No such justification could be forthcoming from Kingsley. He at most would have agreed that Huxley was absolutely right that the agreement in question was but a secondary matter in the confrontation of Bible and Science. The real issue, the *crux* of miracles, touched on a deeper layer of knowledge which Huxley could never clarify. And he sensed it and was at times deeply agitated by it. He was in that respect a far deeper thinker than

---

[9] Huxley's remarks were quoted in full in the Introduction, p. 11.
[10] Ibid.

James Watson, the co-discoverer of the double-helix model of DNA, who on more than one occasion blandly rejected efforts to see some deeper design to human life: "It can all be described in molecules. There is no need to invent anything else."[11]

The deeper layer which, unlike Watson, Huxley at least sensed is not simply the difference between the personal and the impersonal. Many scientists handle that difference with total disdain for the personal. Otherwise, Dawkins would not have earned the applause of many of his colleagues (some of them driven by a very high degree of academic self-seeking) for having reduced even the non-selfish actions of man into a function of selfish genes. How many scientists have remembered that only four hundred years ago science achieved its maturity by depersonalizing nature and its parts?

Far fewer Darwinists dare deny openly man's freedom, although the denial logically follows on a genuine Darwinian basis. Darwin himself knew that, but he tried to dodge the issue as much as possible. Free will is also a merely subjective impression if one takes the view that only quantitative considerations represent truth. It was on that basis that Einstein denied free will, though only in correspondence. Yet he took all the prizes and glories for his great achievements, apparently in the conviction that he fully deserved them, which again is possible only if he did freely what he did.

At any rate, what makes a person is that he or she can act freely. But freedom of the will is a nightmare in a world that admits only scientific truths. Denial of free will in the name of science is a boomerang that hits religion only by hitting science first. Science depends on man's free will and is a manifestation of it. Even to raise the question, Why Science? makes sense only if it is done freely. Further, why is it that science flourishes best in a free society? But can a society be free if its individuals must think themselves victims of delusion whenever they claim that they have acted freely? Is not this most precious freedom

---

[11] The quote is from Watson's Einstein memorial lecture of February 16, 1995, at Princeton University. See *Trenton Times Advertiser*, February 25, 1995, p. 1.

threatened by behavioral psychology? And if E. B. Wilson of sociobiology fame assures us that "there are free will and many choices," how can this be justified if he also assigns to genes the ability to "profoundly" influence those choices?[12] Where is profundity when the rock bottom is kept in the dark?

The rock bottom about free will too, is, of course, God, the Creator. For insofar as free will, or any genuinely free quality in any action, is a reality, it can only exist insofar as God created it. To be free and still to be created remains forever the ultimate natural mystery, though a most luminous one, because one's freedom should be self-evident. Otherwise, one becomes a legitimate candidate for the psychiatrist's ward. Even a determinist must deny freedom freely in order to assure some legitimacy to his arguments. This freedom is not as simple a proposition as the difference between to be or not to be. That difference entails a total disjunction. Of course, only God, the Creator, can bridge that difference. He alone can give reality. Therefore, insofar as that free quality is a reality, only God can make it so. Herein lies the most profound of luminous mysteries. While a free act is fully created, it enjoys, through God's omnipotence, genuine freedom. If not, there could be no moral perspective, let alone eternal moral perspective, which is the ultimate *crux* of miracles.

It is tempting to apply some of this to the futile debates between Thomists and Molinists. They both forgot that the mystery of free will does not begin in reference to supernatural grace. On the purely natural level, free will is a mystery, in the sense that it can only be reduced to God's omnipotence, the only power that, being infinitely free, can give genuine freedom to an entity (the free human act) which, like any other entity, is a creature. Therefore it exists, in every respect, in utter dependence on the Creator. Such is a first step in plain epistemology, a first step no less indispensable in any treatise on grace.

Here let it be considered what this means for God himself. It means above all that the medicine of miracles, those powerful

---

[12] From an Interview in *Modern Maturity* 38 (May-June 1995), p. 70.

supports of faith, will be dispensed sparingly. If not, man's freedom will be overwhelmed and his worship of God will no longer be the kind of "reasoned worship" as demanded by Paul (Rom 13:1). This is why God performed his miracles most of the time, including his *magnalia,* in such a way as to make them appear to be the enhancement of natural processes. Here too, the grace of God merely raises but does not destroy nature.

Moreover, man is free to resist the evidence, in fact any evidence. Every issue of any newspaper is a bulging dossier of proofs of this. Plain criminals claim their innocence without batting an eye. Lawyers get rich by letting crooks get away scot-free on mere legal technicalities or by steering protracted trials into a hung jury. Many politicians think they never lose their innocence. And the media keep suggesting that while everybody is economical with truth, they alone serve truth and nothing but truth, although all too often it is visible only between the lines they print. In all this, the media heavily relies on man's proverbially short memory. The latter is, in good part, but not necessarily for good reasons, due to man's heavy dependence on sensory evidence. Few principles are so valid about epistemology as the dictum that what is out of sight is quickly out of mind. This is true of miracles as well, though this is not what constitutes their real *crux.* What is crucial about miracles is that their recognition demands that man, as St. Paul put it, crucify his body with all its passions so that he may serve his Creator and Redeemer.

The crux of science

Compared with this, all other issues that can turn up about the Bible and Science are relatively minor. One of them relates to the quantitative method of science. For all its power (predictive and industrial), that method cannot probe into what lies beneath the phenomena. For science, which is not about the difference between passions and their absence, is not even about the difference between reality and non-reality. Science is merely about a methodical stance whereby one restricts one's eyes to purely quantitative characteristics and differences. This is science's greatness as well as its poverty. And herein lies its *crux*. For precisely through that methodical stance science disqualifies itself from pronouncing on anything non-quantitative, including the always non-quantitative statements about the very existence of material things. Nor can science reveal what things are. Science, to mention only one example, remains notoriously inept to say what electricity is. Yet it possesses what is nothing short of a wizardry about the quantitative properties of what is called, rightly or wrongly, electricity.

One need not be a theoretical physicist to grasp that it was precisely this self-imposed ignorance of science that H. Hertz tried to convey by saying: "Maxwell's theory is Maxwell's system of equations."[13] Tellingly, he said this after he had demonstrated the reality of electromagnetic waves predicted by Maxwell's theoretical work. While those equations "worked," they said nothing about what it was that worked like electricity. About the same time, another great student of electricity, Lord Kelvin, called attention, though in a witty way, to the even greater ignorance of science as to what are those very things, in this case electricity, which it investigates quantitatively. He did so as he visited, unexpectedly, a major Glasgow plant maufacturing electrical instruments and appliances. Without disclosing his identity he let himself be conducted through the plant by a young foreman who kept explaining to him the rudiments of electrical science. On completing the tour, Kelvin asked him quietly: "What then is electricity?" His guide fell silent. "No matter," Lord Kelvin said kindly, "that is the only thing about electricity which you and I do not know."[14]

Yet, however narrow the range of science may be, by being limited to quantitative considerations, the reach of that range goes as far as things go. For anything real has quantitative properties. But those properties are not merely universally

---

[13] H. Hertz, *Electric Waves, Being Researches on the Propagation of Electric Action with Finite Velocity through Space*, tr. D. E. Jones (London: Macmillan, 1893), p. 21.
[14] See Edmund Fuller, *2500 Anecdotes for All Occasions* (New York: Avenel Books, 1978), p. 192.

present in matter. They are also the very first items grasped by the mind in knowing things material. A scientist, unmindful of philosophy, may turn this fact upside down and declare that, just because he knows those quantitative properties better than anyone else, there is nothing else to know. In doing so, he may lose hold on the question, Why Science? Because, unless one is a naive Platonist, quantities do not make matter, although they invariably inhere in any bit of it.

A theologian sees much farther when he lets himself be instructed by the biblical dictum that the Creator arranged everything according to measure, number, and weight—all quantitative parameters. Seeing things in this light, the theologian can confidently face up to the question: Why Science? For the answer he can safely look to that human mind which, precisely because it is created in the image of God, is bound to find enormous delight in tracing out the quantitative features and correlations of things. And if success with quantities seems to carry the mind away, reflection on its created status—and such reflection alone—can provide it with restraint and balance.

But search for quantities that mind must and will, whether some theologians, foreign to the realm of quantities, like it or not. Latter-day Huxleys will find in that search an ever fresh source of observations with which to needle the theologian. Not that a theologian should try to oppose with rational arguments a stance which is simply willful, if not plainly irrational. For such was Huxley's attitude toward what he declared to be mere anthropomorphism, or the Bible's basic claim that there is a Creator who cares for man.

Nor should the theologian be concerned about those on the outer fringes of exegesis whom Huxley rightly identified as "circle squarers" and "flat-earth fanatics." But the theologian should dissociate himself from all those latter-day Canon Liddons whose thinking appeared to Huxley a sort of a crime committed against the human mind in the name of revealed religion. Examples of that thinking are a dime a dozen. One of them appeared, very recently, in the pages of *Time,* in reference to a cover-story there on the historicity of the Bible,[15] and in particular on some of the *magnalia Dei*. The thrust of the story was, in line with a journalism feeding on false alarm, that some of the *magnalia*, such as the dramatic fall of Jericho and Joshua's campaign, did not take place at all.

That such was indeed that thrust appeared very clearly from the letters to the Editor, published four weeks later. In one of them, which would have brought much grist to Huxley's mill, it is claimed that the Bible is "not a history book as we understand that term in this day and age." There is much truth in this, although one should not present it as "a fundamental point in most sound theology" and leave aside the many ways in which reports of facts can qualify as history. Undoubtedly, it is true that "the text of the Scripture deals with mystery, faith and how God is perceived in dealings with people." But the very rationality of God's saving action is undermined when the same writer adds: "As a trained theologian and pastor, I am not concerned with whether there was an Abraham, a Noah, a 40-year trek in the wilderness or an invasion of Palestine. The stories were created to convey the theological truth that God empowers, guides and saves. Faith is the key."[16] Huxley today would call this a theological cop-out. In a much deeper vein Paul of Tarsus would recall his warning, made, of all places, in his letter to the Romans (12:1), that Christian worship should be a *logike latreia*, or a worship that satisfies all legitimate demands of a human mind created in the image of an infinitely rational God.

Such are some of the basic perspectives of the relation between Science, provided it is not taken for a pseudo-creed, and the Bible, provided it is not waved as a textbook of science. The specifics of that relation have become enriched in the measure in which more was learned about the Bible and more about Science as well. The rock bottom rule is that truth is one, though, of course, with different aspects, simply because the human mind cannot reduce to one set of conceptualizations all those nuances.

---

[15] "Are the Bible's Stories True?" *Time*, Dec. 18, 1995, pp. 64-70.
[16] *Time*, January 15, 1996, p. 8.

Within the set of quantitative conceptualizations of empirical data, the findings of science rule supreme, provided they are securely established. Whatever is outside that set is non-quantitative and is best called philosophy and even metaphysics. There the statements of scientists have no more credibility than the philosophy they use in making them. Those, therefore, who try to specify the relation of the Bible and Science, or rather the Creed and Science, without coming clean as to their philosophies, simply play to the galleries to which fuzzy thinking is the ticket of admission.

Science should be listened to as it argues that the age of the universe is to be measured in at least billions of years, as this proposition is strictly quantitative. But, as was said earlier, no attention should be paid to scientists who claim to know that the universe began, say, twelve billion years ago. The quantitative methods of science simply cannot specify the so-called first moment, and for an obvious reason. There is no empirical way of establishing a given moment as being the absolutely first moment, for such a moment cannot have empirically verifiable antecedents. Those who conjure up an eternal though absolutely inert state preceding that first moment, still have to prove that there is a physical state which absolutely lacks any motion whatever. But whatever their proof, it cannot be empirical. For an absolutely inert matter cannot reflect light, or any radiation, in order to be observed. For an equally empirical reason, science cannot speak of the creation of the universe out of nothing, simply because the word nothing implies utter physical unobservability, or else it stands for something and not for nothing.

Last but not least, scientists contradict their very method when in the name of evolutionary science they deny the reality of purpose in life processes. Those who, because of their Darwinist assumptions, must consider themselves barred from talking about purpose, should not devote their scientific lives to the purpose of proving that there is no purpose. Conversely, readers of the Bible, or devotees of the Creed, should not trap themselves into a similar self-contradiction. The Creed (and therefore the Bible resting on it) predicates divine providence and purpose through all creation. But it does not follow from this that it is therefore possible to find empirical evidences of purpose in the vast domain of flora and fauna. The reason for this limitation is that apart from conscious human action, purpose, being a most metaphysical item, is not something empirically verifiable in beings that lack consciousness. Only insofar as that consciousness is coupled with free will is there on hand a planned and purposeful activity, ready to be verified, though not by the methods of science.[17]

If there is indeed something that commends the Bible, it is the fact that it contains an unparalleled narrative, authenticated by the Church, of the most vast and purposeful process which is an all-encompassing salvation. To cast doubt on that process in the name of a total misunderstanding of what science can do about miracles, biblical or otherwise, is to trade an orchard for a mere apple which may be half rotten. In doing so, one also blinds oneself to perceiving about science itself an all-important point, which is the very vote science casts on behalf of that process.

For science itself owes to firm belief in that narrative the very spark, without which it would not have come into existence. Prior to that spark scientifically useful data kept accumulating without revealing their true usefulness. Time and again, and especially in ancient Greece, science came close to being perfected to the point where it could have handled those most universal among all phenomena: things insofar as they move. Only the spark was missing for making that crucial advance. Tellingly, when the spark came, it proved true to its nature as well as provenance. It was its nature to dart around and produce thereby illuminating considerations. We owe to these considerations the science of motion, the very backbone of all science properly so called. The spark also remained true to its provenance, which

---

[17] For further details, see ch. 6 in my *The Purpose of it All,* referred to in note 6 above. There I also discuss the limits of seeing in animal behavior analogous realizations of purpose.

was from above. Like God's great interventions in history, the *magnalia Dei,* this spark too had to act in an almost natural way. It certainly looked natural to its erstwhile proponents—Buridan and Oresme—animated as they were by the Creed and the Bible authenticated by it. And, like the Gospel, the new science of motion also put, in its own way, things in motion in human history in a truly powerful manner. But when things in motion, fueled by the fantastic inventions of modern science, appear to be on a runaway course—this time not by nuclear chain reactions but by genetic manipulation—the Creed is still there to provide restraint and guidance.

Index of Names

Index of Subjects

(continued from p. ii)

By the same author

The Savior of Science
(Wethersfield Institute Lectures, 1987)

Miracles and Physics

God and the Cosmologists
(Farmington Institute Lectures, Oxford, 1988)

The Only Chaos and Other Essays

The Purpose of It All
(Farmington Institute Lectures, Oxford, 1989)

Catholic Essays

Cosmos in Transition: Studies in the History of Cosmology

Olbers Studies

Scientist and Catholic: Pierre Duhem

Reluctant Heroine: The Life and Work of Hélène Duhem

Universe and Creed

Genesis 1 through the Ages

Is There a Universe?

Patterns or Principles and Other Essays

* * *

Translations with introduction and notes:

The Ash Wednesday Supper (Giordano Bruno)

*Cosmological Letters on the Arrangement
of the World Edifice* (J.-H. Lambert)

Universal Natural History and Theory of the Heavens (I. Kant)

Note on the Author

Stanley L. Jaki, a Hungarian-born Catholic priest of the Benedictine Order, is Distinguished University Professor at Seton Hall University, South Orange, New Jersey. With doctorates in theology and physics, he has for the past thirty years specialized in the history and philosophy of science. The author of over thirty books and nearly a hundred articles, he served as Gifford Lecturer at the University of Edinburgh and as Fremantle Lecturer at Balliol College, Oxford. He has lectured at major universities in the United States, Europe, and Australia. He is honorary member of the Pontifical Academy of Sciences, *membre correspondant* of the Académie Nationale des Sciences, Belles-Lettres et Arts of Bordeaux, and the recipient of the Lecomte du Nouy Prize for 1970 and of the Templeton Prize for 1987.